W9-CKV-153

HOW TO ACHIEVE
A HEAVEN
ON EARTH

HOW TO ACHIEVE
A HEAVEN
ON EARTH

Edited by John E. Wade II

PELICAN PUBLISHING COMPANY
GRETNA 2010

Copyright © 2010
By John E. Wade II
All rights reserved

The word "Pelican" and the depiction of a pelican are trademarks of the Pelican Publishing Company, Inc., and are registered in the U.S. Patent and Trademark Office.

Library of Congress Cataloging-in-Publication Data

How to achieve a heaven on earth / edited by John E. Wade II.
    p. cm.
  Includes bibliographical references.
   ISBN 978-1-58980-597-2 (pbk. : alk. paper)   1.   Social problems. 2. Social action. 3.   Religion and social problems. 4.   Humanity. I. Wade, John E., II.
  HN18.3.H69 2010
  362'.042—dc22

                              2009039137

Printed in the United States of America
Published by Pelican Publishing Company, Inc.
1000 Burmaster Street, Gretna, Louisiana 70053

Contents

Freedom

Democracies

Prosperity

Health

Moral Purpose and Meaning

Individual Paths to Heaven on Earth

Preface

"I will try to love and help create a heaven on earth"—the most important sentence that I have written or may ever write.

Many people already try to live by these simple, yet powerful, words without articulating this explicit promise. I believe that if we—one by one, million by million, billion by billion—would all accept this challenge, the world would progress immensely. Think about the words and use them to motivate yourself to reach out to love and help others.

How did the pledge come into being? The groundwork was laid by years of psychoanalysis and follow-up analysis, faithful attendance at Sunday school and church, much prayer and thought, as well as many varied life experiences.

The world may never really know me, or if it does I may someday be forgotten, as most of us are. But I believe those words and the concept behind them will live on.

"I will try to love and help create a heaven on earth." Think about it.

Such an explicit, personal goal as this can drive humankind forward on a wonderful journey. I want my life to count. Dr. Milburn Calhoun, the publisher of this book, told me that he wants his life to count too. You want your life to count, don't you?

Character is elemental in all forms of human endeavor. Resiliency is also necessary for many of life's greatest challenges. A number of essays in this book convey these essential truths, one being, "A Prisoner's Example: A Study of Nelson Mandela" by Rúna Bouius.

Our very wise founding fathers made a serious pact in the form of our Declaration of Independence. That famous document includes a reference to the pursuit of happiness. Such a concept is an attractive and desirable one, but I believe it can be carried too far if one lives a hedonic life. I once did. Instead of seeking only pleasure, we should, in many facets of our lives, delay gratification and seek to become part of a loving cause larger than ourselves.

The pledge is an invitation to join such a cause, either explicitly or implicitly. To help further this goal of guiding humankind toward a heaven on earth, I founded a charity, Soldiers of Love. This charity will be the beneficiary of half of my royalties from this book. Appendix A outlines the scope and achievements of this nonprofit entity.

Humankind has progressed and relapsed since the dawn of our existence. Yet the expansion of all kinds of knowledge has been rapidly accelerating, especially in the last few decades. Experts estimate that our knowledge is doubling about every ten years.

Our connectivity has expanded with the telegraph, telephone, radio, television, fax machines and the Internet. The computer and the Internet have increasingly allowed us to avoid duplicating knowledge. Now we can avoid searching, researching, inventing, and developing ideas that are available elsewhere within our company, government, organization or the entire base of human knowledge.

This increase in our knowledge has resulted in a doubling of human longevity, although the benefit is unevenly enjoyed around the world. For many of us and in many ways, life is easier than it used to be, from health to recreation to travel to the valuable time saved by modern home appliances. Formerly extremely poor nations, such as China and India, are making giant strides in advancing beyond their past states of abject poverty.

Beyond knowledge comes imagination. Albert Einstein said, "Imagination is more important than knowledge." I firmly concur with this giant thinker's opinion.

What does our enormous capacity for knowledge and imagination mean to a heaven on earth? These two basic ingredients can allow us to progress, but they in themselves are not enough. I deeply believe that since the dawn of humankind each of us and all of us have a little piece of God within us that goes beyond our human knowledge and imagination. Expressed another way, there's a hero inside each of us and all of us. We are made up of mind, body and spirit, with spirit being another way of identifying that little piece of God. Our knowledge, imagination and our little piece of God combined with God Almighty's support will carry us to a heaven on earth.

I believe that God has always intended that humankind achieve a heaven on earth, with the necessary help of His enduring, steadfast love. All the great religions of the world teach the Golden Rule, to "Do unto others as we would have them do unto us." Let us build on that.

The ten elements that I believe are essential to our achieving a heaven on earth are:

1. Peace
2. Security
3. Freedom
4. Democracies
5. Prosperity
6. Spiritual Harmony
7. Racial Harmony
8. Ecological Harmony
9. Health
10. Moral Purpose and Meaning (doing the right thing with regard to word and deed)

Peace: The major keys to peace lie in our ability to prosper and spread democracies worldwide. Going beyond toleration to respect of all loving faiths is also critical. Advancing to general acceptance and appreciation across racial lines will build peace within and between nations.

The lessons of Afghanistan and Iraq, not to mention World War II, show the extreme burden in spreading democracies through military action. As you will see from Michael N. Nagler's and Rodolphe Adada's essays herein, Mahatma Gandhi's methods of nonviolent actions coupled with a more effective utilization of the United Nations can allow us to proceed along a nonviolent path that will be far superior to combat.

In the short to intermediate term, the United States must maintain its military strength, especially to help stop genocide anywhere and aggression by non-democratic nations such as North Korea.

The good news lies in the long term, as the entire globe becomes more integrated on a wholesome economic basis and as governments evolve into stable democracies.

Security: We must strive to gain security from terrorism and crime. It is critical that we stop radical Islamics. History is replete with fanatics such as Hitler who somehow gain power with genocide and aggression. Recognizing the danger and acting internationally through winning minds and hearts without letting up on international pressure are essential to a victory over terrorism. For example see Paul Marek's powerful essay, "A Look at Radical Islam" and James K. Glassman's persuasive contribution, "How to Win the War of Ideas."

Legalizing forbidden drugs can rid us of the failures of Prohibition II including extensive national and international crime. See Walter Wink's essay summarizing this serious problem and a critical part of its solution.

Freedom: Freedom is prized by all humans whether they currently possess it or not. Implicit in the democratic ideal is that free individuals will generally act in their own best interests. And the sum of a free society's actions will allow a greater whole than with nations who repress its people.

We must be careful in exercising our freedom. Consider Chef Paul Prudhomme's essay, "The Lost Art of Family Meals." We must also cherish our freedom as shown by three other essays that examine various aspects of human freedom or the lack thereof. "Undivided Hearts" by Debra Rosenman even addresses the imprisonment of chimpanzees along with a more universal concern of all beings on earth.

Democracies: Democracies worldwide in the long run would be the best kind of government for reaching and enjoying a heaven on earth, for they empower the individual and ultimately societies to make good choices. History has shown that democratic governments are less likely to make war with one another. Additionally, they discourage tyrants who are corrupted by power. Democracies provide for the orderly transfer of power. However, we must realize that elections don't necessarily produce the best leader in every case.

Education and economic well-being lay the groundwork for stable, successful democracies. Democracies thrive with wise, capable and honest leaders as well as citizens who recognize the optimum balance of capitalism tempered with democracy.

Prosperity: Capitalism tempered with democracy and free, fair trade can lead to worldwide growth and wealth, which can benefit each of us and all of us to the degree that our own talents and resources permit. Preparation and opportunity go hand in hand with self-discipline and hard work. Each of us must strive for financial literacy and make it our business to know what we own. We have a responsibility beyond ourselves in our wealth. We are not meant to love money, but to treat it with respect and be generous toward worthy ends.

Education, the rule of law, and prudent, simple tax laws encourage prosperity. Effective, honest and stable governments also promote prosperity. Each democracy can decide on its own form of economic safety nets.

In this section Alice Schroeder presents "10 Ways to Get Rich—On Warren Buffett," which goes all the way from methods to gain a fortune to philanthropy after achieving it.

I believe that a heaven on earth will still find us with varying degrees of personal wealth, yet all will have their basic needs fulfilled. Poverty will no longer exist. Each of us and all of us will be grateful for what God entrusts to us.

Spiritual Harmony: We must move beyond religious tolerance to real respect among all the world's loving spiritual beliefs and practices. Even differing beliefs can lead to similar values, which in turn may lead to behavior that is acceptable to God. Loving religions teach us how to live our lives and how to cope with our own mortality. God's enduring, steadfast love will empower us here, just as I firmly believe that love will allow all the other elements.

Chris Beneke's essay demonstrates how George Washington and Benjamin Franklin practiced real religious civility, a discipline which will be needed globally.

Racial Harmony: While the lack of racial harmony goes back to ancient times, that certainly doesn't mean that we can't overcome this obstacle. Our nation has moved forward largely by peaceful means over recent decades, including the election of an African-American president. Many other nations have also advanced in this march toward racial harmony. In our country we owe much of this nonviolent racial progress to Martin Luther King, Jr. See "Where Do We Go From Here?" in that great leader's own words. The Golden Rule is especially important in treating others with respect.

Ecological Harmony: We must tend to the world's God-given environment—emphasizing natural beauty and perpetual conservation. Concurrently, we must achieve a balance between those worthy goals and the necessity of rescuing those in abject poverty as well as maintaining all nations' economic progress.

Examples in this section include excerpts from Al Gore's Nobel Peace Prize acceptance speech concerning global warming; Michael Gerson's essay about the Prince of Wales' pioneering ecological awareness and earth-friendly practices on his country estate; and "Superstar Brad Pitt Makes It Right" by Renée Peck lauding a charity in the process of constructing futuristic homes for those displaced by Hurricane Katrina.

Health: Technology and medical science are vital to advance the health of the world's population. Additionally, our own physical, mental and spiritual habits must embody disciplines that promote good health. Death is inevitable until God acts to prevent it, but wholesome, active behavior can result in longer and longer lives as medical science, our habits and economic means progress.

The quality of our well-being will eventually be assured not by inefficient and ineffective government programs, but rather by rewarding and continuing relationships between health providers and patients.

Topics presented in this section include emotional healing, the actual health benefits of satisfying sex, and even the possibility of death because of the lack of dental care.

Moral Purpose and Meaning: Moral purpose and meaning is perhaps the hardest element to achieve. We do not always do the right thing day by day. Our DNA and environments are not perfect. We have weaknesses that can result in horrors such as the Holocaust. But our flaws do not mean that a nurturing environment can't lead to success after success until God finally takes over and pulls us out of the misery of our human condition. Examples in this area include Emilie Griffin's essay about Mother Teresa and William Griffin's essay concerning Billy Graham.

Many of the essays, speeches and articles in this book provide practical and useful ways to achieve the above elements, whereas others are more general in nature. But all the contributions reach toward an optimistic, positive outcome. Prior to assuming the presidency, President-elect Obama wrote about his dreams for his presidency. President Bush's presentation described the inspiration he experienced during 2007 from the examples of five outstanding people. One of the most critical aims of this book is to get away from the "noise" in the world, especially the unrealistic pessimism and cynicism that pervade the media.

The whole is greater than the sum of its parts. This applies to all parts of this book including this Preface, the essays, speeches and articles as well as Appendix A and the Additional Reading List. This concept also encompasses each and every life as we strive for one awesome human village. Of course, we will never completely reach our supreme fulfillment until God intervenes.

When I started this quest to seek guidance from others about how to achieve a heaven on earth, I was thinking in terms of each of us and all of us, the whole of humankind. Yet as the essays came in, I realized that it has been and is quite possible to achieve a heaven on earth individually. Thus, in the past and present, many may have essentially attained a heaven on earth in mind, body and spirit.

That does not mean that we can achieve perfection, but rather something spiritual and meaningful that approaches a joyful, contented state, full of purpose. We can't be self-absorbed and do the right thing in word and deed at the same time, and it is doubtful that we could achieve inner peace while ignoring the needs of others anyway. Each of us needs food, shelter, health care, education and certain other basic necessities. Beyond that, much of life can be an unsatisfying accumulation of "things" if we are not grateful to our Maker and don't give back to others.

I believe the above ten elements and the individual paths to a heaven on earth apply to each one of us as well as all of humankind. This book is meant to engender serious thinking about how humankind can do our part to achieve a heaven on earth. If we don't have a worthwhile and definite destination in mind, it is highly questionable that we will ever be able to reach it.

Humankind must reach out for our ultimate destiny. Each of us and all of us must pledge "I will try to love and help create a heaven on earth." We must also seek to implement the ten elements for all of humankind. A heaven on earth. I invite you to think about it, imagine it, dream about it, pray about it, and, ultimately do something to bring it about.

Love to Within, Love to Without, God's Enduring, Steadfast Love to Within and Without

John E. Wade II
Editor

Acknowledgments

First I want to thank the authors who contributed essays, speeches or articles to this ambitious undertaking. Many may have been surprised by or skeptical of a book seeking to achieve a heaven on earth. Yet they were daring enough and of sufficient talent to provide the wonderful pieces within this book. Again, thank you authors, one and all.

I have deep gratitude for my assistant editor, Patricia Livingston. I first started writing about a heaven on earth in the year 2000 on a trip with other Presbyterians to the Holy Land. I met Patricia on that trip and she became not only my editor, but my friend. She edited my book *Deep Within My Heart* which included my account of that trip. As I wrote more and more unpublished essays she kept asking me how humankind could attain a heaven on earth. We worked together to assemble this answer for all. Patricia is an accomplished writer in her own right. She has written a column, "Uptown Line," in *The Times-Picayune* for over twenty years, and contributed the chapter on trout amandine to *New Orleans Cuisine*, published in the spring of 2009. Whatever credit we receive from this book should certainly be shared with her.

Bond PR & Brand Strategy has also enabled this journey. Lauren Lagarde has devoted great effort in promoting the concept to potential contributors. Lauren, Jennifer Bond, Skipper Bond, Ashley Davis, Suzanne Anderson, Jamie Langley, Mathew Bowes, Casey O'Connell and Whitney Plaeger were all instrumental in some phase of researching for potential authors, contacting them and doing many of the logistical matters necessary to assemble these pieces.

Our copyeditor, Marion Stafford, has been a true professional, and I certainly appreciate her fine work.

International Strategy Group, LLC, and especially Suman Naresh have provided intellectual property advice and general guidance from the concept of the book to the negotiations of the book contract.

Pelican Publishing Company has stood behind us throughout the prepublication stages, and I look forward to a long and productive relationship with them. Dr. Milburn Calhoun, the publisher, possesses both intellect and character. Editor in Chief Nina Kooij and Dr. Calhoun's daughter, Kathleen Nettleton, have also helped our book team along the way.

While the spiritual beliefs of some members of St. Charles Avenue Presbyterian Church may not coincide precisely with my own, the clergy, staff and congregation have furnished valuable spiritual food to me through good and bad times.

John E. Wade II

Introduction

... for God, all things are possible.
—Matthew 19:26

"... for God, all things are possible."
Matthew 19:26

By Donald R. Frampton

"I am about to do a new thing; now it springs forth, do you not perceive it?" (Isaiah 43:19)

History is replete with stories of tragedy and disaster. It is particular news to no one that human life necessarily means times of sorrow and joy, failure and success, bitter disappointment and jubilant accomplishment. The biblical poet is at his philosophical best in describing life not as an "either/or," but a "both/and" proposition: "For everything there is a season, and a time for every matter under heaven: a time to plant, and a time to pluck up what is planted . . . a time to break down and a time to build up . . . a time to weep, and a time to laugh. . . ." (Ecclesiastes 3)

The rain falls on the good and the evil, every generation of philosophers has concluded.

"That's life," we, the heirs of this age-old wisdom, have thus learned to say. Laws of nature do not treat everyone alike, nor do they make exceptions for good, as opposed to evil, people.

But simple stoicism in the wake of catastrophe is never the answer, for such only adds insult to the injury of life's tragedies. When "life happens," what matters most is not how we act, but how we *react*.

Hurricane Katrina was a killer storm in every sense. People not only lost their homes, their communities, and their livelihoods; some 1400 persons perished in its deadly waters. The general population remained in various places of exile for nearly two months until it was safe to return. Now, a year and a half after the storm, the city is less than half its pre-Katrina size with the overall situation being too daunting, too depressing, to justify re-establishing roots.

Others, however, remain—have chosen to remain—seeing in the storm's deadly aftermath not the end, but a possible new beginning. Such is the case of the church I serve as senior pastor, a dedicated congregation of folk whose reaction to Katrina was fundamentally shaped by its Christian identity—children of a loving God and disciples of a gracious Lord. Because of our faith, we have been able to hear, even in the cacophony of voices of gloom, God's clear voice of promise and new power—the God who "makes all things new."

Katrina actually gave us new purpose. We fed, clothed, and housed. We cleared and cleaned, and gutted and gutted and gutted. Recently we shifted into building new housing.

And what have we seen for our efforts? Each day, we see God's "new thing" in floor joists, and siding, and fresh landscaping. Each day we see God's "new thing" in the faces of incredibly kind and generous volunteers from all over the country who, van by van, come to our city for an entire week. Each day we see God's "new thing" in the tears and laughter and joy of once hopeless citizens as they watch their new homes going up right before their eyes.

But more than this, every day that we rip out moldy walls or nail down new plywood flooring, we are able to see God's "new thing" reflected in our own faces. In the corporate face of an erstwhile ordinary church now transformed into a full-blown mission center, we see the face of God.

All things are possible for this God, we would testify, the One whom we worship and adore, and who, through us, gives us the power to make all things new.

Katrina was one of the most devastating natural disasters ever to affect the United States. At the same time, however, it has taught us about a God who teaches us never to lose hope—a powerful, providential God who made heaven and earth, and who plainly, plainly is still about the business of making all things new.

Don Frampton, senior pastor at St. Charles Avenue Presbyterian Church in New Orleans, Louisiana, is the son of a Presbyterian minister. In 1975 he received a B.A. in history with a minor in religion at the University of South Carolina. He was elected the National Undergraduate Chairman of Kappa Alpha Order and was active in fraternity affairs.

Dr. Frampton received his D. Min. degree from Columbia Theological Seminary with a faculty prize for biblical scholarship. He has served three Presbyterian churches with outstanding achievements in invoking membership and stewardship as well as community and international benevolences. His church and civic leadership during the aftermath of Hurricane Katrina has been inspiring to many in and beyond St. Charles Avenue Presbyterian Church.

HOW TO ACHIEVE
A HEAVEN
ON EARTH

Peace

It is good that war is so horrible, or we might grow to like it.

—Robert E. Lee

The Role of Faith in World Peace

By Tony Blair

Adapted from Tony Blair's talk at the launch of the Tony Blair
Faith Foundation at the Time Warner Center, New York City, on
Friday, May 30, 2008. © 2008 The Tony Blair Faith Foundation.
All Rights Reserved. Used by Permission of The Tony Blair Faith
Foundation.

Today we launch the first of a series of partnerships to put into
effect the purpose of the Tony Blair Faith Foundation—to bring
dialog among the six leading faiths: Christian, Muslim, Hindu,
Buddhist, Sikh and Jewish.

The world is undergoing tumultuous change. Globalisation,
underpinned by technology, is driving much of it, breaking down
boundaries, altering the composition of whole communities, even
countries, and creating circumstances in which new challenges
arise that can only be met effectively together. Interdependence
is now the recognised human condition.

The characteristic of today's world is change. The consequence
is a world opening up, becoming interdependent. We must make
sense of this interdependence through peaceful co-existence and
working together to resolve common challenges, requiring an
emotional as well as an intellectual response consistent with the
conclusion that we are members of a global community as well as
individual nations. We must be global citizens as well as citizens
of our own country.

All this sounds impossibly idealistic, but if the analysis of the
nature of the world is as I believe, it is in fact the only practical
way to organise our affairs. Idealism becomes the new realism.
This is especially so since the world is changing in other ways

too—power and the centre of political interest are shifting east. The emergence of China and India has been obvious for years with practical impact on our lives.

Consider an institution like the G7, how different it and its membership would be if it were invented today. We must come to terms with the new reality, for the twentieth century is history. Into this new world comes the force of religious faith. I quote from recent Gallup polls, which indicate that most Christians want better relations between Christianity and Islam but believe most Muslims don't. Most Muslims want better relations but believe most Christians don't. Most Americans think most Muslims do not accept other religions. Actually most Muslims say they want greater and not lesser interaction between religions.

In answer to the question: "Is religion an important part of your life," many Muslim countries' citizens answer in the high eighties or nineties as a percentage; in the US it is around seventy percent; in the UK and mainland Europe it is under forty percent. Interestingly, though, even in the UK over a third of people say it is important.

Religion matters and there is a lot of fear among the faiths, but you cannot understand the modern world unless you understand the importance of religious faith. Faith motivates, galvanises, organises and integrates millions upon millions of people. Yet globalisation is pushing people together. Interdependence is reality. Peaceful co-existence is essential. If faith becomes a countervailing force, pulling people apart, it becomes destructive and dangerous. But if it becomes an instrument of peaceful co-existence, teaching people to live with difference, to treat diversity as a strength, to respect "the other," then faith becomes an important part of making the twenty-first century work. It enriches, it informs, it provides a common basis of values and belief for people to get along together.

Even if I had no faith, I would still believe in the central necessity of people of faith learning to live with each other in mutual respect and peace.

There are many excellent meetings, convocations, conferences and organisations that work in the inter-faith area. We do not want to replicate what they do. We do not want to engage in a doctrinal inquiry, or to subsume different faiths in one faith of the lowest common denominator. We want to show faith in action, produce greater understanding among faiths, for people of one faith to be comfortable with those of another because they know what they truly believe, not what they thought they might believe.

The Foundation has four specific goals. First, the Foundation aims to educate. We begin today with the association with Yale University's School of Divinity and School of Management, which will help design a new three-year course called "Faith and Globalisation." I will lead a series of seminars each fall, starting in September 2008. The idea is to create a course which can become an enduring part of Yale's teaching, can be spun off to other universities in different parts of the globe, and can stimulate original research and be a resource for those working in this field.

Secondly, we are announcing the first of our partnerships to mobilise those of faith in pursuit of the UN's Millennium Development Goals. We call on the four billion people of faith in the world to help do more to end the scourge of malaria that has killed so many millions and will kill many more unless eradicated. We are joining with the Malaria No More Campaign, a wonderful organisation whose mission is to end death through malaria in the next five to ten years. The solution lies in distributing bed nets and medicines. The resources are becoming available. But the need to get the bed nets and medicines to the people and see them properly used is where the faiths, who are present in each of the affected communities, can help. Our purpose will be to help mobilise the different faiths in pursuit of this goal.

Thirdly, we believe that inter-faith interaction can benefit from a physical structure to which people can come, to learn, to discuss and to contemplate. We have agreed to partner the proposal initiated by the Co-Exist Foundation to establish Abraham House in London. Though expressly about the Abrahamic faiths, it will be open to those from the wider faith community. It will be a standing exhibition, library and convention centre for the inter-faith world. The extraordinary success of the "Sacred Texts" exhibition at the British Library last year shows the potential for such an initiative.

Finally, we will help organisations whose object is to counter extremism and promote reconciliation in matters of religious faith. Though there is much focus, understandably, on extremism associated with the perversion of the proper faith of Islam, there are elements of extremism in every major faith. It is important where people of good faith combat such extremism, that they are supported.

This is a century rich in potential to solve problems, to provide prosperity to all, to overcome longstanding issues of injustice that previously we could not surmount. But it only works if the values which inform the change are values that unify and do not divide. Religious faith has a profound role to play.

The Right Honorable Charles Lynton "Tony" Blair was Prime Minister of the United Kingdom from 1997 to 2007, the longest-serving Labour Prime Minister. A graduate of St. John's College at Oxford University, he is trained as a lawyer, and upon stepping down as Prime Minister was appointed Middle East envoy to the United Nations, the European Union, the United States and Russia.

The Economics of Peace and Prosperity

By Sir Clive W. J. Granger

There are several types of war and consequently several types of peace. With regard to wars, the simplest division is between "internal" and "external." An internal war is fought, at least partially, within the boundary of the nation, whereas an external war consists of sending troops or some parts of the armed forces to another country.

The Internet lists 175 wars between January of 1945 and March of 2008, each of which is internal for some country and possibly for several. Some, but not all, of those wars also are external for one or several countries.

Generally internal wars will have much greater impact on the economy than will external wars, if one considers the usual measures of production, consumption, inflation and employment. An external war's effect on the economy could actually be a boost to the general economy for a few years, unless and until the cost of the war becomes excessive.

The economics during the peace period after the end of a war depends on the type of war. After an internal war the first few years can be difficult economically unless other countries are generous, as happened with the Marshall Plan after World War II.

The peace period after the end of an external war should be one of gentle recovery for the economy. During any kind of war the uncertainty level, connected with risks, is high, which can be linked with investments in high return projects usually associated with higher interest rates. In contrast, during periods of peace, risks should be lower and projects that give lower returns over long periods of time should also become attractive. Such projects should also be associated with lower risk and lower interest rates.

However, the present structure of the government links the control of inflation with changes in interest rates which are controlled by a government agency. It follows, therefore, that interest rates do not fluctuate from war to peace quite as well.

In any postwar period there will be a variety of economic transitions. Unemployment is usually low during a war but can be much higher in the period immediately after a war, and can fluctuate widely during periods of peace. Gross national product growth can be fairly high during a war because of government investment, and should be steady during a period of peace, provided there is political stability and no difficulties for trading partners.

The happiest and most economically successful countries usually have long periods of peace and stable governments; examples of which are the Scandinavian countries, Switzerland, New Zealand and Australia. All have high or very high standards of living. It is possible for some people to move from a country with an internal conflict and fairly low growth rates to one with no conflict and an exceptionally high growth rate. Ireland is such an example; the removal of the Irish Republican Army (IRA) threat together with its location with the European Union, far-sighted tax rules, and the decline in the importance of the Catholic Church have produced a noteworthy economic improvement.

Individuals do not seek peace primarily for economic reasons, but rather for the safety of their families and their society. But peace can also produce a stable economic environment that enables standards of living to improve steadily. The complicated relationship between peace and various aspects of the economy needs to be studied further.

While world powers, academics and economists examine and attempt to solve these problems, what can the rest of humankind do? Keep as well informed as possible, and let our leaders know our concern. Push them to make good decisions, not for their own self-interest, but on behalf of all of us. Involve everyone you know in the cause of peace and economic stability, and never lose sight of the goal.

Welsh economist Sir Clive W. J. Granger, who died in May 2009, was Professor Emeritus at the University of California, San Diego, where he taught from 1974 to 2003. He was previously on the faculty at the University of Nottingham, 1956 to 1973, where he earned his doctorate and where the building that houses the School of Economics and the School of Geography is named for him. He wrote numerous books on economics and shared the 2003 Nobel Memorial Prize in economic sciences.

Democracy and Peace

By Dan Reiter

Sometimes good things do not go together. Eating donuts does not help you lose weight. Other times, good things do go together. Eating chocolate and drinking red wine can make your heart healthier. In international politics, democracy and peace are two good things that go together. Democracies are very unlikely to fight each other, and the spread of democracy can foster global peace.

The pacifism of democracies is an old idea. Thinkers as far back as the eighteenth-century Prussian philosopher Immanuel Kant have observed that democracies do not fight each other. President Woodrow Wilson supported the United States' entry into World War I because "the world must be made safe for democracy," and democracy in turn would guarantee world peace. President Bill Clinton focused on spreading democracy in the 1990s through expansion of the North Atlantic Treaty Organization and other policies to build a more stable global order.

Why are democracies more peaceful? The most important reason is that citizens hate war because they, rather than their leaders, pay the costs of fighting, in higher taxes as well as spilled blood. If a country's leadership is made answerable to the people through regular, competitive elections, then that leadership will be less likely to launch wars and risk being removed from power by an angry electorate. Conversely, dictators are confident they will not lose power even after starting bloody military ventures. Saddam Hussein kept power even after launching disastrous invasions of Iran and Kuwait. Democracies are also good about establishing international networks that help sustain peace. Democracies join international organizations such as the European Union and the

World Trade Organization. They invest in international trade, and when goods cross borders armies are less likely to. Democracies are more likely to employ international law and mediation to resolve disputes.

There are almost no examples in recorded history of true democracies fighting each other, the 1999 India-Pakistan Kargil War being perhaps the best exception. Moreover, statistical studies have shown that the democracy-peace relationship holds up even after accounting for potentially confounding factors such as trade, geography, military alliances and military power.

The most important foreign policy successes of the twentieth century are closely tied to the spread of democracy. The imposition of democracy on Japan, Germany and Italy after 1945 rapidly turned those imperialist warmongers into peaceful, prosperous and law-abiding members of the international order. More broadly, the spread of democracy in Europe after World War II transformed that region from the world's most war-prone continent into a zone of peace.

That being said, there are two important caveats to this otherwise happy story. First, though democracies do not fight each other, they do fight countries that are not democratic. Democracies such as the United States, the United Kingdom, India and Israel have fought many wars since 1945 against non-democracies, such as North Korea, China, North Vietnam, Iraq, Afghanistan, Pakistan (under dictatorship), Egypt, Syria, Jordan and Argentina. One solution to this problem of democracies fighting non-democracies is to make entire regions democratic, as has been achieved in the past few years in Europe and the Americas. A democracy is generally less likely to go to war if all of its neighbors are democratic, as in Europe, than if it is a lone democracy surrounded by authoritarian neighbors, as is the case for Israel.

Second, though achieving democracy may be desirable, creating robust and enduring democratic institutions is difficult. Though democracy thrived in Germany after World War II, it collapsed in Germany following World War I as Adolf Hitler rose to power. President George W. Bush had grand hopes that installing democracy in Afghanistan and Iraq would transform the Middle East, but, at least as of this writing, robust, stable, and mature democracy seems a remote ideal in both countries. A pressing priority for the global policy community is to identify effective, low-cost tools for spreading democracy around the world.

Sometimes we do not have to choose between virtues. We can be comforted to know that nurturing freedom can also spread peace.

Dan Reiter, PhD, is a professor in and chairman of Emory University's department of political science. He is the author of Crucible of Beliefs: Learning, Alliances, and World Wars; How Wars End; *and coauthor of* Democracies at War.

The Quest for Peace in the Global Village

By Thomas R. McFaul

News Flash: Religion Is Driving the World Toward Global Catastrophe!

In the wake of the destruction of New York's World Trade Towers on September 11, 2001, alarmist images of pending chaos sparked by religious hatreds jumped off the front pages of daily newspapers and circled the planet through instant Internet communication. Anyone who has made even a cursory observation of public events during the past decade might quickly conclude that growing animosity among the followers of the world's diverse religions is an irreversible global trend.

However, this is not the case. Below the flashy headlines, at a deeper level the leaders of the world's religions are searching for ways to overcome their differences and heal a divided planet. All of the elements are in place to move the earth's spiritual communities in the direction of achieving greater moral purpose and meaning, harmony, democracy and long-term security. Underneath the surface of everyday impressions lies one of the world's major long-term macro-trends that is steering the planet toward peaceful solidarity. The signs are readily visible.

For example, prior to the emergence of worldwide electronic communication and mass transportation structures, wide oceans and high mountains isolated the diverse peoples of the planet from each other. This is no longer the case. In the emerging global village, it is not isolation but the deepening interpenetration of pluralistic populations that is the name of the game. In other words, what it genuinely new is that for the first time in human evolution there exists a worldwide technical framework for the creation of a genuinely peaceful planet.

This process of planetary evolution toward peace has been, as the saying goes, a long time "a-comin'." During the past 5,000 years of human history, the earth has been evolving through stages that began with thousands of small and splintered tribes to ever larger and more encompassing social groupings. War and conquest often served as a central driving force that brought together once divided peoples. By the end of the nineteenth century and throughout the twentieth, for the first time the signs of the search for global unity began to emerge.

Many of the leaders of the world's diverse spiritual traditions played a central role in this process. This quest began in earnest in 1893 with the first international assembly in Chicago of the Parliament of the World's Religions. Conference participants gathered to identify ways to overcome their centuries-old divisions and to develop a vision of global unity. Subsequently, many worldwide gatherings emerged out of this initial venture. After World War II, in 1948, the United Nations created the first of many Universal Declarations of Human Rights.

The last two decades of the twentieth century witnessed the development of two important groups, the Institute for Global Ethics and the Center for Global Ethics. Both of these organizations came into existence for one purpose: to identify the common core of human values that can serve as the basis for creating global harmony. Then, in 1993, the Parliament of the World's Religions met to celebrate its one-hundred-year anniversary. Out of this meeting of the world's most important interfaith leaders came one of the most inspiring calls for planetary unity—Toward a Global Ethic—that any worldwide interfaith communion ever created.

The Parliament's vision of global ethics pulls together all of the main spiritual and ethical ideals that various ecumenical and political groups from around the world have been advocating for more than a century. These include the quest for truth, emphasis on kindness, compassion, and the Golden Rule; the search for moral cooperation that sustains harmony, prosperity, security and environmental health; and above all the call for human conduct that is capable of creating and sustaining permanent peace.

Thus, underneath the maze of disconnected day-to-day images, there is ample evidence of a growing worldwide trend toward interfaith cooperation, creating the spiritual and ethical foundation for a lasting peace that will spread throughout the emerging global village. As this movement goes forward into the future, the diverse peoples of the planet will bring heaven closer to earth.

Thomas R. McFaul is professor emeritus in ethics and religious studies at North Central College in Naperville, Illinois. His most recent book is The Future of Peace and Justice in the Global Village: The Role of the World Religions in the Twenty-first Century.

The Way Out:
Gandhi's History and Our Future

By Michael N. Nagler

I want to live in a world—and I am sure you do also—where no woman is trafficked, no child abused, no one imprisoned for his or her beliefs, where crime is almost a thing of the past; a world where most people, especially world leaders, avoid conflicts or solve them with maturity and compassion where they still occur.

I firmly believe that it is possible to build such a world. In fact, Mahatma Gandhi laid out its essential structure. He did not make it easy to follow—no one can do that—but in his fifty years of "experiments with truth," backed by the astonishing success of his struggle against the most powerful empire the world had ever seen, he showed that it could work. It is only because he was so far ahead of his time that so few of us understand this. And that is what we have to change.

Gandhi made the bold claim that "Nonviolence is the greatest force at the disposal of mankind. It is greater than the mightiest weapon devised by the ingenuity of man." Can this be true?

In 2002 the Gujarat Riots broke out in India where, as the mainstream media reported, Hindu mobs fell upon villages and indiscriminately murdered Muslims. This is partly true. But what the media did not tell us is that in more than one case Hindu women brought their Muslim neighbors into their homes to protect them, and some of these women calmly told the enraged rioters, "If you want my neighbor you'll have to kill me first." In the face of that courage, the mob melted away, their violence no match for these acts of truth. Many men were saved, not just in one village, but the district.

We who work in nonviolence often hear, "Oh yes, but it would never have worked against the Nazis," but even this is wrong.

In 1943, in Berlin, when the Gestapo rounded up the remaining Jewish men who had thus far been spared because they had non-Jewish wives, those wives, daughters and mothers spontaneously gathered at the prison and refused to go away without their men. In the course of three days, the Gestapo blinked and set them free.

These were spontaneous, unplanned actions that had no outside support any more than the participants themselves had previous training. Imagine what we could do if we trained and supported people who had the courage to use this power!

In fact, this is slowly happening. New institutions are springing up, like Nonviolent Peaceforce, that puts trained teams into conflict zones like Sri Lanka, and the Center for Advanced Nonviolent Actions and Strategies, that takes experienced activists from successful uprisings—particularly the overthrow of dictator Slobodan Milošević in 2000—and teaches other freedom-seekers around the world what works. The astonishing fact is that over half the world lives in a state that has experienced some kind of major nonviolent action in the last half century or so. The overwhelming majority of these uprisings—Serbia in 2000, Madagascar in 2002, Georgia in 2003, Ukraine in 2004 and 2005, Lebanon in 2005, and Nepal in 2006—succeeded.

Would nonviolent uprisings be enough to bring in the kind of world you and I long for? No, but Gandhi's experiments covered much more. In addition to nonviolent resistance, or Satyagraha, he instituted his Constructive Programme, an ambitious set of eighteen projects that were designed to rebuild Indian society along lines of sustainability and justice. Here, too, he scored considerable success, not only making it easier to get the British to leave but to forestall the backsliding into disorder and corruption that has often followed an otherwise successful insurrection.

What's more, a spiritual renewal was implicit in everything Gandhi thought, said and did, laying the groundwork for a new value system that could elevate the vision of humankind. For without that renewal even an overhaul of our institutions and a widespread introduction of nonviolent methods—both urgently needed—would not bring us a secure, sustainable state. This alone gives us, as I like to put it, "not so much a different kind of people in power as a different kind of power in people." And

Martin Luther King would add, "We must rapidly begin the shift from a 'thing-oriented' society to a 'person-oriented' society."

If we want the kind of world these great men strove for, this is the job we must undertake, with all the dedication and urgency we can muster.

Michael Nagler is professor emeritus at the University of California, Berkeley, where he founded the Peace and Conflict Studies Program and developed its courses in nonviolence and meditation. He is the author of The Search for a Nonviolent Future *and many other works, and president of the Metta Center for Nonviolence Education in Berkeley.*

The UN Is Making a Difference in Darfur

By Rodolphe Adada

Republished with permission of Dow Jones & Company, Inc., from *The Wall Street Journal,* "The UN Is Making a Difference in Darfur," Rodolphe Adada, 2008; permission conveyed through Copyright Clearance Center, Inc.

Editor's note: Many have maligned the United Nations as being a toothless tiger, able to roar but too feeble to put into action any aspect of its noble cause—world peace. We thought this thoughtful comment, by one who has seen the UN in action, has a place in the dialog.

AL FASHER, DARFUR A delegation from the United Nations Security Council recently witnessed the challenges facing the African Union/UN operation in Darfur (Unamid). We are missing forces and the equipment needed to sustain them. Our mandated strength is 26,000, yet six months into our deployment we stand at less than 10,000. We are working to build the infrastructure needed to cope with our increasing troop strength. Our plan is ambitious: We aim to have deployed eighty percent of our forces by the end of the year.

We are not sitting on our hands waiting for the troops and materiel to arrive. I am proud of my peacekeeping forces who risk their lives daily to fulfill our mandate to protect civilians, improve security, facilitate humanitarian aid, and engage the parties to this conflict. Every day our blue-helmeted peacekeepers carry out patrols right across Darfur, an area the size of Texas. They defend thousands of innocent Darfurians, such as women from the camps gathering firewood to cook meals for their families.

47

One of the most disgusting aspects of this conflict has been the widespread rape of women by armed thugs on all sides. Unamid is carrying out more and more night patrols to increase this protection around the clock.

Critics say we are hunkered down, yet the facts speak for themselves: In January, when our mission began, we carried out 271 patrols. Last month, it was 644, or more than 20 a day. Our peacekeepers intervene on a daily basis across the length and breadth of Darfur to calm tensions arising from cattle losses, water distribution and land ownership—issues at the heart of the conflict. These missions are critical, successful and welcomed by Darfurians, but they do not make international headlines.

Some of our more impassioned critics call on us to intervene more forcefully. I would remind them that Unamid is a peacekeeping force. We are here to keep a peace that doesn't exist. It is the duty of the belligerents—and there are many—to make peace. As Gen. Martin Luther Agwai, our force commander, stated recently, even if we were at full deployment our peacekeepers are not here to stand between rival armies and militias engaged in full-scale combat.

The rebel movements have fractured into ever greater numbers. The peace process has stalled, and the parties still demonstrate a greater readiness to settle their disputes with guns than around the negotiating table. Whatever anyone tells you, there is no simple solution to Darfur. Still, we are engaging all parties. The imminent appointment of a new mediator will give renewed vigor to this process.

The word Darfur may conjure up uniform images of misery and insecurity. In fact, it's a patchwork of different situations. There are many areas, such as swaths of North Darfur, which are relatively secure. We are determined to reinforce these gains. In other locations, such as parts of South Darfur, lawlessness and violence remain the order of the day, and we are acting there to calm tensions. Finally, there are some areas, particularly in West Darfur close to the Chad border, that are conflict zones. Here we continue to protect civilians and engage all parties.

In addition to helping to end the suffering of the last five years, Unamid represents a giant step forward for the African Union on the international stage, and an expression of the desire for

African solutions for African problems. It is the first time the AU has partnered with the UN in what is destined to be the largest peacekeeping operation in the world. It cannot afford to fail. As I stressed to the Security Council members during their visit, patience is running thin here and local trust—essential for our mission to succeed—is on the line.

We will work to empower civil society, because the best hopes for peace lie with the traditional tribal leadership. We will expect the government in Khartoum to honor its responsibilities to protect all the citizens of Sudan, and to cooperate fully with Unamid. We will engage the movements, pushing them to commit to a peaceful settlement. Finally, we will encourage the international community to demonstrate equal resolve. Together we can make a difference to the millions of ordinary, peace-seeking Darfurians. Here on the ground we have the resolution to succeed.

Rodolphe Adada, a former foreign minister of the Republic of Congo, is now the Joint Special Representative of Unamid.

The Lessons of Hiroshima

By Ted Turner

Speech delivered at the Peace Memorial Museum, Hiroshima, October 28, 2006. © 2006 R. E. Turner. All Rights Reserved. Used by Permission of R. E. Turner.

To all my friends from Hiroshima—thank you for your kind welcome. I am overwhelmed by your hospitality, and by everything I have seen, in this park and in the museum. I especially want to express my heartfelt respect to the Hiroshima survivors. On that day more than six decades ago, your world was blasted to ashes at 8:15 in the morning. Many lost family members immediately. Some lost them slowly in the weeks and months and years after. But the people of Hiroshima carried on—and you embraced the duty conferred on you—to bear personal witness to the horrifying destructive power of nuclear weapons. You've dedicated your lives so that others will not suffer.

Most important, and most amazing, you have borne witness to this horror with love in your hearts and without vengeance. That love for others is at the heart of every great religious teaching. The Buddha said: "For never does hatred by hatred cease: hatred ceases by love alone; this is an eternal law." This compassion you have shown for other human beings makes your message all the more powerful and inspiring, and it is a message many of us are still learning from.

When I was a young man, my heroes were Alexander the Great and Horatio Nelson. I used to have statues of them on my desk. I wanted to be a war hero. But when I got older, I began to feel more and more the love for humanity that you can see here in this park and this museum. I decided I didn't want to be a war

50

hero. I wanted to be a peace hero. And I put Alexander the Great and Horatio Nelson away. In their place on my desk, I put statues of Martin Luther King and Mahatma Gandhi.

I have spent much of my adult life working for peace, and for the elimination of nuclear weapons. Now that I have visited Hiroshima, I can say only that I wish I had started earlier and worked harder.

I have been very fortunate in my life and was able to fulfill so many of my dreams. Except my dream for a world of peace. Nothing is a greater threat to humanity than nuclear weapons. During the cold war—when the United States and the Soviet Union had tens of thousands of nuclear weapons each, I was scared we were going to destroy ourselves, so I did everything I could to help bring peace between the two countries.

When the cold war ended, I was thrilled. Now, I thought, we could dismantle those horrible weapons and get rid of them. When I learned five or six years later that Moscow and Washington still had thousands of weapons on hair-trigger alert, ready to launch within minutes, I was appalled. We placed the very survival of the world at risk by deploying these weapons at the height of the cold war. So why are we running that risk now that the cold war is over?

When I realized the nuclear threat was still a very real possibility, I wanted to do something to make a difference. So I formed the Nuclear Threat Initiative with some of the most talented, accomplished security experts in the world. We are very honored to count Judge Odawa as one of our board members of this initiative. At NTI, we're determined to do everything we can to reduce to zero the chance that nuclear weapons will ever be used again, either by intent or accident.

We have to destroy nuclear weapons—before they destroy us!

Some very good, well-meaning people I know would like a world without nuclear weapons, but they don't think we can get there safely. They think we have to keep some. I disagree. I believe that if less is better, zero is best.

Beyond eliminating nuclear weapons, I think there is much more we must do to create a better, more peaceful and prosperous world. Most importantly, we must strive to instill in all people the values of mutual respect. The day I launched CNN, I said I hoped it would provide "a better understanding of how people from different nations live and work together."

I remember telling the CNN newscasters they were not allowed to use the word "foreign" on the air. The lines that divide countries shouldn't divide people. That word "foreign" makes one country the center of the world, and everyone else an outsider. That's not a respectful way to look at the world. It's all "us" versus "them." When it comes to big problems like nuclear weapons, there is no "them"; there is only "us"—our world, our children, our future, and our choice.

I want to close my remarks today by thanking all of you for inviting me here today. We share the same heart and the same dream. I have heard the voices of Hiroshima. Having visited this sacred site, I want to make a promise to all the citizens of Hiroshima—past and present: I will never stop my work. I will never lose hope. I will never give up the dream that one day—in your memory—we will eliminate nuclear weapons from the face of the earth.

Robert Edward "Ted" Turner III is a media proprietor and philanthropist. As a businessman, he is known as founder of the cable television network CNN, the first dedicated twenty-four-hour cable news channel. In addition, he founded WTBS, which pioneered the superstation concept in cable television.

Security

The superior man, when resting in safety, does not forget that danger may come. When in a state of security he does not forget the possibility of ruin. When all is orderly, he does not forget that disorder may come. Thus his person is not endangered, and his States and all their clans are preserved.

—Confucius

A Look at Radical Islam

By Paul Marek

A man, whose family was part of the German aristocracy prior to World War II, owned a number of large industries and estates. When asked how many German people were true Nazis, the answer he gave can guide our attitude toward fanaticism. "Very few people were true Nazis," he said, "but many enjoyed the return of German pride, and many more were too busy to care. I was one of those who just thought the Nazis were a bunch of fools. So, the majority just sat back and let it all happen. Then, before we knew it, they owned us, and we had lost control, and the end of the world had come. My family lost everything. I ended up in a concentration camp and the Allies destroyed my factories."

We are told again and again by experts and talking heads that Islam is a religion of peace, and that the vast majority of Muslims just want to live in peace. Although this unqualified assertion may be true, it is entirely irrelevant. It is meaningless fluff, meant to make us feel better, and meant to somehow diminish the spectra of fanatics rampaging across the globe in the name of Islam.

The fact is that the fanatics rule Islam at this moment in history. It is the fanatics who march. It is the fanatics who wage any one of fifty shooting wars worldwide. It is the fanatics who systematically slaughter Christian or tribal groups throughout Africa and are gradually taking over the entire continent in an Islamic wave. It is the fanatics who bomb, behead, murder and honor-kill. It is the fanatics who take over mosque after mosque. It is the fanatics who zealously spread the stoning and hanging of rape victims and homosexuals. It is the fanatics who teach their young to kill and to become suicide bombers.

The hard quantifiable fact is that the peaceful majority, the silent majority, is cowed and extraneous. Communist Russia was comprised of Russians who just wanted to live in peace, yet the Russian Communists were responsible for the murder of about twenty million people. The peaceful majority were irrelevant.

China's huge population was peaceful as well, but Chinese Communists managed to kill a staggering seventy million people. The average Japanese individual prior to World War II was not a war-mongering sadist. Yet Japan murdered and slaughtered its way across Southeast Asia in an orgy of killing that included the systematic murder of twelve million Chinese civilians, most killed by sword, shovel and bayonet.

And who can forget Rwanda, which collapsed into butchery? Could it not be said that the majority of Rwandans were peace loving? History lessons are often incredibly simple and blunt, yet for all our powers of reason we often miss the most basic and uncomplicated of points: peace-loving Muslims have been made irrelevant by their silence. Peace-loving Muslims will become our enemy if they don't speak up, because like my friend from Germany, they will awaken one day and find that the fanatics own them, and the end of their world will have begun.

Peace-loving Germans, Japanese, Chinese, Russians, Rwandans, Serbs, Afghans, Iraqis, Palestinians, Somalis, Nigerians, Algerians and many others have died because the peaceful majority did not speak up until it was too late. As for us who watch it all unfold, we must pay attention to the only group that counts: the fanatics who threaten our way of life.

Lastly, anyone who doubts that the issue is serious and just ignores this lesson is contributing to the passiveness that allows the problems to expand. So, extend yourself a bit—pass this message on, and let us hope that thousands worldwide read this and think about it, and act before it's too late.

Paul Marek has been a teacher, freelance writer and owner of a wilderness lodge. He is an educational consultant in Saskatoon, Canada. His lifelong passion is reading, especially history, and most especially about World War II.

Energy and Security Through Fuel Choices

By Gal Luft

Look around you. What do all the cars, trucks, planes and ships you see have in common? They can all run on nothing but petroleum products. Without oil our food cannot travel from farm to plate, our children cannot go to school and our mail cannot reach its destination. Oil has a virtual monopoly over transportation fuels, and since transportation underlies the global economy, oil has a strategic status second to no other commodity. Our dependence on oil would not be a global security problem if not for the fact that most of the world's oil is concentrated in non-democratic countries which often use their control over our fuel supply as a geopolitical weapon while abusing human rights, supporting terrorism, intimidating their neighbors and spreading radical and hostile ideologies.

The world's growing dependence on oil means that, barring a fundamental shift in our transportation sector, in the future the small club of oil-exporting countries will only wield more power while importers will become increasingly impoverished and beholden to the oil cartel. This problem will be most acute in the developing world, where poor and heavily in-debt nations import growing quantities of oil to power their economies. For such countries, the deliberate manipulation of supply by the oil cartel over the past three decades—OPEC accounts for almost eighty percent of oil reserves and yet just forty percent of oil production—has served as a regressive tax which prevents millions from rising from poverty.

To strengthen global security and enable prosperity among the world's poor, we must break the monopoly of oil in the transportation sector and thereby turn oil from a strategic commodity into just another commodity, something that is bought and sold but has readily available substitutes and thus lacks the power to influence global affairs. We can learn from history: years ago salt was a strategic commodity because of its monopoly over food preservation. Alternatives such as canning and refrigeration made salt irrelevant to world affairs.

The easiest way to open the fuel market to competition is to require that new cars be flexible fuel vehicles which can run on any blend of gasoline and a variety of alternative liquid fuels, such as ethanol, methanol, etc., made from a variety of feedstocks, from agricultural material to waste to coal. Flex fuel technology has been available for many decades, and the process is cheap, about a hundred dollars extra per new vehicle.

In Brazil, where more than eighty percent of new cars sold in 2008 were flex fuel vehicles, sugarcane ethanol can compete at the pump against oil. This fuel competition not only enabled Brazil to break the yoke of its oil dependence, but also insulated the country's economy from the pain of the recent spike in global oil prices. In the United States cars have an average street life of sixteen years, which means that the minute you leave the lot, you're signing up for two decades of oil dependence. So let's remember the old saying: when in a hole, stop digging. And stop digging means stop making cars that can run only on oil.

Opening our market to biofuels imported from developing countries has significant geopolitical benefits. Sugar, from which ethanol can be cheaply and efficiently produced, is now grown in one hundred countries, many of which are poor. Encouraging these countries to increase their output and become fuel exporters by removing import tariffs on alternative fuels could have far-reaching implications for their economic development. Deploying flexibly fueled cars could then greatly reduce global poverty.

Electricity, which in most parts of the world is no longer generated from oil, also has great potential to power cars. Electric cars and plug-in hybrids are entering the market, offering people the option to travel on electrons rather than oil. Plug-in hybrids, which have a liquid fuel tank and internal combustion engine in addition to a battery, offer the same range as gasoline cars. Batteries allow us to make most of our daily commute on a charge and plug in our cars at night when electricity is cheaper. By using electricity instead of oil, we shift from an expensive and depleting resource—owned by some of the world's most unsavory regimes—to a clean, affordable, domestically produced and potentially renewable source of power.

If a plug-in hybrid is also a flexible fuel vehicle powered mostly by alternative fuels, oil economy could reach over five hundred miles per gallon of gasoline, with each gallon of gasoline stretched by electricity and non-oil liquid fuels. By opening the fuel market to competition, such cars will break the oil cartel's stronghold over us, ensuring increased prosperity, security and cleaner air for everyone.

Dr. Gal Luft is co-director of the Institute for the Analysis of Global Security and co-founder of the Set America Free Coalition. In 2007, Esquire Magazine *listed him as one of "America's Best and Brightest."*

How to Win the War of Ideas

By James K. Glassman

Republished with permission of Dow Jones & Company, Inc., from *The Wall Street Journal*, "How to Win the War of Ideas," James K. Glassman, 2008; permission conveyed through Copyright Clearance Center, Inc.

Military action against insurgents, terrorists and those who give them safe harbor is essential. It is working now in Iraq, and has helped keep Americans safe since 9/11. But as President Bush's National Strategy for Combating Terrorism put it two years ago, "In the long run, winning the War on Terror means winning the battle of ideas."

Many of the strongest supporters of ideological engagement can be found in the Department of Defense, starting with Secretary Robert Gates, who reminded senators earlier this year that the Cold War was "as much a war of ideas as it was of military power." Unfortunately, since the rise of Islamic terror, we haven't done enough on this front.

That's changing. Throughout the government and the private sector, the war of ideas is in early renaissance. The enthusiasm is bipartisan, and we have the opportunity to leave a robust legacy for the next administration. But what kind of war of ideas will fit the terrorist threat today? First, we need to get the goal straight.

While educational exchanges and other such efforts seek over the long term to encourage foreigners to adopt more generally favorable views of the United States, the war of ideas today should have a different, specific focus. The aim must be to ensure that negative sentiments and day-to-day grievances toward the U.S. and its allies do not manifest themselves in violence. We want to create an environment hostile to violent extremism, especially by severing links between al Qaeda and like-minded groups and their target audiences.

For starters, we should confront the ideology of violent extremism directly. The most credible voices here are those of Muslims themselves—especially Islamists—who have publicly disavowed al Qaeda's methods and theology. Lately such apostates include Sayyid Imam al-Sharif, also known as Dr. Fadl, who laid the foundation for the movement's bloody ideology and has now repudiated it, and Noman Benotman, a Libyan close to Osama bin Laden who rebuked al Qaeda bluntly last year.

Our public diplomacy efforts should encourage Muslims, individuals and groups, to spread the denunciations of violence by these men and others far and wide. But non-Muslim Americans themselves should not shrink from confidently opposing poisonous ideas either.

A second approach to the war of ideas may, in the long run, be even more effective. Call it "diversion." The ideology that motivates al Qaeda and similar groups is based on the notion that believers have a duty to carry out the excommunication (and execution) of unbelievers, or even of those who collaborate with unbelievers or refuse to resist them. This ideology posits a Manichean world, divided into two camps: one practicing the terrorists' version of Islam, the other not.

This is a fantasy, but a distressingly powerful one. Our vision is a pluralistic world with many peaceful and productive choices on how to order one's life. The task is not to persuade potential recruits to become like Americans or Europeans, but to divert them from becoming terrorists.

We do that by helping to build networks (virtual and physical) and countermovements—not just political but cultural, social, athletic and more: mothers against violence, video gamers, soccer enthusiasts, young entrepreneurs, Islamic democrats. For example, there is an emerging global network of families of Islamic victims of terrorist attacks. While winning hearts and minds would be an admirable feat, the war of ideas needs to adopt the more immediate and realistic goal of diverting impressionable segments of the population from being recruited into violent extremism.

Unlike the containment policy of the Cold War, today's diversion policy may not primarily be the responsibility of government. My own job, as the interagency leader for the war of ideas, is to mobilize every possible American asset—public and private, human and technological—in the effort.

Where does Iran fit in? The pool of future suicide bombers and insurgents is sustained by people like the leadership of Iran. Both of the approaches I have outlined—ideological confrontation and diversion—should appeal to a proud and sophisticated Iranian population that is open to pluralistic ideas.

What we seek is a world in which the use of violence to achieve political, religious or social objectives is no longer considered acceptable, efforts to radicalize and recruit new members are no longer successful, and the perpetrators of violent extremism are condemned and isolated.

Military success is necessary, but it is not sufficient—for the simple reason that we face as an enemy not a single nation, or even a coalition, but a stateless global movement. Without a vigorous war of ideas, as we kill such adversaries others will take their place.

Known for his analyses of investment opportunities, James K. Glassman is a syndicated columnist, co-author of Dow 36,000, *and editor-in-chief and executive publisher of* The American. *He was sworn in on June 10, 2008, as United States under secretary of state for public diplomacy and public affairs.*

Getting Off Drugs: The Harm Reduction Option

By Walter Wink

The drug war is over and we lost. We merely repeated the mistake of Prohibition. The harder we tried to stamp out this evil, the more lucrative we made it, and the more it spread. Our forcible resistance to evil simply augments it. An evil cannot be eradicated by making it more profitable.

We lost that war on all three fronts: destroying the drug sources, intercepting drugs at our borders, and arresting drug dealers and users.

In the first place, we have failed to cut off drug sources. When we paid Turkey to stop the growth of opium, production merely shifted to Southeast Asia and Afghanistan. Crop substitution programs in Peru led to increased planting of coca, as farmers simply planted a small parcel of land with one of the accepted substitute crops and used the bulk of the funds to plant more coca. Cocaine cultivation uses only seven hundred of the 2.5 million square miles suitable for its growth in Latin America. There is simply no way the United States can police so vast an area.

Second, the drug war has failed to stop illicit drugs at our borders. Hard drugs are very easy to smuggle because they are extremely concentrated. All the cocaine imported into the United States in an entire year would fit into a single C-5A cargo plane. As if the flood of imported drugs were not enough, domestic production of marijuana and methamphetamine continues to increase, to say nothing of prescription drugs. Even if we sealed our borders we could not stop the making of new drugs.

Third, the drug war calls for arresting drug dealers and users in the United States. There are already 750,000 drug arrests per year, and the current prison population has far outstripped existing facilities. Drug offenders account for more than sixty percent of the prison population; to make room for them, far more dangerous criminals are being returned to the streets. It is not drugs but the drug laws themselves that have created this monster. The unimaginable wealth involved leads to the corruption of police, judges and elected officials. A huge bureaucracy has grown dependent on the drug war for employment. Even the financial community is compromised, since the only thing preventing default by some of the heavily indebted Latin American nations or major money-laundering banks is the drug trade. Revenues from drug trafficking in Miami are greater than those from tourism, exports, health care and all other legitimate businesses combined.

The war on drugs created other casualties besides those arrested. There are the ones killed in fights over turf; innocents caught in crossfire; citizens terrified of city streets; escalating robberies; children given free crack to get them addicted and then enlisted as runners and dealers; and mothers so crazed for a fix that they abandon their babies, prostitute themselves and their daughters, and addict their unborn. Many of these tragedies also are the result of drug laws.

The media usually portray cocaine and crack use as a black ghetto phenomenon. This is a racist caricature. There are more drug addicts and far more occasional drug users among middle- and upper-class whites than in any other segment of the population. The typical customer is a single white male between twenty and forty years old. Only thirteen percent of those using illegal drugs are African-American, but they constitute thirty-five percent of those arrested for simple possession and a staggering seventy-four percent of those sentenced for drug possession.* It is the demand by white users that makes drugs flow. Americans consume sixty percent of the world's illegal drugs, too profitable a market to refuse.

I'm not advocating giving up the war on drugs because we can't win. I'm saying that so far we have lost because we let drugs dictate the means we used to oppose them. Harm reduction is not capitulation but a better strategy. We must ruin the world market price of drugs by legalizing them. We have to repeal this failed Second Prohibition. The moment the price of drugs plummets, drug profits will collapse—and with them, the drug empires.

No one wants to live in a country overrun with drugs, but we already do. We should at the very least commit ourselves to a policy of "harm reduction." Addicts will be healed by care and compassion, not condemnation. Dealers will be curbed by a ruined world drug market, not by enforcement that simply escalates the profitability of drugs. What is needed is a nonviolent, creative approach that lets the drug empire collapse of its own deadly weight.

* Statistical data courtesy the Lindesmith Center, Drug Policy Foundation, New York, New York, Ethan Nadelmann, Executive Director.

Dr. Walter Wink is Professor Emeritus of Biblical Interpretation at Auburn Theological Seminary in New York City. Previously, he was a parish minister and taught at Union Theological Seminary, where he earned his doctorate, also in New York City, and was a Peace Fellow at the United States Institute of Peace. He is the author of numerous books and articles. With his wife, dancer and liturgical ceramist June Keener Wink, he received the Martin Luther King Jr. Peace Prize, awarded by the Fellowship of Reconciliation for 2006.

Deal or No Deal: The Price of Purchasing Counterfeit Goods

By Alexandra Mack

In the third season of *Sex and the City*, lead character Carrie Bradshaw decides not to buy a fake Fendi handbag, objecting to its cheap appearance, but there's more for customers to ponder than esthetics. It's not illegal to buy designer imposters in this country, only to sell them. These purchases support counterfeiters who deprive governments of billions of dollars. France fights this with vigilance, passing laws against the purchase of fakes, whatever the circumstances. "Most people think that buying an imitation handbag or wallet is harmless—a victimless crime," explains Dana Thomas in her *New York Times* op-ed piece "Terror's Purse Strings." "But the counterfeiting rackets are run by crime syndicates that also deal in narcotics, weapons, child prostitution, human trafficking and terrorism." (August 30, 2007)

Nonetheless, women in the United States continue to buy fakes. Once the ultimate status symbol, designer bags may have recently taken a back seat to sunglasses as the must-have accessory, but a label-emblazoned carryall will never go out of style. "Even liberated women were in Chanel chains as the purse became the most flagrant status symbol of an aspirational society," writes Suzy Menkes for a *New York Times* article. "First Gucci, then Vuitton and Chanel bags were worn like insignia by the fashionable, who were closely followed (in this order) by trophy wives, high-price prostitutes, dress-for-success women, the country-club set, people with funny money and those who bought counterfeits in Hong Kong's Stanley Market or from sidewalk peddlers."

Counterfeiters are thankful. As soon as a handbag becomes an "it" bag, counterfeiters around the globe produce affordable, almost exact replicas by the truckload. Tourists scour booths on

New York's Canal Street for the perfect fake Louis Vuitton or Prada. They descend upon Santee Alley in Los Angeles, department stores in Korea and backrooms in Thailand market stalls looking for imposters that will pass muster at home. And in Florence, Sudanese street salesmen shout, "Bella, Bella!" at American sightseers, then seconds later, as police officers approach, hastily roll up their display mats and flee.

Buying fakes has become so socially acceptable that the contraband is sold door-to-door, explains Caitlin Ingrassia in her *The Wall Street Journal* article "Knockoffs Go Suburban." High-end label lover Jane DeTorre invited friends and neighbors to her home in Middletown, New York, to drink wine and shop. "This was no Tupperware party," writes Ingrassia. "The thirty or so women had come to this 'purse party' to buy fake versions of the season's hottest designer handbags. . . . The bags, in their authentic form, sell in posh stores for as much as $735 for a Louis Vuitton Ellipse bowling bag; the knockoffs in Ms. DeTorre's living room sold for about $40. These illicit yet hugely popular parties have become a lucrative source of income for the suppliers. But it's a dangerous game," claims Ingrassia. "Bag ladies have become the new targets of luxury-goods companies and law-enforcement authorities determined to stop the spread of counterfeiting."

Over the last several years, New York City has accelerated efforts against counterfeiting. In February 2008, the city raided Chinatown storefronts. According to the police commissioner, six thousand summonses were issued, seven hundred felony arrests were made, and seventy-five establishments were closed.

The city also launched an ad campaign to educate about the negative social ramifications of purchasing counterfeits. The ads appear on telephone booths in Times Square and Chinatown and read, "The Real Price of Counterfeit Goods." One of the ads states, "When you buy counterfeit goods, you support child labor, drug trafficking, organized crime and even worse." ("What's 'Even Worse' About Buying Fake Handbags," by Jennifer Lee, *The New York Times*, May 16, 2008). Broad claims of links to terrorism have raised skepticism among some. Critics dispute a connection and tout it as an urban legend created by fashion conglomerates to keep consumers from spending elsewhere. Regardless, the existence of a financial impact on New York City is indisputable, though it's difficult to ascertain exactly how great. Another ad links fake goods to a decline in city services: "The sale of counterfeit goods costs New Yorkers $1 billion in lost tax dollars each year—less money to improve schools, staff hospitals and make our streets safer." It's hard to argue with those figures, and it's clear that buying counterfeit goods affects everyone. How to solve the problem?

Groups like the International Anti-counterfeiting Coalition, an organization whose members include fashion, software, pharmaceutical and other businesses concerned with knockoff versions of their products, can spread their "fight the fakes" message in educational and informative ways ("School of Hard Knockoffs," by Rob Walker, *The New York Times*, September 19, 2008). Groups like these can help explain that imposter handbags are not the only products being sold on the black market. The theft of intellectual property—ideas themselves, books, music, movies—and phony pharmaceuticals contribute to this problem. Most importantly, industry officials must also go after the source— not just the little guys. Much as in the war on drugs, nabbing the bad guys at the top, in this case the manufacturers, is key to snuffing out the entire industry. Traffickers are not likely to be law-abiding citizens in other areas of life.

It comes down to a basic matter of supply and demand. As long as fakes are sought, they will be available in backrooms and dark alleys. However, if we make the choice to stop purchasing designer imposters, fewer will be produced. Eventually the market will dry up, and the counterfeiting rackets, with less access to money, will be forced out of business.

New Yorker Alexandra Mack's work has appeared in Vogue, Fashion Rocks *and* Skirt! *magazines, and she is the assistant managing editor of* Domino *magazine.*

Freedom

Freedom is the last, best hope of earth.
—Abraham Lincoln

The Lost Art of Family Meals

By Chef Paul Prudhomme

Adapted from the Introduction to *Chef Paul Prudhomme's Louisiana Tastes.* © 2008 Paul Prudhomme. All Rights Reserved. Used by Permission of Paul Prudhomme.

To my way of thinking, fantastic meals and great cooking are about more than just putting nourishment into your body, although of course that was food's first purpose. As incredibly important as flavor is to me, good food means more than that—to me it's very emotional, and means sharing love and friendship. Let me explain.

I was the youngest of thirteen children, and when my last sister got married I was appointed to help Mother in the kitchen. I saw first-hand how she used her skills and knowledge to express her love for her family, and some of my happiest memories are of all of us around the table, laughing and talking and sharing the day's events. The kitchen table was where we got to really know each other, where we learned about family history, the give and take of relationships, manners, and how to hold a conversation. It was where we learned about how precious life and family are, and what being a family really means.

I'm pretty sure that people have been eating together since the dawn of civilization. As hunters and gatherers settled down and became farmers, it took the entire family to raise the food and prepare the meals, so of course they all stopped to eat at the same time. There weren't any books or television or schools, so they talked about crops, weather, and family matters, and their conversations further strengthened their sense of family.

We weren't the only ones who regularly gathered around the

table to feed body and spirit—up until the 1960s or so, most families across the country would never have thought of eating separately. But we lost something very precious when other activities became more important—committee meetings, working late, classes, social events, and sports. I don't pretend to be a sociologist, but I think there must be some connection between the loss of the daily family meal and the fracturing of families and their traditional values. I think as a nation we're nearing a crisis with our children because they don't know who they are or what their heritage is.

I wish I could say something like "Use one of my cookbooks and it'll bring your family back together," but there's no magic in the pages themselves. What I can say, though, is "Create some wonderful dishes, and make the effort to bring your family together for a meal." Maybe you can't count on everyone at the table every night, but perhaps you can aim for two or three nights a week to begin with. And if you're a family of one, then think close friends when I refer to family members. We all need love and fellowship, even if we don't have children or a spouse.

Another proof of how important food is to us is the fact that when we want to impress people, the first thing we do is feed them. A young man wants to impress a date—he takes her out to dinner. A lady wants to impress a gentleman—she invites him over for a home-cooked meal. A businessperson needs the good will of a client—takes that person to lunch.

My life's work is about making people happy. When I autograph books with "Good cooking, Good eating, Good loving," it's because I firmly believe that cooking, eating and loving are very closely related.

Chef Paul Prudhomme was the son of sharecroppers, born on a farm near Opelousas, Louisiana. He always knew he wanted to work in the food business, and right out of high school he opened his first restaurant—a drive-in hamburger place. For many years he cooked in other restaurants, in New Orleans and all over the country, before opening K-Paul's Louisiana Kitchen in the French Quarter. He developed blackened redfish and created his own line of dry seasoning mixes as well as marinades and sauces, and has published eight cookbooks. He still travels, but now throughout the world, learning from others and mentoring culinary professionals.

Undivided Hearts

By Debra Rosenman

The greatness of a nation and its moral progress can be judged by
the way its animals are treated.

—Mahatma Gandhi

Heaven on earth becomes an authentic dwelling place when we
live and respond to life with total reverence, a true recognition
that all beings are part of God's astonishing tapestry. I speak
for the animals that are suffering and have no voice in today's
world.

An acute exposure to pesticides collapsed my immune
system in 1999. Overnight, I became a refugee in my own body,
hypersensitive to the fragrances and toxins in the world. Allergic
to gas heat and even sensitive to electricity, I had nowhere safe
to land. I became homeless. The only place to turn was to God. I
prayed for all the broken pieces of my life to be put back together
again. Imagining myself waving a white handkerchief high in the
air, I surrendered.

While walking through the labyrinth of illness, homelessness
and isolation, I had a dream that would move my life in an
extraordinary direction. I was told to be "receptive to the beauty,
grace and deep wonder of the forest, animals and our own human
nature." Animals started to show up in my dreams, chimpanzees
mostly. I vividly remember chimpanzees and gorillas teaching
me how to be in my body, instructing me in the art of proper
breathing and body alignment. The dreams continued for many
years, facilitating my healing and opening me into an extraordinary
relationship with animals and the earth. Chimpanzees changed
my life in the most unexpected way.

73

Immersing myself in the language, history and plight of the chimpanzee, I was broken-hearted to discover the tragic issues confronting them today. In the United States, there are over thirteen hundred chimpanzees imprisoned in federally-owned research laboratories. Many, if not most, of the chimpanzees held in labs for decades exhibit symptoms reminiscent of the same emotional suffering that human prisoners of war and survivors of abuse experience—Post Traumatic Stress Disorder. The chimpanzees suffer through isolation and unrelenting high anxiety, exhibiting panic attacks, crying and depression. Sorrowfully, most often the experiments performed on chimpanzees are not medically beneficial to humans. Their only sin is that their DNA is 98.6 percent identical to ours. I felt the deep pain of their isolation, understanding what it's like to lose everything and become dispossessed. I made a vow to speak on their behalf. We have forced animals to exist in our world with little or no respect for who they are. Every animal has the undeniable right to live free.

It is extremely difficult to witness the abject misery that millions of people and animals endure on a daily basis. In order to recognize and acknowledge others' pain, we must first be able to understand our own. St. Francis of Assisi spoke wisely when he said, "If you have men who will exclude any of God's creatures from the shelter of compassion and pity, you will have men who will deal likewise with their fellow men." Compassion is born out of our open hearts and the willingness to, at times, move out of our comfort zone to meet the needs of others.

Many cultures share an inherent respect for animals that is built into the daily fabric of their lives. Indigenous people of the Americas blessed the animal killed for food and hide. The Jains, members of an ancient religion of India, promote vegetarianism, doing no harm to any animal. While not everyone chooses to be a vegetarian or a vegan—eschewing the use for any purpose of any animal product, including eggs, milk, honey, leather, wool—our moral compass could at least point toward the humane treatment of those animals we raise for our use, from cage-free chickens to grass-fed cows.

The truth is that compassion lives on a continuum of perception and beliefs, with a diverse range of moral principles. Gandhi

promoted peace and understanding for all beings, employing
empathy and tolerance as a way to build our moral character as
a nation. If humankind were to embrace a universal compassion,
giving moral significance to all lives, the world would be a true
heaven on earth.

*Debra Rosenman is the founder and director of Project Sweet Dreams,
a nonprofit organization that teaches children humane ethics and
animal compassion through the study of great apes, focusing on
education, fundraising and community relations. She is a writer,
workshop leader, media consultant and Rubenfeld Synergist. She leads
earth/animal re-visioning councils across the country.*

Women Who Never Give Up

By Sharon L. Davie

Estimations of women's groups in Kenya that come together with serious purpose number in the tens of thousands, with millions of individual women involved. They are not a new phenomenon; in very different forms, these groups have existed throughout Kenya's history. Today women's groups are most often economic self-help organizations; many have informal structures, and most do not meet the approved "best practices" of international micro-finance, but many hold the seeds of social change.

I want to tell you about one such group.

In 2006 I made the long, arduous drive from Nairobi to the town of Migori in the Western Province. Community leader Peter Indalo took me to a nearby village to see the women of Wasio Kinda. The group has been together for ten years, helping each other—and their families—out of poverty.

As Peter translated from our English to the women's Dhluo and back again, we were all a little uncomfortable, stilted. Then I asked if the men could have a cooperative group, an economic collective, like this? The whole group laughed uproariously. They thought that was a ridiculous idea. "They would drink up all the money!" they said.

Comfortable now, the women explained that in their society, most individual women cannot inherit or buy land, so they bought their house as a collective. They began with a rudimentary savings and loan structure, and built up the group fund so that together they could buy a cow—which led to shared milk, calves, then chickens and eggs, and finally a mill to grind their maize and millet.

Later we went outside, again looking at the livestock, then

Grace bent over, raising a machete to chop the tall green stalks to feed her cows. Glancing at me, with a big grin, she said, through Peter's translation, "By myself, I am weak. I am weak. With my group I am strong as a man!"

Back at the house, when asked whether violence is a part of their lives, they told of the woman in the next village who was being brutally beaten by her husband, over and over. She ran away—not something that women do, they said. Men can beat women, and they must stay. They said she was seen as shameful. When she came back to the village after her husband died, Grace said, people were shocked. The townspeople still shunned her for running away, and would not speak to her. The house she had shared with her husband, the land she had worked, by tradition had gone to the eldest brother of her deceased husband.

Grace said that their help made all the difference. "We talked softly to her. Not like the others." The woman next to Grace showed us what the "others" did, looking sideways, her eyes narrowed into slits, and mimicked, "Hummph! What's she doing back here?" Grace said their group then began to build a new house for the shunned widow, and eventually even convinced townspeople to help them.

"What makes social transformation possible is to go back and forth from lived experience to changes in discourse," suggests Begoña Aretxaga in *Shattered Silence*, and then back again "to experience," and then finally "to change in the conditions of possibility."

I think of the ten years that the women of Wasio Kinda have had together, and the way that "lived experience" has shaped them. Grace told me that the real name of their group is "Women Who Never Give Up." The progress of social transformation is not linear, nor does it ever reach closure. But the millions in grassroots women's groups in Kenya sing a song that catches that rhythm of new experience, new discourse, and new conditions of possibility for women. That song of the future is carried on the wind, bearing the seeds of social change.

Sharon L. Davie is the author of a play, My Sister's Hair, *and the editor of* University and College Women Centers: A Journey Toward Equity. *Director of the University of Virginia Women's Center, she is the co-creator of the traveling exhibit "We Have to Dream While Awake: Courage and Change in El Salvador" and author of "Two Stories" in the exhibit booklet of the same name. She is working on a book project on grassroots women leaders' transformative approaches to gender violence.*

Choices and the Mystery of Life

By Jacob G. Hornberger

Looking back over his life just before dying, a man asked, "Now, what the heck was that all about?"

It's the type of question that a person might be wise to ask himself every day of his life: What is my life all about? What am I here for? What was I born to do? While we might not come up with definitive answers to such questions, we can surmise that the mystery of life has something to do with growing, developing, "hatching," becoming the best of whatever we are capable of.

If such is the case, an obvious question arises: What type of social order would be most conducive to promoting each person's discovery of himself and to the development of a person's mind, talents, and abilities? I submit that the answer to that question is one in which every individual is accorded full latitude with respect to the peaceful choices he makes in life. Such a social order would be one in which the law protects, not regulates or punishes, the exercise of any peaceful choice.

"Peaceful" is a critically important adjective here. Obviously we don't want people to be free to make violent choices because those choices would interfere with the right of others to live their lives peacefully. For example, if I have the "freedom" to kill another person, my action deprives the victim of the right to live his life the way he chooses.

But the same reasoning does not hold true for peaceful or nonviolent choices in life. Within this broad realm of human activity, the fact that everyone is free to live his life in the manner he chooses does not interfere, in a violent way, with the right of anyone else to do the same. Obviously, such a social order holds dangers. After all, it's a virtual certainty that some people will choose "wrongly." They will make choices that other people will consider irresponsible, immoral, or unethical.

Nonetheless, despite such a risk, that kind of social order would create an environment in which people could achieve the greatest degree of self-discovery and self-growth. Moreover, I submit that a social order based on freedom of choice would inevitably nudge people in society to greater heights of responsibility, morality, and ethics.

Unfortunately, that's not the social order in which we live. We instead live in a world in which coercion is employed both to ensure that people make the right choices and that they avoid making the wrong ones.

Consider a real-world example: government-imposed smoking bans in restaurants. Under principles of private property and free enterprise, I believe the owner of a restaurant has the moral right to run his business any way he chooses. If he wishes to permit smoking in his restaurant, that is his right. He also has the right to establish a total ban on smoking in his restaurant or divide it into smoking and nonsmoking sections.

By the same token, however, consumers are free to make their own choices with respect to their selection of restaurants. They have the right to choose which restaurants to patronize and which ones to avoid. If a restaurant permits smoking, people are free to go elsewhere, which might well nudge the restaurateur into changing his smoking policy.

Why shouldn't every person be accorded the respect that comes with making his own decisions? Isn't that the essence of individual freedom—the right to choose wrongly? Or, to put it another way, if a person is "free" only to be responsible and caring, then how can he truly be considered free?

This raises an important question: Under what moral authority does anyone use force to impose his values on someone else's peaceful choices in life? Since a person's life is his own, it would seem that so are his choices, even when they are contrary to the choices that everyone else in society is making.

While none of us can truly understand the mystery of life, my hunch is that life has something to do with trying to approach what each of us will be like in heaven. By leaving people free to choose their own way with respect to peaceful activity, this preparatory period from birth to death, while providing no guarantees with respect to outcome, provides the best opportunity we have to come as close as possible to achieving a heaven on earth.

Jacob Hornberger received a bachelor of arts degree in economics from Virginia Military Institute and doctor of jurisprudence degree from the University of Texas School of Law. After practicing law in Texas for thirteen years and serving as an adjunct professor of law at the University of Dallas, he became director of The Foundation for Economic Education. In 1989 he founded The Future of Freedom Foundation, a libertarian education foundation in Fairfax, Virginia. He lectures widely on free-market principles and has written for The Washington Post, The Charlotte Observer, El Nuevo Miami Herald *and other publications.*

Surviving Injustice

By James Douglas Waller

Twenty-seven years ago I was an ordinary person, living an ordinary life, when I was misidentified as the perpetrator of a brutal rape, and found myself in the terrible whirlwind of the criminal justice system. I never doubted that I would leave the system as quickly as I had entered it, but I was convicted of the crime. I always maintained my innocence, but I felt that the justice system was determined to allow me to live out my days on earth in hell.

During my ten years in prison, I struggled to stay positive. I was the biggest proponent of my innocence, but the last person with any real power to change my situation. I sought the Lord's help and guidance. Surrendering to the Lord gave me a peace that surpassed all doubt that truth would actually prevail.

After I was released on parole, I got in touch with the Innocence Project. The Lord used them as intercessors of freedom, hope and change on my behalf. I am certain that they were placed in my life for my restoration. The Innocence Project sought DNA testing in my case and found that only a tiny amount remained after all those years, but, miraculously, it was enough to prove my innocence.

I didn't believe it was possible for someone to go to prison for something that they didn't do. But my experience opened my eyes to the flaws of the criminal justice system. Although there are many people who are rightly imprisoned, it is not accurate to assume that everyone who is convicted is guilty. Every month the Innocence Project receives hundreds of letters from prisoners asking for help and claiming innocence, and so far over two hundred people have been exonerated through DNA testing in the United States.

For most Americans, the criminal justice system represents a great force for good for our society, protecting us from crime and keeping our communities safe, and it is indeed responsible for removing some of the most violent and reckless people from our streets. But we also need a fair system, one that places the burden of proof on the prosecution, not the defense, one that demonstrates racial and socioeconomic equality.

Although DNA testing has also been used to solve cold cases, the crime that I was wrongfully convicted of was never solved. The real perpetrator was never found and may have gone on to commit more crimes. It is impossible to know how many lives, in addition to mine, were affected by the injustice in my case. If there is one person subjected to the unfairness and injustices of the system, then it is a problem for all of us. Through the jury system, every American citizen has an opportunity to participate in the criminal justice system, and therefore an obligation to question it.

Fifty years later, I can still hear the words of my wonderful, wise grandmother, whose mantra was "Always tell the truth, and the truth will set you free." I have been guided by these words as I have been guided by my faith, before I was convicted, during my time in prison, and as an exonerated person.

Can we really have heaven on earth? Yes, when we fight for justice, are truthful, and remain faithful to the promises of God, our days take on a new, exalted view, and when we look carefully, the signs of heaven are right there.

James Waller was wrongfully convicted in 1982 and spent ten years in prison and fourteen years on parole before his exoneration in 2007. He lives in the Dallas area, where he speaks publicly about his wrongful conviction, works with the homeless, and supports people who have recently been exonerated.

Democracies

A government of laws, and not of men.
—John Adams

The Tao of Reagan

By Daniel Agatino

Ronald Wilson Reagan embodied the words of Theodore Roosevelt when he said, "Far better is it to dare mighty things, to win glorious triumphs, even though checkered by failure . . . than to rank with those poor spirits who neither enjoy nor suffer much, because they live in a gray twilight that knows not victory nor defeat." When Americans merely wanted to make ends meet, Reagan delivered prosperity by cutting taxes and slashing regulation. When Americans wanted to avoid nuclear war, Reagan helped deliver the peaceful fall of the Soviet Union, without a shot being fired. When Americans would have been satisfied with simple stability, Reagan delivered inspiration and courageous leadership by reminding us that the great rights we hold come with great responsibilities.

Ronald Reagan became the fortieth president of the United States when a gloomy shadow was cast out over our nation. On his first day in the White House he faced multiple crises—U.S. citizens were being held hostage abroad by extremist zealots, the economy was fragile and deteriorating while the continuing cold war loomed over the nation, robbing us of valuable resources. Perhaps worst of all, Reagan was confronted with a country where general pessimism about the viability of the American dream prevailed. But his faith provided him with great strength when others were ready to give up.

By choosing optimism over despair, resolve over trepidation, and sacrifice over indulgence, he met all these challenges head on with integrity and exuberance. It was not that Reagan believed himself to be a great man capable of handling any problem; he was too humble for such hubris. Instead, he had an unshakable hope in the promise of democracy and the inventiveness of the human spirit, coupled with a personal trust in God. Put another way, Reagan was deeply committed to those famous words of the Declaration of Independence: "We hold these truths to be self-evident, that all men are created equal, that they are endowed by their Creator with certain unalienable rights, that among these are life, liberty and the pursuit of happiness."

For Reagan this meant a trust in a real and personal God who cares about the choices we all make; a recognition that rights don't come down from the government to be generously bestowed on the people, but arise from the people and are held in trust by the government. Reagan also believed that life was to be respected. Not just in a formulaic opposition to abortion and euthanasia, but through his awe-inspiring respect for creation. Lastly, he loved liberty, and worked tirelessly to promote abroad many of the freedoms he so treasured.

Comedian George Burns, a friend of Reagan, once quipped that to make it in acting all you need is sincerity, and if you can fake that you have it made. As a young man, Reagan was an accomplished actor, but even then he was sincere through and through. His sincerity and lightheartedness were contagious. Looking through the countless photos on file of him, it is genuinely hard to find one where he is not smiling, or at least where he is not making another person smile. He was charismatic to the core.

While others thought him childishly naïve or hopelessly unsophisticated, he proved to the country and the world that any free person in a democratic society, who is grounded in a traditional morality and fosters a definiteness of purpose, will inevitably succeed and inspire others to success. It was true then, it is still true today and shall evermore be, so long as men and women aspire to achieve the American Dream.

Many experts scoffed at Reagan's plans. They questioned the sheer scope of his objectives—to rebuild the economy, to end the cold war and transform the Soviet Union, to inspire America and the world. Those cynics vilified Reagan, and history shows them to have been wrong. But part of his greatness was that at that time Reagan did not know he would succeed, but persevered anyway. Despite uncertainty he risked much, made tough choices and accomplished great and lasting objectives. Ronald Wilson Reagan is an exemple of how passion when united with virtue can bring about heaven on earth.

Daniel Agatino, the author of The Tao of Reagan: Common Sense from an Uncommon Man, *is a professor of communication law and is a defense attorney practicing in New Jersey.*

What I Want for You and Every Child in America

By [Then] President-Elect Barack Obama

© 2009 Barack Obama. Initially published in *Parade Magazine*. All rights reserved.

Next Tuesday, Barack Obama will be sworn in as our 44th President. On this historic occasion, PARADE asked the President-elect, who is also a devoted family man, to get personal and tell us what he wants for his children. Here, he shares his letter to them.

Dear Malia and Sasha,

I know that you've both had a lot of fun these last two years on the campaign trail, going to picnics and parades and state fairs, eating all sorts of junk food your mother and I probably shouldn't have let you have. But I also know that it hasn't always been easy for you and Mom, and that as excited as you both are about that new puppy, it doesn't make up for all the time we've been apart. I know how much I've missed these past two years, and today I want to tell you a little more about why I decided to take our family on this journey.

When I was a young man, I thought life was all about me—about how I'd make my way in the world, become successful, and get the things I want. But then the two of you came into my world with all your curiosity and mischief and those smiles that never fail to fill my heart and light up my day. And suddenly, all my big plans for myself didn't seem so important anymore. I soon found that the greatest joy in my life was the joy I saw in yours. And I realized that my own life wouldn't count for much unless I was able to ensure that you had every opportunity for happiness and fulfillment in yours. In the end, girls, that's why I ran for

President: because of what I want for you and for every child in this nation.

I want all our children to go to schools worthy of their potential—schools that challenge them, inspire them, and instill in them a sense of wonder about the world around them. I want them to have the chance to go to college—even if their parents aren't rich. And I want them to get good jobs: jobs that pay well and give them benefits like health care, jobs that let them spend time with their own kids and retire with dignity.

I want us to push the boundaries of discovery so that you'll live to see new technologies and inventions that improve our lives and make our planet cleaner and safer. And I want us to push our own human boundaries to reach beyond the divides of race and region, gender and religion that keep us from seeing the best in each other.

Sometimes we have to send our young men and women into war and other dangerous situations to protect our country—but when we do, I want to make sure that it is only for a very good reason, that we try our best to settle our differences with others peacefully, and that we do everything possible to keep our servicemen and women safe. And I want every child to understand that the blessings these brave Americans fight for are not free—that with the great privilege of being a citizen of this nation comes great responsibility.

That was the lesson your grandmother tried to teach me when I was your age, reading me the opening lines of the Declaration of Independence and telling me about the men and women who marched for equality because they believed those words put to paper two centuries ago should mean something.

She helped me understand that America is great not because it is perfect but because it can always be made better—and that the unfinished work of perfecting our union falls to each of us. It's a charge we pass on to our children, coming closer with each new generation to what we know America should be.

I hope both of you will take up that work, righting the wrongs that you see and working to give others the chances you've had. Not just because you have an obligation to give something back to this country that has given our family so much—although you do have that obligation. But because you have an obligation to yourself. Because it is only when you hitch your wagon to something larger than yourself that you will realize your true potential.

These are the things I want for you—to grow up in a world with no limits on your dreams and no achievements beyond your reach, and to grow into compassionate, committed women who will help build that world. And I want every child to have the same chances to learn and dream and grow and thrive that you girls have. That's why I've taken our family on this great adventure.

I am so proud of both of you. I love you more than you can ever know. And I am grateful every day for your patience, poise, grace, and humor as we prepare to start our new life together in the White House.

Love, Dad

Barack Obama was inaugurated the forty-fourth president of the United States on January 20, 2009. He was born in Honolulu, Hawaii, to a Kenyan father and a mother from the United States. After high school he moved to California, where he studied at Occidental College for two years, then transferred to Columbia College in New York. Obama earned a degree from Harvard Law School and served as president of the Harvard Law Review.

The president worked as a community organizer, civil rights attorney, and constitutional law professor before being elected to the Illinois State Senate and then the United States Senate. He is the author of Dreams from My Father *and* The Audacity of Hope.

What Made My Year Special

By George W. Bush

© 2007 George W. Bush. Initially published in *Parade Magazine*. All rights reserved.

It's been a tumultuous year for President Bush. So when PARADE asked him to share his thoughts on the best and worst moments of 2007, we didn't know what to expect. Would he talk about the war in Iraq, the housing crisis or the California wildfires? The President told us right away that he is "an optimist" and chose to describe five people who inspired him in 2007. Their stories offer a glimpse into what matters to Mr. Bush as he begins his final year in office and his last chance to shape his legacy

Every year about this time, the Christmas decorations come down and Washington gets ready to go back to work. In these quiet moments, Laura and I like to take stock of the year that has passed. Inevitably we find that our most treasured memories revolve around the extraordinary people we have met. These men and women inspire us, they touch our hearts, and they remind us of the true strength of our nation.

Dan and Maureen Murphy are two of these people. In June 2005, their son—Lt. Michael Murphy, a Navy SEAL—was conducting surveillance in Afghanistan when his four-man team came under attack. Lt. Murphy moved into a clearing where he could get a signal to call for help for his men, knowing it would make him a target. As he made the call, he came under heavy fire that cost him his life. In a meeting before I presented Maureen Murphy with her son's Medal of Honor, she spoke of the boy she'd raised to manhood. I came away from that day hoping that Lt. Murphy's story would inspire all Americans to live lives worthy of the sacrifices that have been made for our freedom.

Another leader who inspires me is Francis Collins, director of the National Human Genome Research Institute. His work is important because the more we understand the human genome, the greater the opportunity for breakthroughs in the fight against cancer, diabetes and other diseases. Francis also is a believer in God. At this year's National Prayer Breakfast, I heard him speak about how the work he does helps him fulfill his religious calling to alleviate human suffering. Francis is both a man of science and a man of faith. In November, I was proud to award him the Presidential Medal of Freedom.

Throughout 2007, I also was grateful for the opportunity to meet entrepreneurs like Cordia Harrington. A little more than a decade ago, Cordia was a single mom with a dream of starting her own company. Today, she owns a thriving bakery, employs more than 200 people and calls herself "the bun lady." One hot day last July, I flew to Nashville to see her factory and meet Cordia. I found a strong spirit of enterprise. Risk-takers like Cordia create jobs and opportunities for their fellow citizens and show the world the power of the American Dream.

This year, I've also been deeply touched by the spirit of people from around the globe. One of these is Kunene Tantoh. Five years ago, the future for this South African woman looked bleak: She was HIV-positive and pregnant. But—through a program called Mothers to Mothers, in a center that American generosity helped to fund—Kunene got the medical treatment she needed. Not only did she survive, she delivered a beautiful baby boy who is HIV-free. Laura met Kunene during a trip to Africa and introduced me to her at the White House in May when I proposed to double America's commitment to global HIV/AIDS relief. That day in the Rose Garden, I held her smiling 4-year-old boy in my arms—a living example of the difference America is making for millions around the world.

Finally, I'm grateful for the way America inspires freedom-loving people everywhere. In October, Yamile Llanes Labrada came to visit me in the Oval Office. Yamile is the wife of Jose Luis Garcia Paneque, a doctor who is in a Cuban prison for the "crime" of advocating democracy. Yamile and her children had to flee Cuba after a mob surrounded their home. But she continues to press for her husband's freedom. She told me of her deep gratitude for the way Americans have opened their arms to her and her family. And she stressed how important it is for men like her husband to know that, when others look away, America will speak up for their freedom.

One of the best parts of my job as President is the chance to meet men and women whose stories show the great heart of our country. Ours is a good and decent country, filled with caring, compassionate, hardworking people who use their skills and talents to build a better America and a more hopeful world. Their achievements make us proud. And their determination and character are the reasons I am so optimistic about America's future—in 2008 and beyond.

George W. Bush was the forty-third president of the United States, serving two terms from 2001 to 2009. He was born in New Haven, Connecticut, but two years later the family moved to Texas, living in Midland and Houston. He received a bachelor's degree in history from Yale University and a master's of business administration from Harvard Business School.

He was a pilot in the Texas Air National Guard and with partners purchased the Texas Rangers baseball franchise. Bush was elected governor of Texas in 1994, and became the first governor in Texas history to serve two consecutive four-year terms.

Count Your Blessings: An Attorney's Perspective

By Raya Tahan

God's blessings are easy to take for granted, but by appreciating what you have, you can position the first block in building a heaven on earth.

I practice law. My industry is rife with unhappy people. Plaintiffs have been wronged. Defendants are victims of frivolous lawsuits. Judges are jaded by parties who litigate in bad faith.

Sometimes people renege on their word or falsify their position, causing financial damage to others. In these cases businesspeople turn to their attorneys, expecting a quick-and-clean fix, then become disappointed upon discovering that our system is slow and cumbersome.

I often find myself confounding clients during initial consultations. They have a stack of evidence showing unequivocally that somebody breached a contract with them, costing them a lot of money. It wasn't fair. I must tell them they will have to go through months or years of stressful and costly litigation, just to get a judge or jury to look at this evidence. Understandably they don't think it's fair that we must jump through so many hoops to get a court order granting my clients something they should have had all along.

Clients often lament, "That doesn't seem right. Why is it called the 'justice' system?" Even more frustrating to them is the fact that I cannot promise clients that the judge will rule in their favor. "How can that be?" they ask. "It's so obvious that I am right and he is wrong." Yet sometimes trial judges make mistakes, which is why trial judges' decisions are sometimes overturned by the appellate courts.

The legal systems of developed countries are not perfect, but they are better than any place else, and for that I am exceedingly grateful. Not a week goes by when I don't remind some frustrated person—staff, clients, or myself—that we should appreciate our system, even with its warts and flaws. I feel immensely grateful to be practicing law in the United States, for at least in democracies such as ours, justice is not reserved for the ultra-rich or politically connected. Anyone is able to civilly sue somebody who breached a contract, and chances are good that, if you're right, you will obtain justice. Here, God will meet you halfway if you had conducted yourself ethically and are merely seeking what is fair. The right outcome is not guaranteed, but you have a higher chance of obtaining the right outcome here than you do any place else.

I often wonder why am I here, while others around the globe suffer domestic violence, organized crime, or other social ills while the courts of their countries turn a blind eye to their misery. I will never know why God blessed me with this gift of living in a democracy with the right of free speech and to practice my religion. Even with all of the system's flaws, I appreciate what I have here.

We can take steps to promote justice every day, in simple ways. If you let somebody down, did something wrong, failed to fulfill a promise, or didn't live up to your end of a bargain, then admit it and rectify the situation. Many lawsuits could be avoided if the defendants would simply apologize and take simple and inexpensive measures to cure the situation before letting it spin out of control in a heated court battle. The same holds true for plaintiffs. If you feel that somebody has wronged you, take a deep breath before you march into court "with guns blazing." Acknowledge your share of the blame and how you might have contributed to the problem. Concede that nobody is expected to behave perfectly, but rather the expectation is that people behave reasonably. Practicing this attitude is a step toward justice for all, appreciation of your blessings, and honoring God's Golden Rule.

Raya Tahan, whose parents are Israeli citizens, grew up in Phoenix, Arizona. She earned a bachelor's degree in journalism from the University of Arizona, and a JD from Arizona State University College of Law. She has been a staff writer for the Associated Press, taught English as a second language in Budapest, and now heads a law firm in Phoenix, where she volunteers for several nonprofits and enjoys running marathons.

Africa's Heavenly Surprise?

By Tunji Lardner

There is always something new out of Africa, Pliny The Elder

Africa is about as distant a place from heaven on earth as there is on this planet. The prevailing view from the outside, especially as purveyed by the western media, is that it is an undifferentiated, misbegotten continent plagued by an unending narrative of strife, disease, pain and immeasurable suffering.

While at first blush there are certainly negative events in Africa to justify the pervasive cynicism, Africa through the lenses of unbiased curiosity as well as an understanding of the African concept of Ubuntu—respect for and appreciation of others' worth—reveals startling insights to our common destiny. If this fresh view of Africa is adopted, something remarkable happens instantly. In the subject-object relationship in which the viewer is the subject looking through these new lenses seeing a newer object, in this case Africa, the relativism and distance between subject and object narrows to the point where the archeological truth emerges.

The scientific truth that indeed "we are all Africans" gradually evolves in our consciousness properly to frame a new relationship with our fellow brothers and sisters, with scant regard for the melanin quotient, and cultural, religious and other divisive artifacts that distort our world views.

So one way in which we can achieve a heaven on earth is first to remove the distorted lenses of our acculturated biases and schisms, and wear the Ubuntu spectacles to see the gifts of our common humanity in which there is no "other" but "us." And in acknowledging our oneness we are compelled to safeguard the human family because after all, we are in fact our brother's keepers.

For Africa and Africans, the challenges are manifold even with the possibilities of this new sympathetic and inclusive vision of world. It is one thing to be objectified as a cipher for human compassion and possible action of the type which exculpates collective historical guilt; it is yet another thing for Africa fully to come to terms with its own culpability in its predicament.

There are multiple reasons Africans are deeply religious, some profound and others attributed to the net effects of bad leaders, bad governments and poor accountability processes. For many Africans caught in the withering crossfire of greed, violence, ignorance, poverty and dehumanization, there are truly no atheists in their respective foxholes.

As the world slides further into economic decline with a certain fin de siècle sense of the old order as we know it collapsing, there is increasing space for a new world order to emerge, a truly new and transfigured world. While much has been written about the emergence of a truly transformational global leader in the person of President-elect Barack Obama, it bears repeating that his unprecedented emergence has given the world hope and encouragement that there is truly change afoot.

For Africa, Obama's ancestry should mean more than pride for a native son, it should mean that his personal example of personal sacrifice, call to service, keen intellect as well as the self-possession that belies his deep moral and spiritual underpinnings, should be a veritable model of the kind of leadership that the continent needs for the twenty-first century. Slowly, inch by tenuous inch, Africans, especially young Africans in and out of the continent, are beginning to challenge the old post-independent political order. In the emergent Africa, they see neither the ethnic chauvinism nor the religious intolerance that have been cynically manipulated by inept, rapacious and power-hungry politicians over the last fifty-odd years.

Instead they see the latent promise of a remarkably resilient and adaptive continent that can leap-frog into the increasingly inter-dependent world in which collective action is required to tackle a formidable welter of global challenges, from climate change, through trans-national epidemics, wars, terrorism and now global economic collapse.

Strangely enough, these are not new problems for Africa. Through it all, Africa has maintained its ability to surprise: "Ex Africa semper aliquid novi"—there is always something new out of Africa. Perhaps this time, in this new emergent world of deeper understanding of our shared and collective destiny, Africa might provide the place, opportunity and motivation for mankind to rediscover its humanity and to recreate a heaven on earth, here, there and everywhere.

Nigerian native Tunji Lardner is a journalist, social entrepreneur and development communications consultant with experience in Africa and elsewhere. He has over twenty-five years of media and communications experience, the last sixteen as a consultant to the UN, Ford Foundation, UK Department for International Development, and lately the World Bank. He is the founder of the West African NGO Network.

A Mighty Wind

By Marianne Williamson

© 2008 Marianne Williamson. All Rights Reserved. Used by Permission of Marianne Williamson.

Every once in a while, a mighty wind blows.

The political sentiments now storming America in the form of support for Barack Obama are a mighty wind indeed. For those trying to say this is all just hot air, it's time to point out that so is a windstorm. And storms have a function, in nature and in us. They blow away everything not built on a firm foundation, and make room for a lot of new growth.

I'm a boomer, so I know this feeling. We have been here before. We knew what Bob Dylan meant when he sang, "Something's going on here, but you don't know what it is . . . Do you, Mr. Jones?" And something is going on again. What we're experiencing here is a new conversation—something qualitatively different from the promises of effective problem-solving that pass for an excitement factor in his opponent's campaign. Try to dismiss it though she might, someone who has the capacity to change a society's conversation has the capacity to change the society.

From Bob Dylan to Gloria Steinem to John Lennon to Martin Luther King, Jr., people who use words to foster new thinking are the ones we see in retrospect to have opened doors to a better world. Hillary was right when she said Dr. King couldn't have passed civil rights legislation without Lyndon Johnson, but Johnson couldn't have done it without King, either. Johnson had the presidency, but King had the vision. Today we have the historic opportunity—one that comes around only rarely—to have president and visionary be the same person.

A great national leader does not speak just to circumstances; he arouses a nation's soul. The idea that Obama could not only arouse our soul but also handle our circumstances (has he not handled a pretty formidable circumstance already, giving her such a run for her money?) seems far more probable to me than that Hillary could not only handle our circumstances but also arouse our soul.

Jefferson. Lincoln. Roosevelt. Kennedy. Damn right, their words mattered. Try Googling "great speeches" and see what comes up. Great words and great speeches have changed the world because they have changed the way we see the world. Washington-think is so old-fashioned, so treat-the-symptom-and-pretend-you-healed-the-disease, protect-the-status-quo type of stuff that millions gave up on it a long time ago as an agent of true social improvement. But while few of us are looking to the American government to save the world, we'd prefer that it not destroy it either. Obama was right when he said that we have to do more than just end the war in Iraq; we need to end the mindset that produced it.

At the end of World War II, in the last speech he ever wrote yet died before having a chance to deliver, President Franklin Roosevelt said, "We must do more than end war. We must end the beginnings of all war." The source of the debacle in Iraq was not an event; it was a mindset. The source of our environmental problems was not an event; it was a mindset. The source of every problem is the mindset that preceded it. And only someone who can speak to the source of a problem can eradicate its roots.

The ability to inspire new thinking is a more important ability in a leader today than simply being a "problem-solver." We're always trying to solve something—health care, the economy, Social Security, and so forth. Yet according to Carl Jung, our most important problems cannot be solved; they must be outgrown. Just figuring out who has a better plan with which to treat the symptoms of a problem is not the one who ultimately solves it. What we need is someone with a better state of mind, who will lead us to a better state of ours.

Being swept up in Obama's inspirational ability is not naïve; what is naïve is thinking that inspirational ability doesn't count for much. For in the ability to inspire lies the ability to command the most powerful forces of all. No plan, no piece of legislation, no Washington strategy or political maneuvering alone will be enough to change the probability vector of America's future. For that, we will need a mighty wind. And a mighty wind now blows.

Marianne Williamson is a spiritual activist, author, lecturer and founder of The Peace Alliance, a grassroots campaign supporting legislation to establish a United States Department of Peace. She has published nine books, including four New York Times *number one bestsellers.*

Effective Leadership

By Congressman Anh "Joseph" Cao

What does one need to be an effective leader? In my opinion, one requires four elements: virtue, religion, family and heritage.

Aristotle once said that virtue is the mean between two extremes. This definition was appropriate over two thousand years ago and it continues to be true today. The virtuous character, properly exercised, reacts to circumstances in the appropriate way and to the appropriate degree. I believe that an effective leader must govern from a political spectrum that resonates the mean rather than the two extremes.

What are these two extremes? Consider left-wing liberalism, whose governing stance simply focuses on the immediate with little attention to moral implications and burdens on future generations, and right-wing conservatism, whose rhetoric could be construed as intolerant and offensive, as being the two boundaries from which the mean can be found. The future of the United States is too important for Congress to be embattled in and impeded by liberal and conservative ideologies and political maneuvering. An effective member of Congress must remember whom he or she represents: the average American whose ideology reflects neither left-wing liberalism nor right-wing conservatism, but the struggles of everyday life, such as how will I pay my bills, how can I raise my children to be successful and moral citizens, and how can I freely worship and express my religious faith. An effective leader must use all the knowledge and tools he or she possesses to address the problems of a dynamic and evolving society in the appropriate way and to the appropriate degree. This, of course, requires a delicate balancing act where members of Congress are invited to the discussion table not as liberals or conservatives, but as problem solvers addressing the human needs of the average citizen.

Another element that undergirds effective leadership is religious faith. Today, religion is being attacked from every side and religious faith is viewed as something to be avoided. Yet, for a law to be good law, it must be established on solid moral foundations, and morality is often founded in religious faith. We have seen throughout history the effect of bad laws that are not founded on morality: the Holocaust during World War II, the Killing Fields of Cambodia, the re-education camps of Vietnam, religious persecution, and civil rights violations all over the world.

Today, more than ever, we need more leaders who are religiously conscious, who, in their role as the servant, will put the interests of other human beings over their own. Religious faith has had a central role in forming who I am today and how I proceed in my role as a legislator.

Just imagine an eight-year-old boy who was uprooted from his family and friends, uprooted from his comfortable surroundings and placed in a culture that was completely foreign, around people speaking a language he could not understand, and was forced to face his own fears all by himself. With no one to turn to, the little boy could only turn to his religious faith to obtain the comfort and the strength to survive. Just imagine a twenty-nine-year-old man, having faced extreme poverty in the slums of Mexico, having seen the suffering faces of little children in the refugee camps of Hong Kong, and having no power to promote change, decides to make the leap of faith to leave the security of the religious life, to re-immerse himself in the secular world, strengthened only by his faith and his inner compulsion to try to make a difference in the world. This has been my journey, the journey of uncertainty, the journey of insecurity, a journey of fears and suffering, but a journey that must be taken if we want to find ourselves and really be the person God intends us to be.

Third, an effective leader must put his or her family first. If a leader cannot relate to his family, how can he relate to the people he serves? As a father and husband, I understand the struggles in raising a family; I understand the joys in watching your child walk for the first time; I understand the suffering in the death of a family member. Family humanizes the legislator, grounding his feet and head to the important tasks so that laws, when drafted, are not convoluted and impractical.

Finally, a good and effective leader must be proud of his or her heritage. Heritage informs, influences and diversifies the decision-making process. If every representative in the United States Congress were of the same heritage, laws would simply reflect the history and experiences, and possibly benefit exclusively the particular group. Fortunately, the United States is a melting pot of many races and correspondingly many heritages, each with its own uniqueness. As an Asian-American, I inherited a heritage of family values, a heritage of hard work, and a heritage of loyalty that have empowered me with the strength to overcome many obstacles in my life. And like virtue, religion and family, heritage rightly has its place in forming, and possibly transforming, a person in a leadership position.

Anh "Joseph" Cao left his native Vietnam at the age of eight with an uncle and two of his siblings and settled in the United States. He earned a physics degree from Baylor University, and began to study for the priesthood. Later, though, he decided he could better serve those in need through secular efforts, and moved to Washington D.C. where he became an advocate for refugees seeking citizenship.

He earned a master's degree in philosophy from Fordham University and a juris doctor degree from Loyola University School of Law in New Orleans, and became in-house counsel for Boat People S.O.S., a nonprofit aiding poor Vietnamese and other minorities. In 2002, he was chosen by former Archbishop Alfred Hughes to become a member of the National Advisory Council of the U.S. Conference of Catholic Bishops, addressing women's rights in the Catholic Church, social justice, child abuse and the Catholic response to Hurricane Katrina. In 2007, Louisiana Governor Bobby Jindal appointed Cao to help ensure fair voting as a member of the Board of Elections for Orleans Parish. In 2008 he was elected to represent Louisiana's Second Congressional District in the United States Congress.

Prosperity

Much effort, much prosperity.

—Euripides

10 Ways to Get Rich—
On Warren Buffett

By Alice Schroeder

© 2009 Alice Schroeder. Initially published in *Parade Magazine*, September 7, 2008. All rights reserved.

With an estimated fortune of $62 billion, Warren Buffett is the richest man in the entire world. In 1962, when he began buying stock in Berkshire Hathaway, a share cost $7.50. Today, Buffett, 78, is Berkshire's chairman and CEO, and one share of the company's class A stock is worth close to $119,000. He credits his astonishing success to several key strategies, which he has shared with writer Alice Schroeder. She spent hundreds of hours interviewing the Sage of Omaha for the new authorized biography *The Snowball*. Here are some of Buffett's money-making secrets—and how they could work for you.

1. Reinvest your profits. When you first make money, you may be tempted to spend it. Don't. Instead, reinvest the profits. Buffett learned this early on. In high school, he and a pal bought a pinball machine to put in a barbershop. With the money they earned, they bought more machines until they had eight in different shops. When the friends sold the venture, Buffett used the proceeds to buy stocks and to start another small business. By age twenty-six, he'd amassed $174,000—or $1.4 million in today's money. Even a small sum can turn into great wealth.

2. Be willing to be different. Don't base your decisions upon what everyone is saying or doing. When Buffett began managing money in 1956 with $100,000 cobbled together from a handful of investors, he was dubbed an oddball. He worked in Omaha, not on Wall Street, and he refused to tell his partners where he was putting their money. People predicted that he'd fail, but when he closed his partnership fourteen years later, it was worth more than $100 million. Instead of following the crowd, he looked for undervalued investments and ended up vastly beating the market average every single year. To Buffett, the average is just that—what everybody else is doing.

To be above average, you need to measure yourself by what he calls the Inner Scorecard, judging yourself by your own standards and not the world's.

3. Never suck your thumb. Gather in advance any information you need to make a decision, and ask a friend or relative to make sure that you stick to a deadline. Buffett prides himself on swiftly making up his mind and acting on it. He calls any unnecessary sitting and thinking "thumb-sucking." When people offer him a business or an investment, he says, "I won't talk unless they bring me a price." He gives them an answer on the spot.

4. Spell out the deal before you start. Your bargaining leverage is always greatest before you begin a job—that's when you have something to offer that the other party wants. Buffett learned this lesson the hard way as a kid, when his grandfather Ernest hired him and a friend to dig out the family grocery store after a blizzard. The boys spent five hours shoveling until they could barely straighten their frozen hands. Afterward, his grandfather gave the pair less than ninety cents to split. Buffett was horrified that he performed such backbreaking work only to earn pennies an hour. Always nail down the specifics of a deal in advance—even with your friends and relatives.

5. Watch small expenses. Buffett invests in businesses run by managers who obsess over the tiniest costs. He once acquired a company whose owner counted the sheets in rolls of 500-sheet toilet paper to see if he was being cheated (he was). He also admired a friend who painted only the side of his office building that faced the road. Exercising vigilance over every expense can make your profits—and your paycheck—go much further.

6. *Limit what you borrow.* Living on credit cards and loans won't make you rich. Buffett has never borrowed a significant amount—not to invest, not for a mortgage. He has gotten many heartrending letters from people who thought their borrowing was manageable but became overwhelmed by debt. His advice: Negotiate with creditors to pay what you can. Then, when you're debt-free, work on saving some money that you can use to invest.

7. *Be persistent.* With tenacity and ingenuity, you can win against a more established competitor. Buffett acquired the Nebraska Furniture Mart in 1983 because he liked the way its founder, Rose Blumkin, did business. A Russian immigrant, she built the mart from a pawnshop into the largest furniture store in North America. Her strategy was to undersell the big shots, and she was a merciless negotiator. To Buffett, Rose embodied the unwavering courage that makes a winner out of an underdog.

8. *Know when to quit.* Once, when Buffett was a teen, he went to the racetrack. He bet on a race and lost. To recoup his funds, he bet on another race. He lost again, leaving him with close to nothing. He felt sick—he had squandered nearly a week's earnings. Buffett never repeated that mistake. Know when to walk away from a loss, and don't let anxiety fool you into trying again.

9. *Assess the risks.* In 1995, the employer of Buffett's son, Howie, was accused by the FBI of price-fixing. Buffett advised Howie to imagine the worst- and best-case scenarios if he stayed with the company. His son quickly realized that the risks of staying far outweighed any potential gains, and he quit the next day. Asking yourself "and then what?" can help you see all of the possible consequences when you're struggling to make a decision—and can guide you to the smartest choice.

10. *Know what success really means.* Despite his wealth, Buffett does not measure success by dollars. In 2006, he pledged to give away almost his entire fortune to charities, primarily the Bill and Melinda Gates Foundation. He's adamant about not funding monuments to himself—no Warren Buffett buildings or halls. "I know people who have a lot of money," he says, "and they get

testimonial dinners and hospital wings named after them. But the truth is that nobody in the world loves them. When you get to my age, you'll measure your success in life by how many of the people you want to have love you actually do love you. That's the ultimate test of how you've lived your life."

Warren Edward Buffett is an investor, businessman and philanthropist. He is one of the world's most successful investors and the largest shareholder and CEO of Berkshire Hathaway. He was ranked by Forbes *as the richest person in the world during the first half of 2008, with an estimated net worth of $62.0 billion.*

Alice Schroeder began her career as a certified public accountant, working for Ernst & Young before being appointed as a managing director at Morgan Stanley in the equities division. Schroeder first met Warren Buffett in 1998. Her book The Snowball: Warren Buffet and the Business of Life *was published by Bloomsbury in September 2008. There have been many books written about Warren Buffett that purport to reveal the formula for his investment genius, but* The Snowball *will be the first and only book with his cooperation.*

Why How Matters

By Thomas L. Friedman

From *The New York Times,* October 14, 2008 © 2008 The New York Times. All rights reserved. Used by permission and protected by the Copyright Laws of the United States. The printing, copying, redistribution, or retransmission of the Material without express written permission is prohibited.

I have a friend who regularly reminds me that if you jump off the top of an 80-story building, for 79 stories you can actually think you're flying. It's the sudden stop at the end that always gets you.

When I think of the financial-services boom, bubble and bust that America has just gone through, I often think about that image. We thought we were flying. Well, we just met the sudden stop at the end. The laws of gravity, it turns out, still apply. You cannot tell tens of thousands of people that they can have the American dream—a home, for no money down and nothing to pay for two years—without that eventually catching up to you. The Puritan ethic of hard work and saving still matters. I just hate the idea that such an ethic is more alive today in China than in America.

America's financial bubble, like all bubbles, has many complex strands feeding into it—called derivatives and credit-default swaps—but at heart, it is really very simple. We Americans got away from the basics—from the fundamentals of prudent lending and borrowing, where the lender and borrower maintain some kind of personal responsibility for, and personal interest in, whether the person receiving the money can actually pay it back. Instead, we fell into what some people call Y.B.G. and I.B.G. lending: "you'll be gone and I'll be gone" before the bill comes due.

Yes, this bubble is about us—not all of us, many Americans were way too poor to play. But it is about enough of us to say it is about America. And we will not get out of this without going back to some basics, which is why I find myself re-reading a valuable book that I wrote about once before, called *How: Why How We Do Anything Means Everything in Business (and in Life)*. Its author, Dov Seidman, is the CEO of LRN, which helps companies build ethical corporate cultures.

Seidman basically argues that in our hyperconnected and transparent world, how you do things matters more than ever, because so many more people can now see how you do things, be affected by how you do things and tell others how you do things on the Internet anytime, for no cost and without restraint.

"In a connected world," Seidman said to me, "countries, governments and companies also have character, and their character—how they do what they do, how they keep promises, how they make decisions, how things really happen inside, how they connect and collaborate, how they engender trust, how they relate to their customers, to the environment and to the communities in which they operate—is now their fate."

We got away from these hows. We became more connected than ever in recent years, but the connections were actually very loose. That is, we went away from a world in which, if you wanted a mortgage to buy a home, you needed to show real income and a credit record into a world where a banker could sell you a mortgage and make gobs of money upfront and then offload your mortgage to a bundler who put a whole bunch together, chopped them into bonds and sold some to banks as far afield as Iceland.

The bank writing the mortgage got away from how because it was just passing you along to a bundler. And the investment bank bundling these mortgages got away from how because it didn't know you, but it knew it was lucrative to bundle your mortgage with others. And the credit-rating agency got away from how because there was just so much money to be made in giving good ratings to these bonds, why delve too deeply? And the bank in Iceland got away from how because, hey, everyone else was buying the stuff and returns were great—so why not?

"UBS bank's motto is: 'You and us.' But the world we created was actually 'You and nobody'—nobody was really connected in value terms," said Seidman. "Parts of Wall Street got disconnected from investing in human endeavor—helping business to scale and take up new ideas." Instead, they started to just engineer money from money. "So some of the smartest CEOs did not know what some of their smartest people were doing."

Charles Mackay wrote a classic history of financial crises called *Extraordinary Popular Delusions and the Madness of Crowds*, first published in London in 1841. "Money . . . has often been a cause of the delusion of multitudes. Sober nations have all at once become desperate gamblers, and risked almost their existence upon the turn of a piece of paper. To trace the history of the most prominent of these delusions is the object of the present pages. Men, it has been well said, think in herds; it will be seen that they go mad in herds, while they only recover their senses slowly, and one by one."

And so it must be with us. We need to get back to collaborating the old-fashioned way. That is, people making decisions based on business judgment, experience, prudence, clarity of communications and thinking about how—not just how much.

Thomas L. Friedman has written a column for The New York Times *since 1981, covering financial news and international relations. He is the author of* The Lexus and the Olive Tree, Longitudes and Latitudes: Exploring the World after September 11 *and the bestselling* From Beirut to Jerusalem. *He has won three Pulitzer Prizes.*

Ending Poverty One Loan at a Time: Dr. Yunus and The Grameen Bank

By Julie Burtinshaw

Over thirty years ago, Dr. Muhammad Yunus, a young economics professor in Bangladesh, saw a world morally bankrupt and awash in poverty. Unable in good conscience to continue teaching an economic theory that did next to nothing to help the underprivileged, and in fact ensured they remained impoverished, Dr. Yunus paused for a moment and dared, as do all great humanitarians, to think not with his head but with his heart.

In that moment, he envisioned a world where poverty was a thing of the past; a world where being poor didn't mean being worthless, where every human being had the right to live and prosper in safety, free to earn a living and to raise healthy, educated children.

His dream, in his own words, was that "One day we will create poverty museums. We will take the next generation of children to show them what it used to be like, and they won't be able to believe it. There is no need for anybody to be poor."

His idea was simple, yet radical: he would provide small loans to the poorest people living in the poorest countries on earth, seed money so borrowers could build their own self-sustaining businesses. Preference would be given to women, for his own observations convinced him they were disciplined, hard workers who would go to enormous lengths to first feed and then to better the lives of their children.

Dr. Yunus built the Grameen Bank on the simple concept that people can be trusted to do the right thing. Clients don't have collateral, nor do they have credit ratings or loan guarantors. They have only their word and their desire to be successful and self-sufficient contributors to their families and their communities.

Sounds a bit risky, a bit sub-prime? Not at all. Since its inception, The Grameen Bank has lent billions of dollars to the impoverished and boasts a ninety-eight percent payback rate. Borrowers might be materially poor, but ethically they are rich.

Over a hundred million families are now able to feed, cloth and educate themselves. The children of the original borrowers are graduating from universities all over the world. The dream has become a reality.

The author of three best-selling non-fiction books, Dr. Yunus is the recipient of honorary doctorates from universities around the world. In 2008, he received the James C. Morgan Global Humanitarian Award, and admiring youth groups have given him the title "The Global Agent of Change." In 2006, he received the Nobel Peace Prize for his "efforts to create economic and social development from below."

In spite of all of his accomplishments, Dr. Yunus continues to have big dreams. His latest projects include analyzing the many ways technology can help end world poverty. Because he believes that "rich people should not make money out of poor people," he is also encouraging large companies to form business partnerships in developing countries, with participating corporations investing in start-up social enterprises. Their investments are returned, but instead of financial profits, investors see emotional profits—the joy realized when people help other people, and participating companies continue to witness the tremendous positive social impacts their partnerships have in the lives of the Bangladeshi.

Since vowing to end world poverty, Dr. Yunus has become a champion of women and the poor all over the world. In the United States over twelve percent of the population—some forty million people—live in poverty. Currently there are only a few micro-lending institutions, yet the idea is spreading beyond developing countries. In March, 2008, The Grameen Bank opened in New York City, and has already lent over €100,000 (euros), mostly to women who can't otherwise get the credit necessary to start their own self-sustaining business ventures.

Everyone can be a part of this dream. Volunteers are welcome, or you can donate money through the Grameen Foundation, and designate the recipient country and city. You can encourage your government to support micro-lending in inner cities across the country. Words are powerful—you can spread the word about Dr. Yunus and the Grameen Bank. Most importantly, always remember that there is no correlation between one's credit rating and credibility.

Julie Burtinshaw lives in Vancouver, British Columbia, with her husband, their two children and Kitty. Julie is the author of five novels and is also a web editor. She is an avid cyclist and does her best to minimize her carbon footprint by walking, cycling or using public transit whenever possible. She is also passionate about travel and loves to read.

Protecting the World's Children

By King Duncan

A church worker with a passion for economic justice tells of visiting sweatshops in Southeast Asia where young children slave for fifteen hours a day, sometimes earning less than a dollar for the entire day. He discovered children being fed drugs and caffeine pills to keep them alert during their long shifts. At one factory he met a boy with a long scar down his face. The boy explained that one day he was working too slowly, so the sweatshop foreman began to beat him. During the beating, the boy's face was slashed open, and he began to bleed. The foreman didn't want the child to bleed all over his work, so he took a lighter and burned the wound closed.

The United Nations Children's Fund estimates that hundreds of millions of children worldwide are being exploited in ways that are hazardous to their safety, physical or mental health, and moral development. If we truly are to achieve heaven on earth, we cannot ignore the plight of these young people.

Let's begin by considering the root cause of child labor—deep and relentless poverty. We might wonder how parents of these children can allow them to be exploited. Do they love their children less than we love ours? Of course not. Families do what they have to do to survive. There was a time in the United States when children in rural areas were kept out of school to help with the family farm. Families were large. Children provided cheap labor. At the same time, many children in poorer families in cities also had to work under grueling conditions to help their families get by. A combination of rising family incomes and a campaign to help parents see the value of education enabled millions of American children to have better lives.

The emerging global economy provides us with an unprecedented opportunity to better the conditions under which all the world's people, including its children, can live. However, this will require a careful balancing of four of the Ten Elements—freedom, prosperity, ecological soundness, and moral purpose and meaning.

We must begin by resisting calls in our society, whether from the left or the right, to stifle free trade. Family incomes around the world are rising. Admittedly this has brought on a host of new problems, including a strain on the environment, on food and energy resources, and displacement of workers in industrialized countries. Still, free trade, in the long run, is the best tool we have to lift the majority of the world's people out of poverty. The principle that "a rising tide lifts all boats" has been validated beyond all reasonable doubt.

At the same time, we must constantly monitor the activities of corporations and other business interests, as well as governments, in emerging economies. Most business leaders are responsible human beings, but there will always be individuals who will exploit dire economic conditions. Let's not be naïve. There was a time when people lived and worked in sometimes horrendous conditions in most western nations. Today we enjoy the benefits of a careful balance between the needs of labor and capital. This balance, however, was not achieved without pain and strife. We cannot expect that injustices will not occur in developing countries even as living conditions improve overall.

We can also respond to the problem of child labor by supporting organizations that are raising awareness, and by providing direct help to individual children. There are dedicated people who are sacrificing much to keep us informed about injustices worldwide and to minister to the needs of those being exploited. We need to listen to their voices and respond accordingly. We need to open our hearts and our wallets. We need to advance programs of education that help families in developing countries see the value of educating their young, just as we in western nations came to appreciate that value.

Finally, if we know that people anywhere—especially children—are being exploited, it is our moral responsibility to exert any personal and corporate influence we have to rectify the situation.

Then, and only then, can we say that we have helped in the work of achieving heaven on earth

King Duncan, who graduated from the University of Tennessee, is a professional speaker and the author of several books, including The Amazing Law of Influence: How You Can Change Your World. *He and his wife have four grown daughters.*

The Great Seduction by Debt

By David Brooks

From *The New York Times*, June 10, 2008 © 2008 The New York Times. All rights reserved. Used by permission and protected by the Copyright Laws of the United States. The printing, copying, redistribution, or retransmission of the Material without express written permission is prohibited.

The people who created this country built a moral structure around money. The Puritan legacy inhibited luxury and self-indulgence. Benjamin Franklin spread a practical gospel that emphasized hard work, temperance and frugality. Millions of parents, preachers, newspaper editors and teachers expounded the message. The result was quite remarkable.

The United States has been an affluent nation since its founding. But the country was, by and large, not corrupted by wealth. For centuries, it remained industrious, ambitious and frugal.

Over the past thirty years, much of that has been shredded. The social norms and institutions that encouraged frugality and spending what you earn have been undermined. The institutions that encourage debt and living for the moment have been strengthened. The country's moral guardians are forever looking for decadence out of Hollywood and reality TV. But the most rampant decadence today is financial decadence, the trampling of decent norms about how to use and harness money.

Sixty-two scholars have signed on to a report by the Institute for American Values and other think tanks called *For a New Thrift: Confronting the Debt Culture*, examining the results of all this. This may be damning with faint praise, but it's one of the most important think-tank reports you'll read this year.

The deterioration of financial mores has meant two things. First, it's meant an explosion of debt that inhibits social mobility and ruins lives. Between 1989 and 2001, credit-card debt nearly tripled, soaring from $238 billion to $692 billion. By last year, it was up to $937 billion, the report said. Second, the transformation has led to a stark financial polarization. On the one hand, there is what the report calls the investor class. It has tax-deferred savings plans, as well as an army of financial advisers. On the other hand, there is the lottery class, people with little access to 401(k)s or financial planning but plenty of access to payday lenders, credit cards and lottery agents.

The loosening of financial inhibition has meant more options for the well-educated but more temptation and chaos for the most vulnerable. Social norms, the invisible threads that guide behavior, have deteriorated. Over the past years, Americans have been more socially conscious about protecting the environment and inhaling tobacco. They have become less socially conscious about money and debt.

The agents of destruction are many. State governments have played a role. They aggressively hawk their lottery products, which some people call a tax on stupidity. Twenty percent of Americans are frequent players, spending about $60 billion a year. The spending is starkly regressive. A household with income under $13,000 spends, on average, $645 a year on lottery tickets, about nine percent of all income. Aside from the financial toll, the moral toll is comprehensive. Here is the government, the guardian of order, telling people that they don't have to work to build for the future. They can strike it rich for nothing.

Payday lenders have also played a role. They seductively offer fast cash—at absurd interest rates—to fifteen million people every month. Credit card companies have played a role. Instead of targeting the financially astute, who pay off their debts, they've found that they can make money off the young and vulnerable. Fifty-six percent of students in their final year of college carry four or more credit cards.

Congress and the White House have played a role. The nation's leaders have always had an incentive to shove costs for current promises onto the backs of future generations. It's only now become respectable to do so.

Wall Street has played a role. Bill Gates built a socially useful product to make his fortune. But what message do the compensation packages that hedge fund managers get send across the country?

The list could go on. But the report, which is nicely summarized by Barbara Dafoe Whitehead in *The American Interest* (available free online), also has some recommendations. First, raise public consciousness about debt the way the anti-smoking activists did with their campaign. Second, create institutions that encourage thrift.

Foundations and churches could issue short-term loans to cut into the payday lenders' business. Public and private programs could give the poor and middle class access to financial planners. Usury laws could be enforced and strengthened. Colleges could reduce credit card advertising on campus. KidSave accounts would encourage savings from a young age. The tax code should tax consumption, not income, and in the meantime, it should do more to encourage savings up and down the income ladder.

There are dozens of things that could be done. But the most important is to shift values. Franklin made it prestigious to embrace certain bourgeois virtues. Now it's socially acceptable to undermine those virtues. It's considered normal to play the debt game and imagine that decisions made today will have no consequences for the future.

David Brooks graduated from the University of Chicago, and has written for The New Yorker, The New York Times, The New York Times Magazine, Forbes, The Washington Post, The Wall Street Journal, Newsweek *and the* Atlantic Monthly. *He is the author of* Bobos In Paradise: The New Upper Class and How They Got There *and* On Paradise Drive: How We Live Now (And Always Have) in the Future Tense, *and is a commentator on* The Newshour with Jim Lehrer.

What's the Money For?

By Peter J. Tanous

In my professional life as an investment consultant I often come in contact with individuals who need help in managing their wealth. They come to my firm because they want to grow their assets prudently. We go over the standard litany of questions as we ask about their age, tolerance for risk, and investment objectives. As part of the latter discussion, we also ask: "What's this money for?"

Now most of our clients have more than enough money to retire comfortably, whenever that moment in their lives comes around. They generally have ample resources to put their children through school, to take splendid vacations, and even to own an extra house or two in some part of the world they enjoy visiting. So the question of what the money is for takes on special relevance. After all, the money will last well beyond their lifetimes so what do they want it to do after they are gone? Of course, they could always leave their fortunes to their children, but leaving large sums of money to heirs has lost its cachet among the very wealthy. Few want to leave the fortune they worked so hard to build to a bunch of kids who may opt out of work and devote a career to enjoying the good life without effort or responsibilities. Imagine that you are one of these fortunate individuals. How might you contribute to leaving the world a better place? After all, if you are fortunate enough to have prospered in life, the notion of sharing your wealth with others involves a special challenge that may be just as daunting as the ones you encountered becoming wealthy in the first instance.

In listening to my clients and then advising them on these subjects, I am no longer surprised at the number of different ideas there are about leaving a legacy of shared wealth. For some, homelessness is a major issue; for others it is the fate of undernourished and abandoned children in different parts of the world. I sit on the board of directors of Christian Children's Fund, a charity to which one of my close friends contributes millions of dollars to help needy children wherever the need is greatest. For some, endowing one's alma mater has special appeal. Imagine a building bearing your name on the campus where you spent those happy college years. Still others consider literacy of prime importance, arguing that if we help children become educated, we enhance their ability to find work and support themselves and their families later in life. There are those who consider the beautification of the planet a source of joy to the world, and they endow botanical gardens and other expressions of nature in their communities. Clean air, clean water, going Green—all attract their share of dedicated donors.

Interesting to me is that almost all the wealthy individuals I know really want to leave a mark on the world after they leave it. Many do so as a refection of their profound faith in God, and their obligation to serve Him by following his prescripts to "do unto others." But even those who may be considered "spiritually challenged" often come around to the same desire to help others, motivated no doubt by the concept of giving back to whomever or whatever enabled them to succeed.

But do you have to be super rich to make a difference? Of course not! The same principles apply to every good deed we do. I see it all around me. Many of our employees contribute to various causes in their own ways. One young woman in our office spends nights manning the phones at a sexual abuse hotline. Others volunteer at schools and hospitals. I see a desire to share almost everywhere I look. Rich or poor, we might not as individuals succeed in creating a heaven on earth, but with desire, imagination, generosity of spirit and wealth along with our own personal efforts, we just might come pretty close.

After high school in Paris, a degree from Georgetown University, and two years in the U. S. Army, Peter J. Tanous began a career as an investment banker and counselor. He has served on several corporate boards and has written numerous books on money management and investing.

Changing the Game of Work

By Christine Barnes

Five minutes into our second session, she was in tears.

My coaching client, overwhelmed by fear of challenging the status quo, was also deeply saddened by wasted years of compromise at work, and yearning to claim values she held dear: respect, meaningful work and fulfillment. What made this an atypical coaching session was not that we talked about her values or that she is a corporate client and that I'm an internal coach in a very large technology company. It was that she wanted to be more effective in her job and honor her values.

It's time to change the game at work and redesign the contract between employees and companies. At the very first Spirituality in Business conference (Mazatlan 1995), attendees complained they couldn't "bring their whole selves" to work. As if we hit our spirituality snooze button when we get to work; as if we flick the on/off button of who we are, depending on where we are; as if we have to choose between our work selves and our true selves.

Why can't we bring our whole selves, including our values and our spirituality, to work? All smart, talented, committed people I have come across in twenty-five years of work, regardless of company size, industry or country, have been willing to put one hundred percent of themselves into their jobs, and only ever really wanted to feel engaged.

The Corporate Leadership Council defines employee engagement as "The extent to which employees commit to something or someone in their organization—and how hard they work and how long they stay as a result of that commitment."

A culture of engagement is not just an empty platitude. In a 2004 global survey of fifty thousand employees on employee engagement, CLC found that "By increasing employees' engagement levels, organizations can expect up to a twenty percentile point increase in performance and an eighty-seven percent reduction in employees' probability of departure."

If a culture of engagement makes good business sense, what's the current status? CLC found, in the same survey, thirteen percent of employees were "disaffected," exhibiting very little commitment to the organization, and therefore very little discretionary effort. While seventy-six percent were "moderately committed," only eleven percent exhibited "very strong commitment."

Why such low levels of engagement? For one thing, engagement is difficult to measure, compared to sales figures, earnings per share, or number of units produced. Second, effective leadership is one of the most important reasons employees stay and thrive in companies, yet it is elusive and complex to achieve.

Even so, individuals and companies can build an engagement culture, where employees can feel fulfilled and make huge contributions. You can start at any level. Don't wait for the CEO to build a culture of engagement, but begin creating heaven on earth for your employees now. Ask questions such as:

Do you know what's expected of you at work?

Do you have the materials you need to do your work?

Do you have the opportunity to do what you're best at, every day?

In the past seven days have you received recognition or praise for doing good work?

Share best practices. Compare notes with colleagues at other companies and implement one thing from your research. Identify what you do best, and ask your manager to work with you on how to do more of those things. If you can't talk with your manager, look for those ways on your own. Discuss it with colleagues and team members. If you could implement just one idea to make your job more interesting, more effective and more fun, what would you do?

Mentor someone, inside or outside your company. Ask someone you admire to mentor you (you can be a mentor and a mentee at the same time). Make employee development a measurable goal as important as sales or financial goals, then reward it. Get clear on your life purpose and look for work that honors that purpose.

Finally, participate in a "spirit at work" conference; share best practices with others.

Most people want to make a meaningful contribution to the world and do their best every day. Engaged employees contributing to the success and viability of a company seems like a match made in heaven and should not take an act of God.

Christine Barnes is an organization development consultant and certified coach with a global high tech company. Her version of heaven on earth at work is to create a coaching culture in her company, so that individuals, teams and lines of business will realize their full potential.

The Obligation to Help the Poor

By Kenneth Einar Himma

Poverty is perhaps the most significant cause of conflict in the world today. One billion of the world's six billion people live in life-threatening poverty, earning less than a dollar a day. Two billion more live in potentially life-threatening poverty, earning less than three dollars a day. Still more, who live in poverty in the affluent world, have enough to survive but so much less than others around them that they are treated as having less moral worth. Wherever it occurs, in Sierra Leone or major American cities, the result of dire poverty is suffering and a threat to peace.

Many people believe helping the poor is morally good but not required, that the only moral obligations we have are negative; we are obligated, for example, to refrain from killing, stealing, lying, etc. Charity is optional.

This pernicious view not only perpetuates poverty and strife around the world, but is inconsistent with the ethics of every classical religion. It is clear that Christian ethics entail an obligation to help the poor. In Matthew 22:39, Jesus commands that we love our neighbors as ourselves. It might be argued that someone who spends money on unnecessarily expensive trips is clearly not loving someone in life-threatening poverty as himself or herself because the latter's life is at stake while all the former has at stake is a desire for a nice vacation.

Indeed, in Matthew 25:31-46, Jesus aligns his own interests with those of the poor, distinguishing those whose fate is eternal paradise from those whose fate is suffering in terms of how they responded to suffering. Jesus states here that how we treat the "least amongst us" is how we treat Jesus himself.

Judaism grounds Tzedakah, an obligation to help the poor, in both the Torah and the Talmud. Leviticus 19:18 states the very law that entails the Christian obligation to help the poor: "You shall not take vengeance or bear a grudge against any of your people, but you shall love your neighbor as yourself." Leviticus 23:22 puts the point in terms of agricultural products, but the point remains the same: "And when you reap the harvest of your land, you shall not reap all the way to the edges of your field, or gather the gleanings of your harvest; you shall leave them for the poor and the stranger."

The Talmud is no less specific. Tractate Baba Bathra states: "It has been taught: R. Meir used to say: The critic [of Judaism] may bring against you the argument, 'If your God loves the poor, why does he not support them?' If so, answer him, 'So that through them we may be saved from the punishment of Gehinnom.'" As Rabbi Maurice Lamm sums up the Jewish view, "Support for the disadvantaged in Judaism is not altruism. It is justice." And to do justice, of course, is obligatory; in the case of Judaism, it is necessary to save the Jew from a meaningless death. As such, it is a commandment and an obligation.

Islam defines the obligation to help the poor as one of the five basic pillars or obligations of its faith. These pillars also obligate Muslims to declare that there is no God but Allah and Muhammad is the Messenger of God, to worship in prayer five times daily while facing Mecca, to fast from sunrise to sunset during the holy month of Ramadan, and to make a pilgrimage to Mecca.

People work hard for their affluence, of course, but no one wholly deserves it. Luck plays as large a role as personal merit in determining who has what. Had Bill Gates' parents lived in absolute poverty in sub-Saharan Africa, he would surely not be one of the world's richest people. Although Gates' personal merits obviously played an important role in his success, he was lucky in that he was born into the affluent world instead of the developing world, and that has made all the difference.

Sometimes it is morally permissible to keep all that you have lucked into, but when luck determines the difference between having much more than you need to survive and not having enough to survive, we who have been lucky are obligated to help those who have not. One important step towards realizing something like heaven on earth is to start meeting our obligation to alleviate poverty.

This does not mean that people should be coerced into giving, for that is not a gesture of love. Nor does it mean that people are obligated to give away all disposable income and wealth; surely, God wants people to be happy, allowing them to devote some of their resources to making themselves and loved ones happy. But it does mean that we are sometimes morally required to subordinate our own happiness to help others who are in desperate need. We should do what is reasonably within our means to help people in need, by contributing our time, energy and material resources to organizations committed to reducing poverty, like Habitat for Humanity, CARE, and World Vision. Our efforts should focus not only on alleviating the life-threatening effects of absolute poverty, but also on providing information and technologies that will make poor nations self-sustaining, remembering that someone who is hungry or sick likely lacks the energy and focus to learn.

Kenneth Einar Himma teaches philosophy at Seattle Pacific University and formerly taught in the philosophy department, information school and law school at the University of Washington. He has published more than one hundred scholarly articles in the areas of philosophy of religion, philosophy of law, and information and computer ethics, and presented papers all over the world.

What Isn't Advertised

By Jane Roper

Not many people would characterize advertising as a force for good in the world. Its critics decry it for promoting materialism, greed and excess. Many also rightly blame advertising for perpetuating stereotypes in its depictions of gender and ethnicity. Others lament the growing pervasiveness of advertising; as marketers find more and better ways to get their messages out—from cell phones to virtual billboards to the sides of rickshaw carriages— it's becoming increasingly difficult to escape the onslaught of corporate logos and reminders to buy, buy, buy.

But advertising is also an inevitable—and arguably essential— part of capitalism and, therefore, the prosperity that capitalism can bring. And it's not going away any time soon. For as long as people have sold their services and wares, there has been advertising of one kind or another. Some of it is crass and misleading, but some of it is thought provoking, even artful. The harshest critics would probably, if grudgingly, agree that there's nothing inherently immoral about advertising, as long as it's truthful.

But therein lies the question: is there such a thing as truth in advertising?

Take the hypothetical example of an ad for laundry detergent. Suppose it's scientifically proven that Brand X gets clothes cleaner than Brand Y. So, the makers of Brand X broadcast a commercial showing a happy-looking family using their detergent to get grass stains out of their kids' soccer uniforms and red wine stains off their dress shirts, while an announcer tells us that Brand X is proven to fight stains better than Brand Y. Technically, the Brand X people haven't made any false claims.

But what they have done—subtly, subliminally, perhaps

without even consciously intending it—is suggest that when you buy Brand X, you'll not only get cleaner clothes, you'll get a taste of everything else you saw in the commercial: the big bright house, the healthy children and the means and time to play organized sports, the luxury of red wine and nice clothes to spill it on—the kind of clothes only people with well-paid jobs are likely to have.

In short, Brand X has forged in our minds an association between their product and a prosperous, ostensibly happy way of life. They have caused us to consider if, in fact, it actually does matter what detergent we buy. You might go so far as to say that Brand X wants us to believe their product will bring us one step closer to heaven on earth.

But it's a two-way street: we, the audience, also want to believe them. If we didn't, they would have changed their tactics long ago. All of us, at one time or another, have fallen for the illusory promise of advertising: that success is just a matter of achieving a higher level of wealth, beauty or style; that a more sophisticated computer, a better-tasting cola, or a more powerful detergent will move us toward that elusive happiness we all crave.

Why do we fall for it? Because it is so enticingly simple. Imagine if, instead of through hard work and sacrifice, selflessness and self-awareness, we could create heaven on earth just by spending our money a certain way. Imagine if we really could become better people, and lead better lives, if only we bought Brand X.

Advertisers will always want us to believe that we can. It's the nature of their work, done not with malice or ill intent, but the simple goal of selling. Meanwhile, even the most enlightened consumer will not always be able to resist the temptation to look for contentment at their nearest retail outlet. Indeed, there is plenty to be said for the pleasure and utility of material things.

But in the face of ever more artful and ubiquitous advertising, we should strive to stay mindful of the fact that it is, at least in part, an illusion. We can't let ourselves fall so completely under its spell that we lose sight of what is most essential to creating heaven on earth: kindness, generosity, tolerance, perseverance—things that can't be bought or sold, but that deserve to be better advertised.

Jane Roper is senior copywriter at the Boston marketing communications agency PARTNERS+simons, where she does her best to practice truth in advertising. A graduate of the Iowa Writers' Workshop, Jane writes fiction and essays, as well as "Baby Squared," a narrative blog on the parenting website Babble.com about her experiences as a mother of twins.

Preservation Complements Prosperity: The New Orleans Example

By Patty Gay

Citizens of cities can learn from each other, and New Orleans has an example par excellence for other cities to consider. The lesson is simply this: tremendous long-term economic, cultural and sociological benefits accrue when the historic urban plan and built environment are preserved. Put another way, it is not an economic hardship to preserve historic buildings. The opposite is true.

The evidence is quite apparent and obvious for all to see, in the thriving Vieux Carré, the original 1718 city of New Orleans. The ultimate goal was to build a beautiful city, defined by standards that had evolved over thousands of years and remain true today. That is exactly what happened. Within a few decades visitors were remarking on the unique charm and beauty of the city, as they still do today.

Since 1936, New Orleans has officially protected its original city, the Vieux Carré, an area of approximately eighty-five square blocks with two thousand properties. While the area is dense, with most buildings having common walls, most of the buildings are one, two and three stories. To repeat, it has not been an economic hardship to preserve these buildings. The Vieux Carré anchors one of the strongest tourism industries in the United States, one that is important to the city and the state.

But certainly the benefits go beyond tourism. In assessing economic impact of the tourism industry, one should count not only the number of visitors and dollars spent; because the area is attractive to visitors, it is also attractive to business investment and prospective residents. The culture and quality of life of a place, something visitors seek out, is a major determinant in decisions to locate a business or residence. Visitors, residents, business investment—all are attracted to areas that are visually appealing and culturally interesting, and authentic and unique. This is accomplished through preservation and protection of a historic area.

Tourism is not an industry to ignore. It is said that tourism is the largest industry in the world. The competition is great, but a city can compete by preserving at the very least a portion of its historic built environment, ideally by also adopting a city plan that includes historic preservation as a key element, requiring development that is sensitive to its context and that reflects the identity of the area.

Tourism, of course, as with any industry, must evolve appropriately and only complement what is there to enjoy, preserve and protect. The adage "Don't kill the goose that laid the golden egg" is appropriate when pursuing tourism development. Careful planning and strong enforcement of regulations are called for. For example, preserving the Vieux Carré not only was so economically successful that by the 1960s the entire area was on the verge of becoming a collection of hotels, certainly not what visitors came to New Orleans to see. Legislation was passed that prohibited any additional hotel development in the Vieux Carré. Was this an economic hardship for the city? Not in the least. The integrity of the Vieux Carré was preserved, and there soon was major hotel development outside the area. There is also the threat of cultural degradation in order to attract visitors. Measures can be taken to avoid this problem as well. The pressure is still on, in spite of successful legislation, to make exceptions and to lower standards, yet many understand the importance of maintaining the Vieux Carré as an authentic tourist attraction, as opposed to a resort or theme park.

There could be no stronger visual statement about a community than that reflected in well-preserved historic commercial and residential areas: the statement is loud and clear that here is a place that is thriving, where people care and are civically involved. The opposite is true when new buildings, inappropriate in scale and design, detracting from the surrounding environment, are erected in the place of the authentic. Often demolition takes place simply because of the argument that, for example, construction of a ten-story building will "generate jobs." This thinking only reflects an understanding of the short-term—genenerally such buildings are obsolete within a few years, and their construction has destabilized and even destroyed the area around them—and fails to consider the tremendous economic potential of appropriate economic development. Had the historic buildings in the Vieux Carré been replaced, there would be no tourism industry in New Orleans today; worse, the city would have no heart, no identity, and would have lost even more of its urban populations in other neighborhoods.

Which leads to the most important point: vitality of the heart of the city is essential to the quality of life of its residents. If the heart has been destroyed, surrounding neighborhoods begin to languish and decline. The "broken window" theory takes effect, as house after house, street after street, and entire neighborhoods are destabilized and abandoned. By assuring the preservation of the Vieux Carré, New Orleans, unlike so many other American cities, has seen its older neighborhoods resist typical urban decline, and even thrive with their own unique identities and loyal residents. In fact, this has been a major factor in the recovery effort in New Orleans, post-Katrina. Evacuated residents were determined to come home to their unique neighborhoods and rich cultural heritage.

Many historic areas are run down and in need of revitalization measures. Cities should take heart. It is worth every incentive and every bit of other public assistance to preserve a historic area. Proof is in the Vieux Carré, which in fact was very much in decline when the legislation was passed to preserve it in 1936. Worse began to happen to urban historic areas across the country after 1945, when federal programs involved federally-funded demolitions and subsidized suburban development that caused urban populations to decline. First, protection is essential to avoid loss of irreplaceable historic building stock and neighborhoods, but that was not enough. In the National Preservation Act of 1966 provisions were made for a review process, for incentives and for the development of preservation programs which have reversed urban decline in many cities. For example, a federally-funded overhead expressway that would have walled off the Vieux Carré from the riverfront was stopped as a result of this legislation.

More needs to be done, but the most important point is that strategies have worked, and in no case were not worth it. While success often brings new problems, a civic consciousness that older neighborhoods generate is the best platform from which to address these problems.

Examples abound around the world where cities that have protected their historic built environments enjoy prosperity and a rich quality of life. Yet with the advent of globalism and the pressures of short-term "economic development" trends in many countries, cities are very much threatened with the loss of identity and culture, and with destabilization that inappropriate new construction generates. New Orleans presents a special case study, having established protection of its original city with positive results. It is documented that the Vieux Carré is today critical to the economy of the city. Not so easy to quantify but even more important is the positive impact on older neighborhoods, and the perpetuation of the city's rich culture that is recognized around the world but means the most to its residents. The same benefits would accrue to any city willing to take this path to a richer future for all of its citizens.

Since 1980, Patty Gay has been executive director of the Preservation Resource Center of New Orleans, a citywide not-for-profit organization with a staff of forty-six and numerous volunteers. An important voice at the state, local and federal levels, she supports legislation to protect historic resources and promote neighborhood revitalization.

Society's True Wealth

By Thomas Höhenleitner

After the Berlin Wall came down in 1990, I spent most of my money on books, books I never had been allowed to read, some I had never even had heard of. One of them was *Chaos: Making a New Science* by James Gleick. He explained why chaos is creative and the better choice instead of order. On reflection, I first decided that his idea is only one side of the coin; then I concluded that his statement is true if your system borders are infinite. The closer the limits of a system, the more order is necessary. Imagine you are with some friends on a boat enjoying a days-long party. Then suppose a storm knocks out the radio and electrical system. You're stranded with just a few soft drinks and a bit of food. You have no idea if help will arrive or if so, how long it will take. Until the storm the system limits had been wide and everyone could do what he or she liked. Afterwards the system borders are very close, and the best thing for all is to establish a strong order, hard rules, just to survive.

Or consider a baby. From its point of view, the system borders are infinite, and the best it can do is chaotic behavior, constantly experimenting. As the child becomes older, he needs more and more order. And when a person is elderly, his system limits are very close and he needs much more order to live a bit longer, perhaps a daily nap and a glass of wine. So we can see a lifetime as a change-over from chaos to order.

A hundred years ago nobody was talking about environmental pollution. Why is it different today? One hundred years ago environmental resources seemed infinite, but now we see how limited they are. The rain forests are disappearing, there is global climate change, forcing society to establish ever-increasing rules for everyone. So we are in a process of rising global order, evident in the political world as well as the commercial world.

What about government—is our system of elections the best one? Most people I talk with agree that this system can be improved. I'm not sure how, but I have some ideas to toss out there for consideration. Let us imagine we have no parties anymore and no elections at all. We have a parliament whose members are selected by chance, as members of juries are determined in the United States, resulting in a body that truly represents a cross-section of the public. Filling offices, from the president down to the most minor local one, would be the responsibility of the parliament.

As an alternative, nations would still have elections, but not to elect persons or parties. Voting would be through a questionnaire, on which everyone would give his opinion, and the more detailed the answers, the more heavily those results would be weighted statistically. Perhaps my ideas sound a little bit strange, but these are just ideas to encourage thought and discussion.

An American scientist—whose name I don't remember—wrote an article on which of the world's people consider themselves the luckiest. Citizens of more than fifty countries responded to a series of questions, including "Do you fear the future?" Surprisingly, the result of the study was that people of Bangladesh, one of the poorest countries in the world, are thought to be the luckiest people in the world. The paper concluded that people in poor situations are luckier than people in rich countries. This result is identical with the impressions I got during my travels. I met rich, even very rich people, and I met poor, very poor people. I lived with them in slums and in huge houses, and I found all the time that poor people are luckier than rich people. I did not understand why, but as I read the article and followed the author's thinking, I came to see that people in poor regions live together in big families, helping each other, forming close networks of love and cooperation.

My great-grandfather gestured in a way that symbolized money, and said, "If you have it, then the world is yours." Then came inflation and all was gone. My grandfather gestured to indicate the land, and said, "If you have it, then the world is yours." Then came the war and all was lost. My mother pointed to her head to indicate knowledge, and said, "If you have it, then the world is yours." I think her idea is closest to the truth, but still not completely correct. I place my hand over my heart and say, "If you have love, then the world is yours." What my little daughter will say later on I do not know, but knowledge combined with love for the rest of mankind must be in everybody to make the world better.

I ask myself, What is society's true wealth? Is it money? No, if we accept that poor people are indeed the luckiest. Is it infrastructure—streets, houses, power stations, computers and so on? Well, let us imagine that a magician can put us in the world as it was millions of years ago. Probably many people would die from lack of technology, including medicine, but I assume after a few generations mankind would again rise to a high level. But if the magician left the environment untouched but put our brains as they were millions of years ago, chaos would result. I think this mental exercise shows that society's true wealth is in our brains, our knowledge. And where does it grow? Mainly in the minds of our children. So for me, making the world a better place means first to give the best you can to the children. Give them your love, your knowledge, and help them collect experiences, for they are our future.

Born in Leipzig, Germany, Thomas Höhenleitner studied electronics engineering at Humboldt University in Berlin. His career has included research and design, project management, hardware development, software systems testing and market analysis. Besides German, he is fluent in English and conversant in Russian. He traveled around the world in 1991 and 1992, immersing himself in the cultures of the countries he visited.

Home Is Where the Spirit Is

By Emily Adams

In a more agrarian past, man kept in constant communication with his natural surroundings, aware of how the rhythms of nature affected the crops, the animals and the family. With the rigorous demands of our technological era, we have lost contact with the natural world, creating our own disharmony. Yet our relationship with our world is an inseparable aspect of our personality, and interior design provides an opportunity for rejuvenation of that original spirit within the home environment.

The process begins with an examination of oneself—self-reflection, one's natural responses to surroundings, including feelings about light, space, form and color. Interior design is about natural elements—wood, marble, granite, linen, cotton and silk—and combining these elements with light and texture within the sheltered walls of a home. Good design is about comfort, healing and inspiration. A designer's responsibility is to identify a healing influence by blending balance, harmony and renewal to create spaces that reflect the inner self.

If you find yourself expressing your creativity in your home with dramatic and interesting focal points, surrounded by photos or paintings you have produced yourself, you are an outgoing, love-of-life person, an extrovert. You likely would be comfortable in well-managed conversation areas, with textured sofas and chairs in casual fabrics of deep reds or greens. Perhaps you would have a fireplace or butcher block counter in your kitchen, for when entertaining you are probably in the center of the group.

As the romantic, you treasure deep relationships, dine by candlelight, and surround yourself with flower colors and delicate fabrics. Your home no doubt elicits warmth and coziness. You tend to prefer small scale furniture, perhaps in velvet or silk. Beautiful old jars and many cookbooks may fill your kitchen. A great day for you might be a day in the country or a long walk.

An exciting room for the natural achiever has lots of light and space with yellows or electric blues. Your furnishings might include modular units for seating, with paintings of athletic events or western action. Add in electrical gadgets. Your home must be a convenient, comfortable environment from which to initiate action and lively conversation.

If you are constantly experimenting and enjoy striking color combinations, abstract paintings or sculpture, you probably fall into the trendsetter category. Your most exciting rooms have surprises or eye-catching effects amidst lots of wall and floor space. Your bathroom might include a TV screen while your kitchen of unusually vivid colors might incorporate an indoor barbeque pit. The trendsetter is a forward-thinking person.

The character of the interiors I design is always different for each client, a direct response to his particular requirements, yet with a common thread: sensitivity to human needs, expectations and aspirations. The more sensitive I am in my work, the more inspired are the spaces and the people who live in them.

If I can create a paradise for individuals or families, then there is a spiritual awakening, as our essential human nature is not separate from the outside reality of beauty, balance and harmony.

I believe that most people desire love, comfort and creativity. True interior design enhances that potential by validating from the outside all that is within. If you are in touch with what is within yourself, you can enhance your surroundings with the elements— style of furniture, texture, color, light and accents—that make you happy and serene while at the same time energizing you, thus creating your own little heaven on earth.

The work of New Orleans-based interior designer Emily Adams has been featured in House & Garden, Metropolitan Home, Walls and Windows, Homes & Lifestyles, New Orleans Magazine, Southern Women *and* The Majesty of the French Quarter. *Her expertise in French and English design of the seventeenth through the nineteenth centuries assures a historical approach to her designs.*

Bringing Hearts Together

Reconcile New Orleans

New Orleans' Central City neighborhood is no different from low-income areas of any large city, with violence, drugs, apathy, hopelessness and lawlessness the prevalent themes, punctuated by graffiti, absent fathers, substandard housing, teenage pregnancy, and young people who think dropping out of school before graduation is the norm. But with vision and perseverance, a small group of dedicated, passionate individuals is working diligently to change all that, one group of young people at a time.

Craig Cuccia—in the midst of an exciting life of international travel, lucrative oil field work, a brief career in the hospitality field, and construction—became involved with a charismatic community and its leader, Father Emile LaFrance, a priest zealous about his vocation. Cuccia had seen poverty before, of course, but during a mission trip to Jamaica, he toured with a group of missionary nuns and visited people who literally lived on a garbage dump. Upon his return he worked in a bargain store and soup kitchen to help people get back on their feet. "The Lord was working in my life," he said.

After Father Emile died in 1995, Father Harry Thompson assumed the role of mentor and inspiration, and described his idea of a parish that promotes outreach and involvement, encouraging spiritual growth and mutual assistance. About this time Cuccia's brother-in-law was experiencing his own spiritual call, so the two met with Father Harry, and from that meeting sprang the concept of Reconcile New Orleans.

The men first opened Kids Café in 1998, a once-a-week ministry for inner city children and their families to provide a fine dining experience in a five-story building that had just become available.

Ignoring the murderers, prostitutes and drug dealers who peopled the neighborhood, the children learned how to wait tables and prepare meals, for which they received a little stipend. They learned how to have dinner conversations. They were introduced to outstanding role models—African-American doctors, firemen and policemen—breaking down barriers and perceptions and building trust with the neighbors, members of the immediate community, and many others throughout the city.

That first venture developed into Café Reconcile, a real working restaurant, open to the public, serving staples of New Orleans' Creole and soul food, from traditional Monday red beans and rice to gumbo, jambalaya, baked chicken, po-boy sandwiches, fried catfish, potato salad, macaroni and cheese, and even vegetarian plates. At any one time, sixteen young people between the ages of sixteen and twenty-two rotate among kitchen and front-of-house assignments, training for careers in the city's famed restaurants.

Café Reconcile now also operates a catering service, offering the same kinds of down-home, well-seasoned dishes "like eatin' by your Mama's." The building is in the process of renovation to house a holistic training center, which will include the Emeril Lagasse Foundation Culinary Training Institute, and serve as a catering hall to provide another level of training.

An outgrowth of the original program is a similar one, begun in the summer of 2006, to train youth for construction jobs, including framing, plumbing, roofing, and electrical and heating/air conditioning installation. As well as education, the project also helps combat the city's dearth of affordable housing; one of the first houses built is now owned by Café Reconcile's own Chef Joe Smith and his family.

Besides job training, participants are given assessments to determine any special needs. They receive life skills training, such as job readiness, employment retention skills, teamwork and leadership skills, anger management and conflict resolution, self-esteem issues, and diversity issues. Literacy and numeracy skills are a part of the program, with a strong emphasis on obtaining a GED. The whole person is the client.

When Cuccia first visited Central City, he might have been forgiven for not recognizing the exact nature of God's call, but he certainly felt the pull. And thanks to his efforts and leadership, more than 450 young people have benefited. After all, one definition of "reconcile" is "to bring together"; the projects of Reconcile New Orleans bring together a spectrum of New Orleanians for the good of all. Surely God smiles on this work.

Sister Mary Lou Specha, a member of Sisters of the Presentation, has been the executive director of Reconcile New Orleans since June 2008. Originally from Chicago, she has served as teacher, youth minister and most recently as a director of campus ministries. Cuccia remains responsible for the completion of the holistic training center, and also plans to develop a social entrepreneurship institute, with the Office of Social Entrepreneurship of the Louisiana lieutenant governor's office, to formalize the numerous, ongoing collaborations with nonprofits from around the country that seek to replicate the Reconcile model.

Spiritual Harmony

There are many paths up the mountain, but the view of the moon from the top is the same.

—Ancient Japanese saying

Liberty and Civility: What Benjamin Franklin and George Washington Taught Us About Religious Peace

By Chris Beneke

Religious peace, or spiritual harmony in the broad sense, can be achieved in a number of ways. We can construct walls, live in segregated enclaves, and even divide ourselves into different nations. Separation works as long as the animosity can be kept on opposite sides of the wall, and as long as the weapons are all short range. Authoritarian regimes, such as Marshall Tito's Yugoslavia and Saddam Hussein's Iraq, have also proven successful at keeping hostile factions from killing one another. They are effective, as the philosopher Thomas Hobbes might have said, because they make people afraid of the state, rather than other groups.

There is another foundation for religious peace, which has been around for at least as long as the United States. It was built to promote the coexistence of different religious groups within the same national community. This American model combined two notable features. First, there were the much celebrated provisions for religious liberty that protected equal rights to religious belief, worship and speech, and kept the civil government out of church affairs. A second, less celebrated feature consisted of something that might be called religious civility.

Better known than the principle itself were the two eighteenth-century leaders who probably best embodied it—Benjamin Franklin and George Washington. Neither man was a conventional Christian, though neither ever said so publicly. In fact, Franklin and Washington kept most of their religious opinions to themselves. Some of their reticence was undoubtedly because of the worry that they would endure disrepute, if not worse, because of their deviation from orthodox Christianity. But their approach to the expression of religious opinions also had something to do with the

151

conviction that conflict could be avoided through the exercise of virtues that Franklin and Washington worked tirelessly to achieve themselves, namely restraint in speech and generosity in action.

From a young age both Franklin and Washington taught themselves to be circumspect and to display courtesy toward opinions and practices other than their own. For Franklin, demonstrating such respect meant, as he put it in his *Autobiography*, striving "to avoid all Discourse that might tend to lessen the good Opinion another might have of his own Religion."

Washington had his own methods. A favorite urban pastime in colonial America was the November fifth Pope's Day celebration, in which crowds wheeled misshapen effigies of the pontiff around cities such as Boston and New York. Washington would have none of it. Aware of the particular need for French Catholic support in the war and the general need for religious harmony, Washington forbade Continental soldiers from participating, writing in his orders: "At such a juncture, and in such Circumstances, to be insulting their [Catholic] Religion, is so monstrous, as not to be suffered or excused; indeed instead of offering the most remote insult, it is our duty to address public thanks to these our Brethren. . . . "

If restraint in their opinions was one mark of the civility that Washington and Franklin exemplified, generosity in their actions toward those of other faiths was another. Both men assisted, praised and worked with men of many different denominations. Franklin was renowned as a patron of Philadelphia churches, long subscribing to the view that doers of good works would find a way to heaven, no matter what their particular religious creeds. He could not resist contributing to the charities of the legendary evangelical preacher, George Whitfield, with whom he had many disagreements.

Washington acted with equally inclusive grace. Not long after becoming the first president of the United States, he wrote supportive letters to groups with long histories of persecution, such as the Jews of Rhode Island, the Catholics of Maryland and the Quakers of Philadelphia. Washington assured them, in a way that no head of state had ever done, that they would enjoy not just toleration, but religious liberty, in the newly created nation.

These were remarkable gestures for an age when men and women were still scarred by searing memories of religious wars and religious oppression, of hangings, whippings, and widespread bigotry. We cannot expect everyone to be as philanthropic as Franklin or as polite as Washington. A republic, after all, needs to leave some room for principled expressions of incivility. But if we are to build religiously integrated national, even international, communities, where trust prevails over suspicion and prejudice, we will have to overcome our own searing memories of religious violence. Following the examples of Franklin and Washington might be a good place to start.

Chris Beneke is an associate professor of history and director of the Valente Center for the Arts and Sciences at Bentley College in Waltham, Massachusetts. He is the author of Beyond Toleration: The Religious Origins of American Pluralism *(Oxford University Press, 2006) and co-editor of* The First Prejudice: Religious Tolerance and Religious Intolerance in the Making of America *(University of Pennsylvania Press, forthcoming).*

True Democracy in the Twenty-first Century

By Mike Farrell

This is adapted from the concluding chapter of *Just Call Me Mike: A Journey to Actor and Activist* by Mike Farrell and is reprinted by permission from Akashic Books, New York (www.akashicbooks.com).

All fundamentalism is dangerous: Christian, Jewish, Muslim, Hindu, or any other. The need to believe in something that gives meaning to life is understandable, and, per the learned Rabbi Leonard Beerman, fundamentalism provides "the comfort of being so much neater than the subtleties and nuances of everything that is human . . . [It] brings the illusion of certainty."

Struggling with the subtleties and nuances of life is the road to humility; the goal is becoming fully human. Religious certitude brings moral arrogance, and with it the fundamentalist Jews' expulsion of Arabs from their land; the fundamentalist Hindu's slaughter of Muslims; the Islamic Jihadists' suicide attacks; the fundamentalist Christians' bombing of clinics and assassination of family health providers. The belief that one speaks for God and can force his beliefs on another is a soul-destroying lie.

Today, a hyper-moralist triumphalism has gained ground in America, slipping in up the sleeve of imperialist zealots. Fundamentalist beliefs are insinuated into American life in Christian versions of *madrassas* that inculcate young Muslims. If a religious belief or practice helps one deal with life's important questions, it is certainly of value, but it is a personal value. To impose a belief system on those who choose to find their answers in another way is to deny their basic human right—their "unalienable right"—to determine their own journey.

There are many different views of the proper ways to express one's faith, and I applaud those who wrestle with the questions. I particularly appreciate the seekers. This seems to me closer to the concept of true faith than that of extremists who claim to have all the answers and, content in their settled wisdom, judge and condemn those who see things differently.

I've come to believe there is a divine spark in all of us, and it is this element of common humanity that we must honor and preserve, no matter the faith proclaimed. Decency and honor and compassion and hope can be the primary sacraments in our lives, respecting ourselves and the gifts we've been given in a way that empowers—rather than demeans—those around us. Honest pursuit of a meaningful, constructive, and productive life in ownership of such qualities is a purposeful way to honor and acknowledge whatever God may be out there—or in here.

In the meantime, we Americans have work to do. Making this nation live up to its principles requires the involvement of its citizens. It's a job that will either be taken seriously or taken away. If we want the nation we love to exemplify principles that made us proud to be Americans, we have to be true to those principles—and require that our leaders do the same. "All men are created equal" can't mean only men, can it? Or only white people? Only rich people? Only heterosexuals? Only Americans? If we're "endowed by [our] Creator with certain unalienable rights," among which are "Life, Liberty and the Pursuit of Happiness," can we be stripped of them by the powerful? By whoever happens to be the majority at a given moment? Should a government "instituted among Men" and deriving its "just Powers from the Consent of the Governed" lie to the very people who gave it power? Should it manipulate its powers secretly to limit or take away people's sovereignty? Can "liberty and justice for all" and "equal justice under law" mean anything in a nation that imprisons people on suspicion, tortures them, holds them for years without charge, and denies them access to a court or a lawyer? Doesn't "Congress shall make no law respecting an establishment of religion, or prohibiting the free exercise thereof" say clearly enough that we're free to practice our chosen faith—or lack of faith—and that we will not allow the government to impose one on us? Just for fun, look up the word "fascism" in the dictionary.

The spirit of America is the vision of human possibility that inspires people across the world to reach higher. The American experiment is the attempt to achieve the goals set out for us hundreds of years ago. To pretend that we've already reached these goals—fully reached our potential—is to lie to ourselves and shirk our duty to our children.

The lessons taught me . . . so many years ago . . . have stood the test of time. They have since been underscored and validated for me by impoverished, illiterate peasants, caring angels of mercy, guerrillas, prisoners, care-givers, the abused, survivors, victims, criminals, the shamed, the hopefuls, and the hopeless. Love, respect, and attention are necessary food for the human soul.

The opportunities and experiences noted above—and many not included—have provided an extraordinary education for this citizen, and I'm profoundly grateful for having been afforded them. My life is rich, made so by experience, by friendship, and mostly by love. And it will, I now understand, only get richer.

Through it all I've come to believe we are on a journey, you and I, a journey from the caves to the stars. There will always be those who choose to live in fear and try to frighten, force, or lure us back to the caves, but our future, our salvation, the realization of our potential, is in the stars. And love will light the way.

Mike Farrell grew up in eastern Los Angeles. After a stint in the Marine Corps, he embarked on a career as an actor, eventually securing roles as the affable and eminently moral B. J. Hunnicut in the popular television series M*A*S*H and later Providence, as well as working as a writer, director and producer. Over the years his social conscience developed, and he devotes time and effort to fighting poverty, the death penalty, torture and war.

Peacemaking in Northern Ireland

By Elizabeth Crawford Watt

Editor's note: Ulster Project International seeks to promote peace among Roman Catholics and Protestants affected by the violence of the decades-long "troubles" in Northern Ireland, through encouraging dialog among future leaders there by bringing groups of teenagers, evenly matched by gender and faith, for month-long stays with families in the United States who have at least one teen of the same gender, close in age and of the same faith. The Irish teens are encouraged to participate in regular family activities, but most of their days are spent fellowshipping with the entire group of youth from Ireland and the United States, in encounter sessions, social activities, community service projects and worship.

Peace in Northern Ireland once seemed a hopeless dream. Sure, you can change the political atmosphere, but the daily issues in the community are what will ultimately determine whether peace will prevail. That is why the grassroots efforts of the Ulster Project—offering the key to social change within the community—are important.

I was just fourteen years old the first time I went to Northern Ireland. I had participated in the project as a host teen twice before. I was young enough to be impressionable but old enough to know the implications of The Troubles, which is why the project works with those around that age.

On that three-week visit to Castlederg, New Orleans' sister city, I saw a town divided, with a Catholic grocery store on one side of town and a Protestant one on the other, a Protestant gas station on one side of town and a Catholic one on the other. But I also saw something new—the teens who had participated in the Ulster Project were having "mixed" house parties to continue the fun they had had in New Orleans.

I participated in the Ulster Project three times as a host teen and two years as an adult "Breakthrough Leader," and my two younger brothers participated as host teens. Each year we saw the teens more relaxed with each other, with less desire to wear sectarian clothing or sing sectarian songs, and more intermingling. There were house parties and signs of people of different faiths mixing socially, significant because generally Protestants and Catholics do not go to the same schools, play the same sports, or enjoy similar extracurricular activities. There has even been a marriage between a Catholic and a Protestant Ulster Project participant there. One reason this marriage is so indicative of the Ulster Project's effects, besides the obvious, is that the two participated in different years, meaning they had not gone to America together, so likely would not have socialized together had it not been for the project.

In Castlederg today, there are mixed grocery stores, mixed pharmacies, and most interestingly for the social aspect, mixed pubs. Siblings of those who participated in the Ulster Project, who once were more hard-lined, are now mixing. There have been other mixed marriages. And during the Christmas season in 2007, there was actually a community-wide carol service with everyone in a single church!

As in the old adage, "what goes around comes around," Castlederg has reciprocated in holding out its hand to New Orleans. When Katrina hit, this town of fewer than three thousand inhabitants immediately began fundraisers that resulted in over $16,000—divided equally between Catholic Charities and Church World Service, the umbrella Protestant relief organization—for the relief of storm victims in the New Orleans area.

The Ulster Project has given me back much more than I put into it. I saw my city and my country from an outsider's perspective and learned more about them. I worked in service projects that benefited my own community alongside Northern Irish and other New Orleanian teens, giving me a glimpse into sides of the city to which I would have otherwise never been exposed. I became interested in cultural differences, which led to my degree in anthropology. I realized I was a part of something special when every college and scholarship for which I interviewed spent most of their time asking about my Ulster Project experiences. I decided to go to England for my master's in archaeological science and there met again a Northern Irish Ulster Project graduate I had first met in 1994. Andy was studying at Manchester Metropolitan University to become a teacher and rugby coach. We married in 2004, now live in England, and have a daughter. I have since decided to go to medical school. My interview at the University of Newcastle focused on my work with the Ulster Project, even more than my academic record, for doctors work with patients from many backgrounds, and England has become a multicultural country.

My brothers have also benefited from participating. One says that the Ulster Project made him much more outgoing and a people person. He is finishing his master's degree and will be a licensed family counselor. The other considered going to seminary to become a Presbyterian pastor after one of the breakthrough sessions where teens get to ask Protestant and Catholic clergy questions about faith and the church (this is an amazing session). After earning his undergraduate degree at Louisiana State University, he graduated from Princeton Theological Seminary, worked as a pastor in Scotland for two years, and is now interested in going to medical school with the hopes of opening a faith-based medical clinic.

Now when I visit Castlederg, I'm no longer a tourist, but a member of the family. My daughter goes to see her Granny and Granda and I get to see the changes in the town, which continue on a more and more peaceful route.

The Ulster Project affects individuals, families, and friends, eventually spreading to the whole town, then the whole country. Ultimately, it shows the world what can be accomplished by people of goodwill on issues and in places worldwide. This kind of effort gives us not only a solution to one problem, but hope for problems beyond.

***

In spite of the fact that only six of Ulster Province's counties are in Northern Ireland—the other three are part of the Republic of Ireland—the name Ulster informally refers to the whole of Northern Ireland, and the name of the Ulster Project is now so well known that it's not likely to be changed.

One of three children, Elizabeth Crawford Watt was born in a suburb of New Orleans, and through her Presbyterian church became involved with the Ulster Project in her early teens, serving as a host to visitors from Castlederg, and traveling to that town. She graduated from Tulane University with a degree in anthropology, earned a master's degree in archaeological science at the University of Liverpool, and has completed her first year of medical school at the University of Newcastle. She and her husband, Andy, have a two-year-old daughter, and if she had time, she would enjoy oil painting, playing the guitar, and possibly napping.

Racial Harmony

I'm concerned about a better world. I'm concerned about justice; I'm concerned about brotherhood; I'm concerned about truth. And when one is concerned about that, he can never advocate violence.

—Martin Luther King, Jr.

A Prisoner's Example: A Study of Nelson Mandela

By Rúna Bouius

All of us face some kind of adversity, some form of suffering, at one point or another in our lives. The question is how do we deal with these challenges? The "how" indicates that we have choices when we suffer. The choices are two: the familiar road followed by most of humanity through the centuries, and the road less traveled.

The road we most often choose in hardships could be called the road to hell. This hell is not the scalding fire of an afterlife, but rather the Buddhist hell-realm that we create by allowing our negative reactions to difficulties to metastasize into resentment, self-pity and other negative illusions that we then drag through life.

In June of 1964 Nelson Mandela was stripped of his freedom and imprisoned in the notorious Robben Island prison after fighting for democracy, opposing the ruling whites, and denouncing apartheid. It would have been easy for Mandela to slip into bitterness and victimhood. He had plenty of reasons. He had been removed from his loved ones and forced to live for close to twenty-seven years in the constrictions of a tiny cell where the floor was his bed and a bucket his toilet. He was fed food barely fit for human consumption and forced to do hard labor in a quarry.

But Mandela made a choice other than self-pity and resentment. He chose the road of peace, reconciliation and forgiveness. His biographer, Anthony Sampson, who had known him since 1951, was once asked in a PBS interview how he saw Mandela change during his prison time. Sampson said that in his younger years Mandela was not a naturally reflective person. He was considered by many impatient, hot-headed, and volatile, and given to extremism. But in that tiny prison cell, in which he had ample time to reflect and consider his choices, he chose to still his mind, and to practice physical and emotional self-control. He chose to cultivate patience and inclusiveness. He chose to listen carefully to his fellow prisoners—and to his jailors. He chose relationships instead of divisions. He chose shared learning instead of squandering his energy. He saw his prison community as a microcosm of a bigger whole. He learned not to take conflicts and negativity personally, but to lift himself above that and see the bigger picture. He became a wise leader by going inside and reaching for something that for me is a heaven. Not the heaven of God and angels, but the heaven that exists in all of us when we connect to our inner being, and to something greater than our small selves. When we go within this way we automatically open up to the world outside of us, and we can let go of our contracted state of being. When Mandela did this, and opened his heart, he released courage and love, and fashioned a lasting inter-connectedness with his fellow humans. He went on to light up the world with his radiant heart.

This larger self within us—this larger consciousness—is what I call a heaven on earth. Do we have to be Nelson Mandela to achieve it? No, we all have that capacity. What it takes is a choice, a choice to let go of our smaller selves, and to come home to something greater than any of us, something that was there all along. The choice is ours.

Rúna Bouius is an Icelandic entrepreneur, leadership mentor and trainer, speaker and writer. She runs her company, Rúnora LLC, from Santa Fe, New Mexico.

Reaching Out Across Our Borders

By Joshua Kucera

People from faraway countries can look very strange and foreign when you see them on television. They always seem to be doing things we don't do in the United States: throwing rocks at a tank, rioting, starving with distended bellies. It can be hard to relate. It's not until you get up close that you learn that those people on the other side of the television screen are, in the end, not too different from us. I've been fortunate to have the opportunity to travel all over the world as a journalist, often to some of the poorest or conflict-ridden countries on the planet—Iran, Iraq, Afghanistan, Congo, the Balkans. And probably the most important thing I've learned is that underneath the different colors of skin, political systems, clothes and food, most of us have very similar human desires and values.

The taxi driver in Serbia may have seen his country torn apart by ethnic conflict, but instead prefers to talk about how proud he is of his son, who is going to college in Germany. The boy in Kyrgyzstan may consider sheep eyes and fermented horse milk to be delicacies, but he also dreams of taking his girlfriend to the Eiffel Tower. Most people around the world love sports and soap operas and the movie *Titanic*. They want to provide for their children and make sure their children can provide for their children even better.

It's not possible for everyone to travel as I have. But it is possible to make meaningful contact with other cultures even when you stay at home. One day several years ago, when I was working in South Dakota at my first journalism job, my boss saw some people carrying a mattress down the street one day—not something that people ordinarily do here. But instead of rolling

165

her eyes, she stopped her pickup and asked if they needed help. They turned out to be recent immigrants from Bosnia, and after she gave them and their mattress a ride to their house, she offered to help them learn English. She invited me along because she knew I was interested in the Balkans, so every Sunday afternoon we went to their house and helped them practice English and ate their delicious Serbian barbecue. They ended up becoming good friends, all because she made a quick decision to reach out instead of staying in her bubble.

These may sound like banal observations, but when you can really absorb them, they become quite profound. Conflict depends on a belief that the "enemy" is substantially different from us. And even well-meaning people can find themselves feeling as if what goes on in another part of the world—including something that our country is doing, or could be helping to stop—doesn't have anything to do with us. It does. Those people who are fighting or demonstrating or starving are, in the end, pretty similar to us. So, what do we do to help them? How do we start on the path to bring peace to the world?

We can't work toward getting along with people from different cultures unless we understand them—we need to get a clear, nuanced picture of the world outside our borders. Your church may have an immigrant outreach program, or you can host foreign exchange students or volunteer to teach English to new arrivals to the United States. And when you do have the opportunity to travel, you can choose to spend some of your time off the beach or away from the castles. You can get out into the small towns and neighborhoods—the farther you venture off the tourist track, the more likely you are to have good encounters with real people, and be able really to understand what it's like to live in that country.

Joshua Kucera is a freelance journalist who has reported from the Balkans, the Middle East, Africa and the former Soviet Union. His work has been published in Time, Slate, The New Republic, The Nation, Jane's Defence Weekly *and many other publications. He lives in Washington, D.C. and writes about military and foreign affairs.*

Where Do We Go From Here?

By Martin Luther King, Jr.

Extracts from Dr. King's address at the convention of the Southern Christian Leadership Conference, Atlanta, August 16, 1967. Reprinted by arrangement with The Heirs to the Estate of Martin Luther King Jr., c/o Writers House as agent for the proprietor New York, NY.

Copyright 1967 Dr. Martin Luther King Jr; copyright renewed 1991 Coretta Scott King.

Ten years ago during the piercing chill of a January day and on the heels of the year-long Montgomery bus boycott, a group of approximately one hundred Negro leaders from across the South assembled and agreed on the need for an organization that could serve as a channel through which local protest organizations in the South could coordinate their protest activities. It was this meeting that gave birth to the Southern Christian Leadership Conference.

Ten years ago, racial segregation was still a structured part of the architecture of southern society. Negroes with the pangs of hunger and the anguish of thirst were denied access to the average lunch counter. The downtown restaurants were still off-limits for the black man. Negroes, burdened with the fatigue of travel, were still barred from the motels of the highways and the hotels of the cities. Negro boys and girls in dire need of recreational activities were not allowed to inhale the fresh air of the big city parks. Negroes in desperate need of allowing their mental buckets to sink deep into the wells of knowledge were confronted with a firm "no" when they sought to use the city libraries. Ten years ago, legislative halls of the South were still ringing loud with such words as "interposition" and "nullification." All types of conniving methods were still being used to keep the Negro from becoming a registered voter. A decade ago, not a single Negro entered the legislative chambers of the South except as a porter or a chauffeur. Ten years ago, all too many Negroes were still harried by day and haunted by night by a corroding sense of fear and a nagging sense of nobody-ness.

But things are different now. In assault after assault, we caused the sagging walls of segregation to come tumbling down. During this era the entire edifice of segregation was profoundly shaken. It is no longer possible to count the number of public establishments that are open to Negroes. Ten years ago, Negroes seemed almost invisible to the larger society, and the facts of their harsh lives were unknown to the majority of the nation. But today, civil rights is a dominating issue in every state, crowding the pages of the press and the daily conversation of white Americans. In this decade of change, the Negro stood up and confronted his oppressor. He faced the bullies and the guns, and the dogs and the tear gas. He put himself squarely before the vicious mobs and moved with strength and dignity toward them and decisively defeated them. And the courage with which he confronted enraged mobs dissolved the stereotype of the grinning, submissive Uncle Tom.

He came out of his struggle integrated only slightly in the external society, but powerfully integrated within. In short, over the last ten years the Negro decided to straighten his back up, realizing that a man cannot ride your back unless it is bent. We made our government write new laws to alter some of the cruelest injustices that affected us. We made an indifferent and unconcerned nation rise from lethargy and subpoenaed its conscience to appear before the judgment seat of morality on the whole question of civil rights. We gained manhood in the nation that had always called us "boy." It would be hypocritical indeed if I allowed modesty to forbid my saying that SCLC stood at the forefront of all of the watershed movements that brought these monumental changes in the South.

Last year as we met in Jackson, Mississippi, we were painfully aware of the struggle of our brothers in Grenada, Mississippi. After living for a hundred or more years under the yoke of total segregation, the Negro citizens of this northern Delta hamlet banded together in nonviolent warfare against racial discrimination under the leadership of our affiliate chapter and organization there. The fact of this non-destructive rebellion was as spectacular as were its results. In a few short weeks the Grenada County Movement challenged every aspect of the society's exploitative life. Stores which denied employment were boycotted; voter registration increased by thousands. We can never forget the courageous action of the people of Grenada who moved our nation and its federal courts to powerful action in behalf of school integration, giving Grenada one of the most integrated school systems in America. The battle is far from over, but the black people of Grenada have achieved forty of fifty-three demands through their persistent nonviolent efforts. Slowly but surely, our southern affiliates continued their building and organizing. Seventy-nine counties conducted voter registration drives, while double that number carried on political education and get-out-the-vote efforts.

***

We must reaffirm our commitment to nonviolence. There is something painfully sad about a riot. One sees screaming youngsters and angry adults fighting hopelessly and aimlessly against impossible odds. And deep down within them, you perceive a desire for self-destruction, a kind of suicidal longing. Occasionally, Negroes contend that the 1965 Watts riot and the other riots in various cities represented effective civil rights action. But those who express this view always end up with stumbling words when asked what concrete gains have been won as a result.

And when one tries to pin down advocates of violence as to what acts would be effective, the answers are blatantly illogical. Sometimes they talk of overthrowing racist state and local governments and they talk about guerrilla warfare. They fail to see that no internal revolution has ever succeeded in overthrowing a government by violence unless the government had already lost the allegiance and effective control of its armed forces. Furthermore, few, if any, violent revolutions have been successful unless the violent minority had the sympathy and support of the non-resisting majority. Castro may have had only a few Cubans actually fighting with him and up in the hills, but he would have never overthrown the Batista regime unless he had had the sympathy of the vast majority of Cuban people. It is perfectly clear that a violent revolution on the part of American blacks would find no sympathy and support from the white population and very little from the majority of the Negroes themselves.

I'm concerned about a better world. I'm concerned about justice; I'm concerned about brotherhood; I'm concerned about truth. And when one is concerned about that, he can never advocate violence. For through violence you may murder a murderer, but you can't murder murder. Through violence you may murder a liar, but you can't establish truth. Through violence you may murder a hater, but you can't murder hate through violence. I have also decided to stick with love, for I know that love is ultimately the only answer to mankind's problems. I've seen too much hate on the faces of sheriffs in the South. I've seen hate on the faces of too many Klansmen and too many White Citizens Councilors in the South to want to hate, myself, because every time I see it, I know that it does something to their faces and their personalities, and I say to myself that hate is too great a burden to bear. I have decided to love. If you are seeking the highest good, I think you can find it through love. He who hates does not know God, but he who loves has the key that unlocks the door to the meaning of ultimate reality.

Martin Luther King, Jr., was born in 1929 in Atlanta, the son and grandson of ministers. He earned a BA in sociology at Morehouse College, and a bachelor of divinity from Crozer Theological Seminary, winning numerous honors and awards. He studied at Harvard and earned a PhD in theology from Boston University. He served as pastor and co-pastor at several churches, and besides his civil rights work also fought against poverty and the war in Vietnam, winning the Nobel Peace Prize in 1964. He was assassinated in Memphis in 1968 while working to organize sanitation workers.

See With Thy Eyes, Hear With Thy Ears, Listen With Thy Heart

By Robert L. Perez, Jr.

In June of 2007 I was asked by a client to participate in a two-day workshop designed to improve safety in the workplace. Even though my job was as corporate safety director for a large commercial construction firm, the workshop didn't sound exciting.

The exercise included employees of various disciplines, educations and levels of professionalism from approximately seven companies. Some forty participants meandered and mingled in a small hotel ballroom, until a woman's voice penetrated the din with a request for everyone to form separate groups of co-workers. These groups varied in size from three to eight members, with one notable exception: one man stood alone across the room from my group of five. When asked to introduce himself, he spoke fluent English, though with a pronounced Hispanic accent. My speculation was that he was a migrant worker, here in south Louisiana in response to our labor shortage following Hurricane Katrina. After introductions, new groups were formed homogenously, and the activities began.

At noon, a cafeteria-style lunch was served in the hotel lobby, and we were instructed to return to the ballroom in thirty minutes. Among the last in line, I found my four workmates occupying all of the seats at a four-top table. I scanned the room for a second choice and saw the Hispanic man I had seen earlier, again alone, beginning to eat his meal. I approached and asked permission to join him, which was quickly and graciously granted. We introduced ourselves, and I asked him his place of birth and how long he had been in the United States. Luis, a thirty-four-year old immigrant from Nicaragua and eldest of three, had been in our country for four years. He hoped to move to the United States

171

and bring his younger siblings so they could enjoy a life their ailing mother was unable to provide. At the behest of maternal relatives, who pledged support while he established his new life, he left Nicaragua alone and arrived legally in Louisiana. At the end of a tedious journey choked with red tape, he learned his family had retracted their offer, and Luis was left to fend for himself on his first day in a strange country. He was suddenly homeless except on the occasional night that he was able to find a mission or a hostel that would accept him. Able to speak fewer than ten English words, employment opportunities were scarce, but after three weeks he got a job as a dishwasher at a greasy spoon in New Orleans. He enrolled in a free immersion course to learn to speak English, and soon escaped the kitchen to become a laborer at a specialty glass company. As we spoke, he was a supervisor for the same company, several rungs above his starting level. His family had joined him here. He had achieved his dream.

As I listened, awestruck, silent, I realized that his professional advancement was no accident. I also realized that I was learning a critical lesson about social worth. Personal value has traditionally been measured by pedigree, conventional education or financial success. This man had none of those. What he had, though, were far more valuable—courage, loyalty, love, self-esteem, dedication and determination. These elements together were responsible for his success in life. That success was defined by him, achieved by him and treasured by him. I realized that I was in the presence of someone truly great, and my definition of success was forever altered.

We human beings are naturally inclined to see greater value in people similar to us than in those who differ greatly. We sometimes view a person who appears different or speaks a foreign language as less intelligent, less educated and less important than those who more closely resemble us. By learning something about these different people, we can understand how truly similar we all are to one another. One of the most valuable lessons I have learned in my entire life was taught to me by a "mere migrant worker," who turned out to be anything but mere. In half an hour, I learned something that I hadn't known in all my thirty-eight years, and I learned it because I decided to talk to someone who was different, and see our similarities. I decided to spend some time with an open mind and learn something new. I resolved to take to heart the admonition from Ezekiel and listen with my heart. I vowed to try to be a better person, and someday find a way to make the world a better place.

Robert L. Perez, Jr., is a health and safety consultant in South Louisiana. He enjoys fine wine, fine dining, concerts and collecting small exotic animals.

We're More Than Our Race

By Leonard Pitts, Jr.

I want you to look at this. Tell me what you see. It's a going-away party, some years ago. My wife and I are leaving Los Angeles after a lifetime and some family and friends have gathered to say goodbye.

Do you see our Mexican neighbors gathered together in one corner of the room? Do you see my white co-workers huddled together in another? Do you see our African-American siblings and friends sitting together in yet a third?

Do you see, in other words, America in microcosm, a nation of nations, a set of subsets, separated by immutable lines of race and culture? And if that is what you see, look again.

Do you see the white couple laughing and talking now, having moved to the kitchen where the other married folks have congregated? Do you see the young Mexican men and the young African-American men getting together to make a run to the store in the conviction that this party is beer deficient? Do you see the immutable lines proving themselves mutable after all, shifting and re-forming according to marital status and love of beer?

There is a lesson in that.

We tend to think of race as the line that supersedes all others, the one which can never be erased, altered or crossed. But human beings exist in multiple dimensions, are defined by manifold characteristics. Race is usually the most obvious and readily visible, yes. But there is also marital status and beverage choice, also city of origin and favorite sports team, also education and economic class, political party and age, preference for art house films or summer blockbusters.

Most of us would never presume to judge another person in his

174

or her totality based on what sort of movies she liked. But race is different. Indeed, race is the difference that defines.

Or at least it is so long as it's the only thing we see. But what happens when we learn to see more? That's not easy. It does not happen incidentally or accidentally. In a culture riven and driven by racial consciousness, seeing past race takes an intentional choice.

I used to correspond with a white preacher who once stood as a guest speaker before a black congregation and said, "Sometimes I think my world is too white." Pause. Then he added what he regarded as the dangerous coda, "And maybe you'll agree that your world is too black." He was braced for murmurs of disapproval. He received applause instead.

In Dallas, meanwhile, they have a thing they call the Dallas Dinner Table. This is an annual program where people are invited to dine across the line, breaking bread with others of different races and cultures for the express purpose of talking through their differences.

The idea isn't that we must learn not to see race, any more than we should learn not to see gender or religion. Rather, the idea is that we should learn to see more than race. There is nothing inherently negative about one's skin color that should require someone else to pretend it doesn't exist. What is inherently negative is when people think a color is all you are.

The preacher and the Dinner Table organizers understand that we exist in multiple dimensions. They know that race is one of them, but only one.

So that if you ever meet that young black minister I know, the one with the elaborate cornrows and the hip-hop attitude, you might not be so surprised to learn that he is absolutely mad for Frank Sinatra.

Or if you meet that middle-aged white storeowner I know, the towering good ol' boy with the country accent, you might not be so surprised to hear that he once offered to defend me from some white supremacists.

And if you look back at that going-away party I had, you might see America in microcosm; yes, you might see immutable lines proving mutable after all. Or you might simply see me, laughing in the company of friends.

Leonard Pitts, Jr., whose column appears in roughly 250 newspapers across the country, won a Pulitzer Prize for commentary in 2004. His book Becoming Dad: Black Men and the Journey to Fatherhood *became a bestseller.*

Saints on the Playing Field

By Charlotte Livingston

Can sports help create a heaven on earth? Ask the people of the Gulf Coast, devastated and divided by the aftermath of Hurricanes Katrina and Rita in 2005, and they will tell you that the New Orleans Saints did much to lighten the spirits and bring together citizens from diverse backgrounds.

Racial tension has historically been a problem in New Orleans. Although numerous organizations have made strides towards balancing racial harmony, I've personally never witnessed the coming together of all citizens—regardless of race—to the extent that they did in support and celebration of this team.

As a New Orleans native, I was deeply affected by this storm and the water that inundated this city following the levee breaches. Like many others, of all races and socioeconomic levels, I lost my home, most of its contents, my car and my job. Even as I returned to my beloved hometown, many others scattered across the country and beyond. Life was turned upside-down, and no one was sure whether New Orleans—and its inhabitants—could be saved, much less reunited.

For as long as I can remember I have been a Saints fan. I have experienced their highs and more frequently their lows. I have traveled to see them play, participated in fan contests, worn my lucky jersey, and cheered my heart out during each game. Since the team's inception, fans have had a completely irrational, and entirely passionate, love affair with this team.

"Who Dats," as Saints fans are known, are a spirited and diverse bunch. You can find at least one image of the team's symbol—the fleur de lis—in every New Orleans home. This symbol represents more than just our team, though; it represents our region. In fact, it is incorporated into New Orleans' official flag. After Katrina, the fleur de lis was ubiquitous. We were scattered all over the country and didn't fit in anywhere, so perhaps we needed something to identify us. Our beloved team even relocated. Much as we were grateful for San Antonio's hospitality, we wanted and needed them back.

I really don't recall the 2005 football season. It started just as Katrina laid us to waste, and progressed as we were evacuated. We had too many real worries to consider whether our team was playing, much less winning.

Despite the letdowns of our government and insurance companies, by 2006 many Gulf Coast residents had returned home. "Home" might have been a FEMA trailer or our mama's house, but many came back, and on September 25, 2006, the Saints returned. Nearly a year and a month after Hurricane Katrina released her wrath on the city, the Saints released theirs on the rival Atlanta Falcons, for a lopsided victory on national television. Throughout that season, the Saints continued to deliver win after win, and eventually played in the divisional championship game.

Finally, we had something to cheer for. Our community had something to embrace and a reason to celebrate. Fans gathered to cheer, and somehow this jubilant feeling evolved into optimism about the community. People got along better with one another. Strangers, wearing the jerseys of their favorite players, greeted one another like old friends, regardless of race. Fans of all colors cheered side by side. Drivers, with vehicles sporting fleur-de-lis magnets and flags, honked and waved to one another in traffic. People connected. God may not have had a direct hand in the team's many victories, but it was surely with His good grace that we were able to enjoy that memorable season.

On a wider scale, despite the egregious slaughter of Israeli participants in the 1972 Olympics in Munich and the all-too-frequent outbursts of violence at British soccer games, athletics more often fosters cooperation between groups who might not otherwise meet. For example, in July of 2008, American and Iranian fans put aside political differences and cheered the Iranian Olympic basketball team at an NBA summer league game in Salt Lake City. Israeli and Palestinian youth sometimes meet on the playing fields between their lands, with the approval of the

Palestinian general delegate to the United Kingdom and Israel's Minister of Culture, Sports and Sciences. And there were reports of sporadic games between youth from Bosnia and Kosovo, even as gunshots rang out.

Sometimes the only place people can get along is on the playing field or in the stands, but perhaps we can use those experiences to build a process of getting along in other venues.

Charlotte Livingston attended Louisiana State University and graduated from the University of New Orleans. She received her juris doctor degree from Loyola University, and is a practicing attorney in New Orleans. Her articles have appeared in nolababy, The Junior League of New Orleans' Lagniappe, *and* Louisiana Cookin'.

Of Colors, Cultures and Popcorn

By Mary S. Rich

When I was young, I was not allowed to go to the new movie house in my hometown of Ocala, Florida. "Colored" people were not welcome there. I, of course, was embittered. I took my hostility out at the town's older theater where, from the balcony where I was permitted to sit, I threw popcorn at the white kids below.

Years later, as president of the city council, I was an invited guest speaker at the reopening of the old theater where once I had been banned. It had undergone many reincarnations over the years, but now it was being reopened as a cinema and performing arts center. And there I was, front and center, participating in the ribbon cutting.

The irony did not escape me. The world has changed.

In our community, part of that change is manifested in a yearly observance called One Ocala, One America. The weeklong observance, which I have the great honor of chairing, is dedicated to promoting racial harmony and cultural understanding. And while it is intended to help us appreciate our differences, it, more often than not, drives home the point that we are more alike than we realize.

Who doesn't want a comfortable place to live, sufficient and nutritious food, a decent job, safe neighborhoods, quality education for our children, and freedom? Who doesn't want their children and grandchildren to have economic opportunity secure from outside threats? Who doesn't want their children free from verbal and physical abuse because they are of a different color, or they speak with a different accent? Who doesn't want respect? These things are universal.

Our celebration focuses on these things. Over the years we

180

have witnessed through testimonials, food, song and dance the many delights that the world's people have to offer.

We see the pride in the eyes of Hispanic kids as they sing songs of their native countries.

We are amazed at the skill and grace of young Indian women as they use their eyes and hands to tell a story through dance that is unlike anything you will encounter in Western culture.

We listen as a black poet speaks of offering a foe a hand of friendship and praying for those who offend him.

We are entertained by the skill of a Japanese magician who creates candy figurines in much the same way a glassblower crafts a vase.

We savor the taste of baklava, that wonderful Greek dessert.

We take delight in an Irish jig.

For a time, at least, we let down our guard against the insecurity of being around people and cultures different from our own. We celebrate our differences and come to realize our similarities. We take joy in what each culture has to offer and begin to understand why people are so devoted to preserving their heritage. Once a year we step out of the darkness—at least a little.

Each year the celebration lifts my heart. It helps me erase the scars of my past. It makes me wonder what scars I might have caused. It motivates me to search for ways to put things right. Perhaps at next year's observance I will challenge my white colleagues on the city council to a popcorn fight.

Mary Rich has served on the Ocala City Council since 1995. She is a retired correctional probation senior supervisor for the Florida Department of Corrections. As chair of the Ocala Racial Harmony and Cultural Awareness Task Force, she often is called upon to speak to local groups about diversity.

Homeless Meals and Racial Harmony

By Barbara Rogoski

There is a "Meals for the Homeless" project in The Hague, run by a small group of English-speaking people who serve local Dutch homeless people and illegal aliens. As coordinator of this initiative, I experienced firsthand what racial harmony means on several levels.

Our team consists of about twenty volunteers who want to do something hands on with a direct impact on someone in need. We are American, British, Irish and South African, but also Sri Lanken, Italian, Filipino, Columbian, Dutch and other nationalities.

Even if we don't realize it, we are striving for heaven on earth. We prepare hot three-course meals in our own kitchens and bring them to the center where, with love and commitment, we offer our meals, illustrating racial and spiritual harmony.

Our guests, as we respectfully call them, are homeless people from many nationalities, drug addicts, disturbed in different ways, in trouble with the local police or illegal aliens. They come from The Netherlands, of course, but also from other European countries, as well as Iraq, Iran, Indonesia, Israel, Africa and Sri Lanka. Because of their circumstances, some appear and then are gone again, but many have become our friends.

They live on the streets and have to fight for everything. They have told me they can trust no one. There is no friendship, as it is always betrayed. It is a hard life, filled with despair, but during the two-hour dinners they have with us every other Friday, they sit together for a meal and conversation with each other and with the volunteers.

This is another type of racial harmony that naturally occurs when people are willing to share experiences and trust each other.

The love our volunteers show in everything they do affirms that we have no hidden agendas, but want to serve, help and make a small difference in their lives.

When our project began, there was a high level of fear and uncertainty between the volunteers and the homeless people, but over the last two years, a subtle change occurred—they began to trust us and open up to the kindness shown them. The fact that we're good cooks and serve delicious meals helps, but it is not just that. We look in their eyes. We know their names and they know ours. We celebrate birthdays and give them toiletries we collect from hotels as we travel.

On many occasions, they have taken me aside and said, "You treat us with kindness and respect and want nothing in return but kindness and respect. You share a meal with us and want nothing but to touch our hearts with your love. This is hard to accept, as everyone always has an agenda to get something, but you don't."

Now when they leave, they kiss us on the cheeks in gratitude and the men jokingly offer marriage proposals to the women who cook. They shake our hands or thank us. They leave with full stomachs and happy hearts and look forward to our next meals together. In a way, our meals help them face the world a bit stronger, knowing someone cares.

We also leave with happy hearts and contented spirits, for we believe we are Jesus's hands to reach out to help the poor, His feet to bring us to those who need our love and kindness, and His heart to connect with the downtrodden and give them hope.

Our program contributes to racial harmony in the middle of a bustling city, seeming to bring heaven down to earth, down to our table for a few hours on a Friday afternoon.

Barbara Rogoski, an ordained minister, is the former coordinator of the St. Egideo meals for the homeless project in The Hague. Her spiritual development company, Authentic Matters, ministers to the international and expatriate community in Europe.

Ecological Harmony

Everybody needs beauty as well as bread, places to play in and pray in, where nature may heal and give strength to body and soul.

—John Muir

We Must Act Now to Avoid a Carbon Summer

By Al Gore

© The Nobel Foundation 2007. Adapted from his speech in Oslo, December 10, 2007, as he accepted the Nobel Peace Prize. Used with permission.

Sometimes, without warning, the future knocks with a precious and painful vision of what might be. One hundred and nineteen years ago, a wealthy inventor read his own obituary, mistakenly published years before his death. Wrongly believing the inventor had just died, a newspaper printed a harsh judgment of his life's work, unfairly labeling him "The Merchant of Death" because of his invention—dynamite. Shaken by this condemnation, the inventor made a fateful choice to serve the cause of peace.

Seven years later, Alfred Nobel created this prize and the others that bear his name.

Seven years ago tomorrow, I read my own political obituary in a judgment that seemed besides premature, harsh and mistaken. But that verdict also brought a precious and painful gift: an opportunity to search for new ways to serve my purpose. And that quest brought me here.

We, the human species, have a choice between two different futures, for we're confronting a planetary emergency, a threat to the very survival of our civilization. But we have the ability to solve this crisis and avoid the worst, though not all, of its consequences if we act boldly, decisively and quickly. However, despite a growing number of honorable exceptions, too many of the world's leaders are still ignoring the evidence.

So today, we dumped another seventy million tons of global-warming pollution into our planet's thin atmosphere, as if it were an open sewer. And tomorrow, we will dump a slightly larger amount, with the cumulative concentrations trapping more and more heat from the sun. As a result, the earth has a fever. And the fever is rising. The experts have told us it is not a passing affliction that will heal by itself. We asked for a second opinion. And a third. And a fourth. And the consistent conclusion, restated with increasing alarm, is that something basic is wrong.

We are what is wrong, and we must make it right.

Last September 21, as the Northern Hemisphere tilted away from the sun, scientists reported that the North Polar ice cap is constantly melting. One study estimated it could be completely gone in less than twenty-two years, and another study warns it could happen in as little as seven years.

In the last few months, it has become ever harder to misinterpret the signs that our world is spinning out of kilter. Major cities in North and South America, Asia and Australia are nearly out of water because of massive droughts and melting glaciers. Desperate farmers are losing their livelihoods. Peoples in the frozen Arctic and on low-lying Pacific islands are planning evacuations of places they have long called home. Unprecedented wildfires have forced a half million people from their homes in one country and caused a national emergency that almost brought down the government in another. Climate refugees have migrated into areas already inhabited by people with different cultures, religions and traditions, increasing the potential for conflict. Stronger storms in the Pacific and Atlantic have threatened whole cities. Millions have been displaced by massive flooding in South Asia, Mexico and eighteen African countries. As temperature extremes have increased, tens of thousands have perished. We are recklessly burning and clearing our forests and driving more and more species into extinction.

We never intended to cause all this destruction, just as Alfred Nobel never intended that dynamite be used for waging war. He had hoped his invention would promote human progress. We shared that same worthy goal when we began burning massive quantities of coal, then oil and methane. Even in Nobel's time, there were a few warnings of the likely consequences. One of the very first winners of the Prize in chemistry worried that "We are evaporating our coal mines into the air."

Seventy years later, my teacher, Roger Revelle, and his colleague, Dave Keeling, began to precisely document the daily increasing CO2 levels. But unlike most other forms of pollution, CO2 is invisible, tasteless, and odorless—which has helped disguise the truth about what it is doing to our climate. Moreover, the catastrophe now threatening us is unprecedented, and we often confuse the unprecedented with the improbable. We also find it hard to imagine making the massive changes now necessary to solve the crisis. And when large truths are genuinely inconvenient, whole societies can, at least briefly, ignore them.

In the years since this prize was first awarded, the entire relationship between humankind and the earth has been radically transformed. And still, we have remained largely oblivious to the impact of our cumulative actions. Indeed, without realizing it, we have begun to wage war on the earth itself. Now, we and the earth's climate are locked in a relationship familiar to war planners: "Mutually assured destruction." More than two decades ago, scientists calculated that nuclear war could throw so much debris and smoke into the air that it would block life-giving sunlight from our atmosphere, causing a "nuclear winter." Now science is warning that if we do not quickly reduce the global warming pollution, we are in danger of creating a permanent "carbon summer." We must quickly mobilize with the urgency and resolve previously seen only when nations mobilized for war, when leaders found words at the eleventh hour that released a mighty surge of courage, hope and readiness to sacrifice for a mortal challenge. When they called upon the courage, generosity and strength of entire peoples, citizens of every class and condition who were ready to stand against the threat once asked to do so. Our enemies calculated that free people would not rise to the challenge; they were, of course, catastrophically wrong. Now comes the threat of climate crisis, a threat that is real, rising, imminent and universal. Once again, it is the eleventh hour. The penalties for ignoring this challenge are immense and growing, and at some near point would be unsustainable and unrecoverable. We still have the power to choose our fate, and the question is only if we have the will to act vigorously and in time, or will remain imprisoned by a dangerous illusion.

We must adopt principles, values, laws, and treaties that release creativity and initiative at every level of society in multifold responses originating concurrently and spontaneously. This new consciousness requires expanding the possibilities inherent in all humanity. The innovators who will devise a new way to harness the sun's energy for pennies or invent an engine that is carbon negative may live in Lagos or Mumbai or Montevideo. We must ensure that entrepreneurs and inventors everywhere have the chance to change the world. The generation that defeated fascism in the 1940s found that they had gained the moral authority and long-term vision to launch the Marshall Plan, the United Nations, and a new level of global cooperation and foresight that unified Europe and facilitated the emergence of democracy and prosperity in Germany, Japan, Italy and much of the world.

By facing and removing the danger of the climate crisis, we have the opportunity to gain the moral authority and vision to vastly increase our capacity to solve other crises. We must understand the connections between the climate crisis and the afflictions of poverty, hunger, HIV-AIDS and other pandemics. As these problems are linked, so too must be their solutions. We must begin by making the common rescue of the global environment the central organizing principle of the world community. Fifteen years ago, I made that case at the Earth Summit in Rio de Janeiro. Ten years ago, I presented it in Kyoto. This week, I will urge the delegates in Bali to adopt a bold mandate for a treaty that establishes a universal global cap on emissions and uses the market in emissions trading to efficiently allocate resources to the most effective opportunities for speedy reductions. This treaty should be ratified and brought into effect everywhere in the world by the beginning of 2010—two years sooner than presently contemplated. The pace of our response must be accelerated to match the accelerating pace of the crisis itself.

Heads of state should meet early next year to review what was accomplished in Bali and take personal responsibility for addressing this crisis. It is not unreasonable to ask, given the gravity of our circumstances, that these heads of state meet every three months until the treaty is completed. We also need a moratorium on the construction of any new generating facility that burns coal without the capacity to safely trap and store carbon dioxide. And most important of all, we need to put a price on carbon—with a

CO2 tax that is then rebated back to the people, progressively, according to the laws of each nation, in ways that shift the burden of taxation from employment to pollution. This is by far the most effective and simplest way to accelerate solutions to this crisis.

The world needs an alliance, especially of those nations that weigh heaviest in the scales where earth is in the balance. I salute Europe and Japan for the steps they've taken in recent years to meet the challenge, and the new government in Australia, which has made solving the climate crisis its first priority.

But the outcome will be decisively influenced by two nations that are now failing to do enough: the United States and China. While India is also growing fast in importance, it should be absolutely clear that it is the two largest CO2 emitters—most of all, my own country—that will need to make the boldest moves, or stand accountable before history for their failure to act. Both countries should stop using the other's behavior as an excuse for stalemate and instead develop an agenda for mutual survival in a shared global environment.

These are the last few years of decision, but they can be the first years of a bright and hopeful future if we do what we must. No one should believe a solution will be found without effort, without cost, without change. Let us acknowledge that if we wish to redeem squandered time and speak again with moral authority, then these are the hard truths: The way ahead is difficult. The outer boundary of what we currently believe is feasible is still far short of what we actually must do.

I want to end as I began, with a vision of two futures—each a palpable possibility—and with a prayer that we will see with vivid clarity the necessity of choosing between those two futures, and the urgency of making the right choice now. The future is knocking at our door right now. Make no mistake, the next generation will ask us one of two questions. Either they will ask: "What were you thinking; why didn't you act?" Or they will ask instead: "How did you find the moral courage to rise and successfully resolve a crisis that so many said was impossible to solve?"

We have everything we need to get started, save perhaps political will, but political will is a renewable resource. So let us renew it, and say together: "We have a purpose. We are many. For this purpose we will rise, and we will act."

Albert Arnold Gore, Jr., served as the forty-fifth vice president of the United States from 1993 to 2001. He began his political career in 1977, representing Tennessee in the U.S. House of Representatives, and served in the U.S. Senate from 1985 to 1993. Along with the Intergovernmental Panel on Climate Change, he was awarded the Nobel Peace Prize in 2007. The film An Inconvenient Truth, *in which he appeared and for which he wrote the text, won an Academy Award.*

A Prince's Green Sensibility

By Michael Gerson

From *The Washington Post,* June 14, 2008 © 2008 The Washington Post. All rights reserved. Used by permission and protected by the Copyright Laws of the United States. The printing, copying, redistribution, or retransmission of the Material without express written permission is prohibited.

TETBURY, ENGLAND At Highgrove House, Prince Charles's country estate, the wild minks are once again eating the large koi in the ornamental pond. But the plentiful birds, often fed by the prince's own hand, are keeping the snails on the hostas under control. These are among the trials and triumphs of modern royalty.

The Highgrove gardens are a marvel of this very British art. In the gnarled wildness of an area called the Stumpery, among the moss-clogged foundations, amid cozy clearings and wildflower fields and tumbled walls of discarded cathedral carvings, order is coaxed by craft, not imposed by pesticides. At the Prince of Wales's nearby organic farm, rare breeds of British cattle graze on grass instead of the enriched feeds that would increase their size and shorten their lives. The farm manager, greeted by the cows like an old friend, explains his preference for homeopathic veterinary remedies and warns about the overuse of antibiotics. Vegetable and grain fields are renewed by crop rotation instead of nitrogen-based fertilizers, which change the nature of the soil and reduce the immunities of some plants.

Few places on earth more distinctly bear the mark of a single personality than this green and pleasant corner of the Cotswolds. When Prince Charles began his organic experimentations two decades ago, he was abused as a crank—the battiest of the royals. Now the question arises: Is such battiness the future of the world?

Charles, it turns out, was a pioneer in a field that now includes Whole Foods and organic sections at every grocery store. (He sells his own brand of organic products called Duchy Originals; the oat biscuits are particularly tasty.) Many experts now argue that small-scale, sustainable agriculture, not a chemical or genetic green revolution, is the key to food security in developing countries. The surging price of oil and natural gas has raised concerns about nitrogen fertilizers—a fuel-intensive product that has made the global food supply dependent on the energy industry.

I admit that some elements of the organic worldview make me uncomfortable: its occasionally pharisaical intensity, the endless lists of symbolic and impractical "steps I can take to save the planet," the nearly universal mania with bird watching (I refuse to get excited about all the indistinguishable little brown ones).

But in the fidgety busyness of modern life, this intensity has a spiritual cause. Indifference to nature is a kind of blindness and deadness and poverty. And the rediscovery of the physical world leads us toward harmonies beyond it.

Wrote the poet Wendell Berry:

> I come into the peace of wild things
> who do not tax their lives with forethought
> of grief. I come into the presence of still water.
> And I feel above me the day-blind stars
> waiting with their light. For a time
> I rest in the grace of the world, and am free.

The organic worldview also has political consequences. Out of a justified fear of the inherent irresponsibility of journalists, the prince's conversation with me was not on the record. But it is safe to say that he thoughtfully defends an older, small "c" conservatism: a suspicion of unbounded technology, consumerism and agribusiness; a disdain for the kind of cinder-block architecture that dehumanizes those it shelters. A conservatism of place, of tradition, of the land, which honors the awesome givenness of both nature and human nature. There is a deep and neglected connection between conservation and conservatism. It has often been a scientifically minded liberalism that has proposed the planning of society and the manipulation of nature. "In many important respects," observes the impossibly bright Yuval Levin, "environmentalism is deeply conservative. . . . The movement seeks to preserve a given balance which we did not create, are not capable of fully understanding, and should not delude ourselves into imagining we can much improve—in other words, its attitude toward nature is much like the attitude of conservatism toward society."

According to traditional conservatism, politicians should be like Highgrove's British gardeners, clipping and pruning society to reveal inner harmonies not always evident on the surface—instead of uprooting and replanting in, say, the severe order of a French formal garden. And there is every reason to apply this same conservative philosophy to the physical environment as well. Depending on your view of climate science and agriculture, this organic conservatism may be increasingly urgent. But there is little doubt it would allow us to rest more easily in the grace of the world.

Michael John Gerson served as President George W. Bush's chief speechwriter for five years, was a senior policy advisor from 2000 until 2006, and was known as "the conscience of the White House." An evangelical Christian, he is an op-ed columnist for The Washington Post *and a senior fellow at the Council on Foreign Relations.*

Searching for Eden, USA

By A. Robert Smith

The quest for a heaven on earth stems from Adam and Eve's expulsion from the Garden of Eden. Most efforts to recreate heaven on earth are led by churchmen convinced that God is guiding them. Pilgrims who came to New England, William Penn's Quakers who launched his "Holy Experiment" in Pennsylvania, and Joseph Smith's Mormons who settled Utah exemplify a noble purpose that set them apart from commercial settlements such as Jamestown, Virginia.

Nobility of purpose is essential to achieving a heaven on earth, though that's not to say the sponsorship must be religious. Indeed, a non-sectarian effort may have greater stability and certainly have wider appeal.

Ephrata, a monastic community in Lancaster County, Pennsylvania, was founded by Conrad Beissel in the mid-eighteenth century. He broke away from his parent church, encouraged celibacy but welcomed families, and drew a population of several hundred Anabaptists. They established farms, shops, a paper mill, a publishing center, a bookbindery, meetinghouses, dwellings and mills. As did many utopian communities, they thrived under their inspirational leader but dwindled after his death in 1768, leaving a museum-like campus that attracts tourists who can only imagine what this version of heaven on earth was like.

Washington Grove, Maryland, a village on the outskirts of the nation's capital, was founded as a summer camp by the Methodist Church in 1873. Starting with rented tents for a ten-day gathering, it evolved into a summer-long retreat, its tents replaced with cottages. When church sponsorship lapsed in 1937, the cottages were remodeled for year-round occupancy.

When the leader's death created a vacuum, Washington Grove transitioned from church ownership to an incorporated town that owns half its acreage but turned residential lots over to private owners. It elects a mayor and council, all serving as unpaid volunteers, and boasts a nature-loving population of about six hundred who are determined to keep out tract housing and strip malls. It is the only municipality in Maryland that owns its own forest.

The Grove benefits from an inspired design, its houses facing grassy walkways and bike trails, with roads behind; its parks, woods, a swimming pond, and community center within a few minutes' walk of all the houses; convenient to commuter trains and public schools.

For the eleven years my family lived in the Grove, we considered it the most heavenly community we could imagine. There was no crime, no corruption, and scant social pretense, and we enjoyed trustworthy neighbors, participation in civic matters, and convenient access to commercial services, medical facilities, churches and cultural opportunities in adjacent towns and Washington at the end of the Metro. And it levied no taxes beyond those of Montgomery County and the state of Maryland.

While Washington Grove has no industrial plants (there is a sizeable IBM plant in next door Gaithersburg), non-polluting industries are situated in the area, affording short commutes between home and office.

Reston, Virginia, is a more modern and much larger example of a non-sectarian community with a noble purpose and superior design. It had an idealistic founder, Richard E. Simon, whose family had owned Carnegie Hall, whose sale allowed Simon to establish Reston. Its stylish modern homes share a natural setting of trees and lakes with a commercial town center that features high-rise office buildings, shops, restaurants, amusements, a hotel, bike and hiking trails, and public transportation into Washington to serve its population of sixty thousand.

There are several requirements to achieve such a fortunate blend of benefits. First, there must be a viable overall urban design that rejects suburbanitis, an ailment first detected in Levittown, on Long Island, when a developer introduced tracts of one-story ranch-style houses in huge residential zones far from industrial or commercial zones. Residents were protected from undesirable pollution and noise, but obligated to drive miles to work, play or shop. Levittown became a model for suburban bedroom communities all over America, and the cause of rush-hour commuter traffic jams. Less drive time reduces air pollution, and offers more family time.

Other necessities include leaders who uphold the town's ideals, reflect the will of the residents, and avoid autocratic edicts; commercial interests that adhere to the plan without seeking variances at odds with the community's interests; and residents who volunteer their time and talents to preserve the community's livability.

Heaven on earth takes high ideals, hard work, and cooperation, but it is attainable.

A. Robert Smith, who lives in Virginia Beach, is the author of No Soul Left Behind *and a forthcoming historical novel* Ben Franklin's Secret Love.

Superstar Brad Pitt Makes It Right

By Renée Peck

© 2008 The Times-Picayune Publishing Co. All rights reserved. Used with permission of The Times-Picayune.

Editor's note: The Make It Right Foundation builds houses for those displaced by Hurricane Katrina who could not manage the financing without assistance.

Brad Pitt's Make It Right houses in the Lower 9th Ward have stirred a lot of talk—not only because of their megastar backer, but also for their futuristic designs and cutting-edge green components, such as rain gardens and solar cells.

Most people either love 'em or hate 'em.

The current issue of *Architectural Digest*, which hit the stands this week, explores both the project and Pitt's philosophy behind creating it. In the article, writer Gerald Clarke takes a stroll with Pitt through the first of the Make It Right houses to be occupied— the persimmon-colored raised cottage featured in *InsideOut* at Thanksgiving. Along the way, Pitt talks about his love of architecture, his concept for rebuilding and life in the paparazzi lane. ("We're big bounty for them. They make a good living off us," he commented as half a dozen aggressive photographers stalked him outside the residence.)

Pitt bases his solution to this country's overly consumptive society on William McDonough's "cradle to cradle" design philosophy, which calls for low-maintenance homes built of planet-friendly and recyclable materials. "It's radical thinking— zero waste—but actually very simple," Pitt tells Clarke. "Simple in the sense that it follows the ecosystem of nature. Why can't we redefine how we do things?"

Against this backdrop of twenty-first-century thinking, Pitt seems to understand the sense of place and tradition that defines New Orleans and its neighborhoods. It is a place, he realizes, where people want front porches. "New Orleans has its own mind, its own thing," he is quoted as saying. "It has a real spirit. It's the most authentic of all American cities."

Pitt has been busy these past few weeks promoting his new film, "The Curious Case of Benjamin Button," filmed in New Orleans and opening Christmas Day. He also has used the opportunity to promote New Orleans in general, and Make It Right in particular.

In a *Los Angeles Times* piece published December 5, he says of the Lower 9th Ward, "It will be great to see barbecues in the backyards and kids riding their bikes on the streets again." According to the article, the actor sees the film as a "love letter" to New Orleans: "There's a sense of magic here, so it made this fantastic story almost believable."

It's nice when someone sees the magic, and nicer yet when someone with influence expresses it. As Pitt tells Clarke, people tend to answer his phone calls. Perhaps this will be the good-news story of 2009: Stars who make headlines for philanthropy rather than bad behavior.

The Los Angeles Times thinks so: Its recent article reports that members of Barack Obama's circle of advisers are floating Pitt's Make It Right project as a model for the kind of celebrity activism that his administration would like to encourage.

Here in New Orleans, we've seen the way that anyone—youth celebrities, everyday residents—can make a difference. Perhaps the country soon will see that too.

William Bradley "Brad" Pitt is an American actor and film producer, who first achieved stardom in several successful films in the mid-1990s. He has been cited as one of the world's most attractive men, and his off-screen life is widely reported. In 2006, Pitt created the Make It Right Foundation New Orleans and gathered a group of housing professionals together in the Hurricane Katrina-stricken city with the goal of financing and constructing 150 new houses in New Orleans' Ninth Ward.

Renée Peck was a feature writer and editor at The Times-Picayune *from 1977 to 2009. She covered, at various times, food, entertainment, parenting, the Internet and television, and was most recently the editor of* InsideOut, *the newspaper's Saturday home and garden magazine. When the levee beaches from Hurricane Katrina inundated 80 percent of the city's housing stock in 2005, "I lost my beat," she says wryly. After that she focused on rebuilding issues, from mold remediation to green construction, volunteer efforts to spray-foam insulation. For her efforts, she received awards in consumer journalism from The Associated Press and New Orleans Press Club.*

Envisioning a Green Middle East

By Levi Ben-Shmuel

Although the roots of the Arab-Israeli conflict are ancient, having lived in Israel for nine years and broken bread with Palestinians who were working towards peace, I saw firsthand the possibility of transforming enemies into friends. I do not dismiss old wounds and the impact they can have on a person or a nation. Yet at some point, wounds must heal and forgiveness be granted to the perpetrators of them. Anything less locks one into a pattern that is ultimately destructive to the self and to a people.

It is up to the Israeli, Palestinian and Arab nations to find their way to peace. To date, the efforts supported by the global community to achieve peace have fallen short. Yet change is in the air. The climate crisis and a new U.S. president have created an opportunity to shift to a new paradigm. Perhaps there is something very practical we can do to help them get there. Our dependency on oil has poured trillions of dollars into the region, thus helping fuel the war and hate machines. If the West makes a serious commitment to create a renewable energy-based economy now, we might help defuse the road to Armageddon.

We can send a message that in the near future, the playing field will be shifted in a dramatic way. By saying goodbye to oil and the revenue it generates, financial support for terrorist organizations will shrink. If we shift our energy policy, a window will be opened for dramatic change in the region. With proper pressure, we can help the regional players see that it is time for a new mode of relating, one based on shared human interests rather than age-old conflict.

Imagine this: we create Green technologies so appealing and practical that even the oil-rich countries in the Middle East see the wisdom of adopting them. We talk to our enemies and help them go Green. New jobs sprout up to create the infrastructure for the Green economy. The abundant Middle Eastern sunshine is harnessed to power energy-efficient schools, hospitals and other buildings. Inefficient means of production are transformed to invigorate traditional industries.

This new, Green path encourages Israelis and Palestinians to try real cooperation. Borders open so people and goods can flow. This leads to trusting that this time, forgiveness and reconciliation are the way forward. Building a better future for the children becomes a shared passion. Ordinary people's lives are changed for the better. The extremist elements that refused to see peace as a desirable option become marginalized. War becomes an outdated thing of the past. The world is inspired, and a global revolution for peace is sparked by seeing that the impossible is indeed possible.

For many, the idea of heaven on earth hinges on peace in the Middle East. Going Green is no guarantee of success, but I am confident that it improves the odds that we don't have to end the world to get there.

Levi Ben-Shmuel is a dual citizen of the United States and Israel. A Massachusetts Institute of Technology graduate with a master's degree in economic development, he has devoted his life to fulfilling a spiritual vision of people coming together through his music, writing and speaking.

Creating Gardens of Paradise

By William E. Barrick

As a professional horticulturist for over thirty years, I have often tried to articulate my motivation for working in public gardens. While listening to NPR one Saturday morning in 1995, I was mesmerized by the winning Thanksgiving essay on "Why We Give Thanks" from avid gardener and listener Hillary Nelson. In describing the peace she derived from gardening, Ms. Nelson summed up my career of trying to recreate Heaven on Earth in Callaway Gardens and now in Bellingrath Gardens and Home by stating, "I believe that the Garden of Eden is real and everyone has a right to live there.... We are made to find joy in unexpected places. That is why I plant a garden and that is why I give thanks." Gardens do indeed provide environments where human beings can develop physically, intellectually, emotionally and spiritually.

In Genesis 2:8 we read, "And the Lord God planted a garden eastward in Eden, and there he put the man whom he had formed." Perhaps that verse alone provides us with the undeniable truth that there is a spiritual link to gardening. English philosopher Francis Bacon wrote in 1625, "God almighty first planted a garden. And indeed, it is the purest of human pleasures." Similarly, Sir William Temple, an English scholar, wrote in the late 1600s, "If we believe the Scripture, we must allow that God Almighty esteemed the life of man in a garden—the happiest he could give him, or else he would have not placed Adam in that of Eden." Our third president, Thomas Jefferson, eloquently opined that "They who labour in the earth are the chosen people of God."

Equally I think that the love of gardening results from three other powerful forces: gardening reinforces our bonds to people, connects us to our senses, and, above all, restores our souls and gives us eternal hope.

From early childhood, I can remember being influenced by neighbors who gardened, but perhaps the greatest influence on my life was my grandfather who farmed until age 101. Granddaddy Ivey taught me in his own special way that "If we lose the soil, we lose the source of all our wealth." But wealth is not always measured in dollars and cents, but from the riches we receive by being stewards of God's creation. The love of gardening binds us to each other, for we delight in sharing our knowledge and passion for gardens.

In the age of technology and reliance on mechanical systems, it is clear that we are constantly being disconnected from the rhythms of nature. As a culture we deal with facts, figures, deadlines, cell phones, emails and the reality of the pace of our lives. Gardening offers us the ability to reconnect to our senses and to imagine visions of paradise.

Eleanor Roosevelt once said, "Where flowers bloom so does hope." Without question, most Americans garden or visit gardens to restore their souls and offer hope for the future. In my early career at Callaway Gardens, Mr. Callaway was noted for saying, "I don't know what the soul is, but surely beauty and goodness must be at the heart of it." Walter Bellingrath along with his wife, Bessie, spent a lifetime creating their sixty-five-acre garden along the Fowl River in Theodore, Alabama. In his epitaph is written, "If a grain of corn will die and rise again in so much beauty, why may I not die and rise again in infinite beauty and life."

Hillary Nelson was indeed correct when she said, "The Garden of Eden is real and everyone does have a right to live there." By planting a garden, we are connecting to people and our senses and offering hope for peace on Earth.

William E. Barrick received BS and MS degrees from Auburn University and a PhD in landscape horticulture from Michigan State University. After graduation, he served as an assistant professor of ornamental horticulture at the University of Florida. He was executive vice president and director of gardens at Callaway Gardens in Pine Mountain, Georgia, for almost twenty years before becoming executive director of Bellingrath Gardens and Home in November 1999. Barrick is a past president of the American Association of Botanical Gardens and Arboreta, past chairman of the American Horticultural Society and a recipient of the Arthur Hoyt Scott Medal. He serves on the board of the Mobile Bay Convention and Visitors Bureau, Advisory Committee Spring Hill College, Visiting Committee of the University of Mobile, Providence Hospital Foundation, and Infirmary West Advisory Board and trustee of Dauphin Way United Methodist Church.

Saving Small Friends

By Annette Aungier

Even though I live and work in Ireland and had never visited New Orleans, I have always had affection for that intriguing city, so in August, 2005, I watched in dread as Hurricane Katrina headed its way. In between tasks at work I checked online news sources to keep up-to-date about the storm and its aftermath.

The United States has always been a great friend to Ireland, and my heart ached to see the people outside the Superdome and Convention Center. I turned to the *Times-Picayune* nola.com forums to see what was happening and if there was anything I could do to help. To my amazement, there were many posts from people who had to leave their pets behind when they evacuated. There seemed to be thousands of pets trapped, many in flooded houses, running out of food and water.

There was a pet rescue forum, and, thanks to the Internet and common language, I thought there might be something I could do. I couldn't help trapped people, but it would be a great consolation to pet owners to know that someone cared about their trapped pets, especially if they had lost everything else.

Throughout September, for some six hours each night, I posted "rescuer" details to people who posted messages about trapped pets, and "trapped pet" details to the rescuers, saving both groups from having to scroll through literally hundreds of posts, for time was critical. Even a month later some animals emerged from darkened homes, only skin and bones, but alive.

I know very well how much a pet can mean to a family, because we have Skippy. She was only about seven weeks old when her mother, part of a feral colony, was run over by a truck. It took my

207

sister, Paula, two hours to catch the kitten, even with the help of her workmates.

She brought her home in a cardboard box punctured with air-holes. When the box was opened in our back garden, Skippy immediately jumped out, ran down a side passage, crawled under an inch-high gap under our side door, and ran into the front garden and straight to the engine of my car.

When I got home, Paula told me what happened. I could see the shadow of a tiny cat behind the grille, but the kitten was too frightened to come out. This was a Friday evening, but I canceled plans to go out.

I spent the whole next day by the car. Neighbors came and went, strangers offered their advice. She came out a few times to play with a toy mouse I bought, but ran back under the car if I went near her. We gave her some food, so she was happy enough. Any time I went away, she meowed very loudly. One of the times I left that night, she meowed so loudly that I came back, and she was halfway from the car to the side passage. I retreated a bit and she followed, hugging the wall. When I retreated again, she followed a bit closer.

Eventually, she came into the back garden. I alerted my sister inside the house, so she ran out to secure the door so Skippy would stay inside. That night our new kitten slept on my dad's gardening glove, curled up on the palm.

We had never had a cat before, but we quickly grew to love Skippy, who provided us with fun, affection and distraction from day-to-day woes.

Many people who lost everything else after Katrina said that the return of their pets gave them back at least part of their old lives. I can't help but think that the peace and happiness one feels in the presence of a beloved cat or dog—or hamster or canary for that matter—promotes the feeling of goodwill toward other people. If you're happy, you're better able to help others and make a contribution to peace and harmony in the world.

Annette Aungier, a native and resident of Dublin, Ireland, is a money market dealer for an agency that serves the national government. Single, she counts her cat as a valued family member. Besides her work, she enjoys sailing, walking, listening to music, socializing and reading a wide range of writers. This is the first piece she has written for publication.

The Amazon Rainforest Cries for Help

By Jana Carvalha

The Amazon rainforest—at 5.5 million square kilometers, by far the largest tropical rainforest in the world—is located within parts of nine nations: Brazil, Colombia, Peru, Venezuela, Ecuador, Bolivia, Guyana, Suriname and French Guiana. Amazonia represents over half of the rainforests left on earth, and contains more species of flora and fauna than any similar region. I have read that this region has twice as many species of birds as the United States and Canada, even though only ten percent of the forest has been studied. There are many species yet to be discovered, and sadly, no doubt some that have gone extinct without our knowledge of them.

Some sixty percent of the rainforest is within the boundaries of my country, Brazil, so it is natural that I have grown up thinking about Amazonia, and developing a concern for its future. This important region is now crying for help. Dealing with the natural resources in a sustainable way is a challenge to all of humanity, and should be our homework in every corner of the globe.

There are many interests involved—governments, non-governmental organizations, national and multinational companies, small farmers—but who is considering the needs of humanity as a whole? The farmers want empty land on which to raise cattle or to start a soybean plantation, and after they cut down the trees to make room for their enterprises, they sell the wood that had covered the area for centuries to wood companies to make gorgeous furniture that will appear in posh malls all over the world. As an example of the devastation of the forest, in February 2008, some 725 square kilometers were cut down, contrasted with 266 square kilometers the same month three years before.

Nowadays there are countless laws regarding the environmental issues, and there have been useful discoveries based on good science, but there has not been enough action taken in the Amazon area. We concede that it is difficult to know exactly where the problem is, and how exactly to find the best solution. Where do we even start? Of course the world needs food and the farmers need to support their families, but the world also needs good air and climate, not just for now, but into the future.

Scientists believe that, apart from the rainforest being the "lungs" that purify the air over a huge area and a vital part of the planet, if the Amazon rainforest disappears or even if it becomes too greatly reduced, global warming will rapidly increase and a huge precipitation imbalance will occur all over the world. We cannot know the effect on agriculture, but we do know that significantly less rain will have a negative impact on the water level that maintains Brazil's hydroelectric power plants, as well as the rivers that supply the whole region and many other countries.

The human race has been forced to learn how to deal with so many catastrophes—drought, earthquakes, flooding, hurricanes, landslides, solar flares, tsunamis, wildfires, the depletion of the ozone layer and other natural disaster—that surely we can learn how to solve the critical problem of Amazonia. We can start by coming together and looking in the same direction—rich and poor, black and white and Indians, specialists and the uneducated, Brazilians and foreigners, governments and nongovernmental organizations, and all kinds of companies. We must put our ecological knowledge into practice in our daily lives. Items we use every day can be made from recycled materials. When we consider buying new furniture, we can be sure the wood is from a reforested farm; after all, if no one buys wood from endangered rainforests, the manufacture will stop and the trees will no longer be cut down. Boycotting woods from the Amazon rainforest can be effective, as was the recent action by several members of the European community, who imposed restrictions against purchasing cattle from Amazonia. Besides its biodiversity, the area is rich in gold, silver, rubies, diamonds, emeralds, oil, manganese, copper, iron and zinc, all of which, if mined with respect for the land, can add to the wealth of the local population and nation as a whole.

The government will have to provide sufficient enforcement

personnel, and managing the huge area will be an unwieldy task, but our very lives and those of future generations depend on our success.

Jana Carvalha is a Carioca, one who is a native of Rio de Janeiro, where she earned a degree in tourism and hotel management from Estácio de Sá Universidade. She is a professional tour guide and self-trained ecologist. Besides the Amazon rainforest, her particular interest is in the flora and fauna of her home city.

Ecology Matters

By Adrienne Froelich Sponberg

You would probably not believe me if I told you that not knowing what a sea lion eats nearly robbed the United States' economy of $2 billion. And you would be just as dubious that a study called *The Sexual Behavior of the Screw-worm Fly* has relevance to your daily life. Yet both statements are true.

Ecological soundness is a cornerstone of achieving a heaven on earth. With the inevitable conflicts between society and nature, how do we achieve ecological soundness? While one could write volumes on how to live alongside nature, all paths to ecological soundness start at the same place: a firm understanding of ecology.

While ecology is often associated with the conservation movement, its roots actually trace back to early studies of agriculture. Much of the original work on food webs in the 1880s was conducted to provide a scientific basis for the practice of agriculture. The screwworm fly study mentioned above first gained public notoriety in the 1970s after being awarded a "Golden Fleece Award" by Senator William Proxmire. Years later, however, Proxmire publicly conceded the study's significance in forwarding the field of biological control of pests in agriculture.

Basic knowledge about the environment has improved our ability to manipulate and live alongside nature. Food web studies have revealed that altering which types of fish are present in a lake can stop algal blooms, which are unsightly and unhealthy. Botany has taught us that many plants take up heavy metals, which led scientists to the development of phytoremediation: the use of plants to remove toxic chemicals from the environment. One of phytoremediation's biggest success stories involves the use of sunflowers to remove radioactive materials from contaminated ponds following the accident at Chernobyl. In just ten days, sunflowers removed ninety-five percent of the radioactivity in a pond near the reactor.

What happens when we don't know enough about our environment? In 2000, the Alaskan pollack fishery—the world's largest fishery and one valued at $2 billion—was temporarily shut down because we did not know enough about the diet of an endangered sea lion. Concern existed that the fishery was depleting their food source. Since the conflict, Congress has shuffled millions towards research on the Steller sea lions' diet. Studies have since concluded that a variety of factors have contributed to the sea lions' decline, but that the pollack fishery most likely does not have a significant impact on their populations. Hindsight is 20/20, of course . . . how many taxpayers would have thought a $200,000 study on the feeding preferences of a sea lion would be a worthy investment?

Seemingly ridiculous questions can—and have—provided answers and solutions to a harmonious existence between society and the environment. Unfortunately in the budgetary tug of war, scientific research on the environment has repeatedly lost out. In the past decade, politicians have lauded the National Science Foundation—the home of basic research on the environment— and garnered significant increases to its research program. The catch? The programs that fund environmental research have increased at only half the rate of the overall portfolio, barely keeping pace with inflation. The United States is home to many of the world's top-notch environmental scientists, who now find themselves competing for a shrinking pool of research funding. As a result, policymakers are finding that scientists often do not have the information they want—and need—on which to base their decisions.

In the end, ecological soundness is unattainable without the information necessary to make informed decisions. Without information, environmental conflicts turn into arguments over values, leaving little to no basis for real solutions. A heaven on earth implies society proceeding alongside the natural resources that are necessary for life and survival. With a little more understanding, we'll be firmly on the path to achieving that goal.

After receiving her Ph.D. in ecology from the University of Notre Dame, Adrienne Froelich Sponberg moved to Washington, D.C. to pursue her goal of making science accessible to policymakers. Following a year-long stint as a congressional fellow in the United States Senate, she began working as a public policy specialist for professional scientific societies.

An Earth-Friendly Mission

By Whitney Parker Scully

Adapted from an article in Delta Gamma's *Anchora*. Reprinted with permission.

Editor's note: Recycling is certainly nothing new and is practiced in communities across the nation. But its prevalence is spotty and someone must propose and encourage its adoption in each venue.

In 2005, when Kristin Strobel served as her sorority's director of wellness, she knew she had a modest budget to tackle projects for the betterment of the chapter and its members. And one thing really bothered her: although students who lived in dormitories recycled, those who lived in sorority and fraternity houses didn't.

Majoring in political science and pre-law at Ohio University in Athens, Ohio, Strobel added an environmental science minor to learn more about the process, and along with the school's manager of refuse and recycling, researched waste and recycling companies. They learned that trash pickup was priced per bag, while a recycling service had a flat monthly rate, just $2 at the time. After recycling bins were put into use at the Delta Gamma house, Strobel began to realize that doing her part to save the planet meant her chapter would actually save money. In fact, with the implementation of the recycling program, the chapter saved more than half of the money it had been throwing away each month for trash collection.

"Who knew helping the environment would also be significantly cheaper?" she asked.

Participating in the program wasn't mandatory, but Strobel

made it easy. She and her sisters placed large recycling bins in the kitchen and smaller ones in the each of the fifty members' rooms, and asked the house manager to add weekly recycling to members' chore rotation. Separating recyclables soon became second nature. Even the house cook got in on the game, recycling the house's industrial-sized cans and other kitchen containers.

"The ultimate goal of the program," Strobel said, "was to show that off-campus, multi-unit housing communities could not only recycle, but could also reduce costs in their budgets." The program's success was tough to ignore. The ease and cost-savings convinced three more sororities and two fraternities at OU to adopt similar programs.

Strobel was awarded the University's 2006 Dean of Students Citation, she received Delta Gamma Foundation's Ruth Billow Memorial Scholarship and she was nominated for *USA Today's* 2007 All-USA College Academic Team. Her efforts were also featured in *Planet OHIO*, Ohio University's Office of Sustainability publication.

"I learned a great deal about the environment, leadership and myself during this process," Strobel, who graduated in the spring of 2006, admitted. "I believe our environment can only be altered by human influence."

Strobel is now pursuing her master's degree in political science at OU, and she continues to monitor the program she created. She hopes her dedication and enthusiasm will grow as awareness spreads, recycling programs expand and the eco-bug that bit her continues to make his rounds.

Some Green (and not-so-green) Facts

- The highest point in Ohio is "Mount Rumpke," a mountain of trash at the Rumpke sanitary landfill.
- Incinerating 10,000 tons of waste creates one job; landfilling it creates six jobs; recycling it creates thirty-six jobs.
- Recycling aluminum uses less than five percent of the energy used to make it new.
- Recycling one aluminum can saves enough energy to run a one hundred-watt bulb for twenty hours, a computer for three hours or a TV for two hours.

- An aluminum can that is thrown away will still be a can five hundred years from now.
- There is no limit to the number of times a can can be recycled.
- Recycling a single run of the Sunday *New York Times* would save 75,000 trees.
- The amount of wood and paper we throw away each year is enough to heat 50,000,000 homes for twenty years.
- Producing recycled paper requires about sixty percent of the energy it took to make it new.
- Recycling plastic saves twice as much energy as burning it in an incinerator.
- The energy saved from recycling one glass bottle can run a one hundred-watt light bulb for four hours.
- A modern glass bottle would take four thousand years or more to decompose.
- The U.S. produces more trash than any other country. Five percent of the people generate forty percent of the world's waste.
- Motor oil never wears out. It can be re-refined and used again, reducing our reliance on imported oil.

Sources: the National Recycling Coalition, EPA and Earth911.org

Everyday Ways to Live Green

In your home
- Check out www.freecycle.org. You can offer that old futon/lamp/pile of books, or search your city's group for "new" treasures of your own.
- Go online to find how easy recycling can be. Search for your city and "curbside recycling." Services are often a few dollars per month.
- Turn lights off when you leave a room.
- Whenever possible, wash using cold water. It takes a lot of energy to heat water.
- Use a broom to clean outdoor surfaces instead of a hose.
- Take a shower instead of a bath, which takes four times the energy. Use low-flow showerheads, which are cheap and provide the same comfort.

At work and school
- Turn your computer off instead of leaving it in stand-by mode.
- Pack your lunch in a reusable bag/box.
- Reuse paper and print on both sides.
- Save electronic files instead of printing.

On the move
- Start a carpool. Do it just two days a week and reduce your carbon dioxide emissions by 1,590 pounds a year.
- Clean out your car and lighten up. Extra weight means you use more gas.
- Have your car serviced regularly.
- Carry a reusable shopping bag.
- Check the parking lots of grocery or home improvement stores. Many offer free recycling dumpsters.

Sources: SEPA, Environmental Working Group, Living Sustainably, Global Warming Facts

Whitney Parker Scully, who earned a bachelor's degree in English from Denison University, is the editor of Delta Gamma's award-winning quarterly publication, the Anchora, which has a circulation of nearly 150,000. She lives in Columbus, Ohio, with her husband, two young, tireless sons and two (also tireless) dogs.

The Evolution of the American Dream: Sustainable Neighborhoods and Heaven on Earth

By Brian Skeele

Living by the Golden Rule and Being our Brothers' Keeper aren't just nice ideas; they're pragmatic ways of taking care of ourselves. After the dust from 9/11 settled, we realized we are not an island, that injustice and suppression in Saudi Arabia and extreme poverty in developing nations breed desperate, deep resentment.

What if, by changing the way we live in our neighborhoods we not only contributed to reversing global warming but impacted the planet's nations in a way that created good will and an abundant future for all?

It might look like this: neighbors meet on a Saturday morning at a Designing Sustainable Neighborhoods workshop, and watch a PowerPoint presentation on alternatives to suburban sprawl. Their imaginations begin to fill with best practices from around the planet—mixed use, mixed-income neighborhoods with profit sharing and cooperation around shared facilities. And it's not all talk; they're out of their seats laughing and playing group problem-solving games. Over lunch, the big fun begins. Teams of four to six, armed with colorful markers and large sheets of paper, start sharing their ideas on sustainable redesigns for specific parts of town.

Neighbors are working toward a better life, with pedestrian-friendly, prosperous, wholesome, connected, enjoyable places to live; a more affordable, lower consumptive lifestyle, based on renewable energy and local food production. They see how they can have more time and less commuting. They can grow old, stay active and included if their neighborhood is redesigned to support aging in place. Kids can safely ride their bicycles everywhere and nature is nearby. The new and improved American dream is emerging.

It can feel risky, sharing from the heart, putting one's needs and dreams out there, and yet the deep respect and dynamic results of the group wisdom is exhilarating. Working moms dare to ask for help and dream of a nature-filled courtyard, surrounded by affordable homes, their children absorbed in play in a safe and nurturing environment at one end of the courtyard. In the evenings, parents gather at the other end of the courtyard, take turns cooking, and have adult conversations as the evening meal is put together. This, for working single parents, is heaven on earth.

After my grandmother died, and my grandfather was loosing his eyesight, he just wanted to garden and be around babies. He had a hard time asking for help with daily tasks, as he felt he wasn't contributing. Imagine a neighborhood where youngsters would bring him a hot meal while he's listening to a ball game, or escort him to the nearby day care center so he can hold babies for the afternoon. And his heirloom tomatoes are the cause for celebration. This would be heaven on earth for my Grandpa.

Through the sustainable redesigning process, existing suburban neighborhoods get transformed by the addition of commercial and community facilities. The new, smart incorporation of shops, businesses and residential structures remodeled to add a second or third floor to make those businesses successful creates new square footage. Who owns this new square footage? From best practices comes the answer, "The neighbors!"

Imagine, a democratically redesigned neighborhood, where neighbors put together a mutually beneficial redevelopment plan, and then profit share off of the well-thought-out mixed use design. This too is heaven on earth. "We are all in this together" isn't just a Utopian philosophy, but a day-to-day evolving, profitable experience.

By creating ecologically sound mixed-use, mixed-income neighborhoods with lifelong learning and open spaces everywhere, the United States can become a true world leader. Once we are demonstrating a sustainable lifestyle built on the needs and dreams of our citizens, we can then share our experience around the planet with pride, our love manifest.

Brian Skeele, who lives in Santa Fe, New Mexico, is a general contractor, pragmatic visionary and co-facilitator of Designing Sustainable Neighborhoods Workshops.

Health

Healing is a matter of time, but it is sometimes a matter of opportunity.

—Hippocrates

Friends for Life: An Emerging Biology of Emotional Healing

By Daniel Goleman

From *The New York Times,* October 10, 2006 © 2006 The New York Times. All rights reserved. Used by permission and protected by the Copyright Laws of the United States. The printing, copying, redistribution, or retransmission of the Material without express written permission is prohibited.

A dear friend has been battling cancer for a decade or more. Through a grinding mix of chemotherapy, radiation and all the other necessary indignities of oncology, he has lived on, despite dire prognoses to the contrary.

My friend was the sort of college professor students remember fondly: not just inspiring in class but taking a genuine interest in them—in their studies, their progress through life, their fears and hopes. A wide circle of former students count themselves among his lifelong friends; he and his wife have always welcomed a steady stream of visitors to their home. Though no one could ever prove it, I suspect that one of many ingredients in his longevity has been this flow of people who love him.

Research on the link between relationships and physical health has established that people with rich personal networks—who are married, have close family and friends, are active in social and religious groups—recover more quickly from disease and live longer. But now the emerging field of social neuroscience, the study of how people's brains entrain as they interact, adds a missing piece to that data.

The most significant finding was the discovery of "mirror neurons," a widely dispersed class of brain cells that operate like neural WiFi. Mirror neurons track the emotional flow, movement and even intentions of the person we are with, and replicate this sensed state in our own brain by stirring in our brain the same areas active in the other person.

Mirror neurons offer a neural mechanism that explains emotional contagion, the tendency of one person to catch the feelings of another, particularly if strongly expressed. This brain-to-brain link may also account for feelings of rapport, which research finds depend in part on extremely rapid synchronization of people's posture, vocal pacing and movements as they interact. In short, these brain cells seem to allow the interpersonal orchestration of shifts in physiology.

Such coordination of emotions, cardiovascular reactions or brain states between two people has been studied in mothers with their infants, marital partners arguing and even among people in meetings. Reviewing decades of such data, Lisa M. Diamond and Lisa G. Aspinwall, psychologists at the University of Utah, offer the infelicitous term "a mutually regulating psychobiological unit" to describe the merging of two discrete physiologies into a connected circuit. To the degree that this occurs, Dr. Diamond and Dr. Aspinwall argue, emotional closeness allows the biology of one person to influence that of the other.

John T. Cacioppo, director of the Center for Cognitive and Social Neuroscience at the University of Chicago, makes a parallel proposal: the emotional status of our main relationships has a significant impact on our overall pattern of cardiovascular and neuroendocrine activity. This radically expands the scope of biology and neuroscience from focusing on a single body or brain to looking at the interplay between two at a time. In short, my hostility bumps up your blood pressure; your nurturing love lowers mine. Potentially, we are each other's biological enemies or allies.

Even remotely suggesting health benefits from these interconnections will, no doubt, raise hackles in medical circles. No one can claim solid data showing a medically significant effect from the intermingling of physiologies.

At the same time, there is now no doubt that this same connectivity can offer a biologically grounded emotional solace. Physical suffering aside, a healing presence can relieve emotional suffering. A case in point is a functional magnetic resonance imaging study of women awaiting an electric shock. When the women endured their apprehension alone, activity in neural regions that incite stress hormones and anxiety was heightened. As James A. Coan reported last year in an article in *Psychophysiology*, when a stranger held the subject's hand as she waited, she found little relief. When her husband held her hand, she not only felt calm, but her brain circuitry quieted, revealing the biology of emotional rescue.

But as all too many people with severe chronic diseases know, loved ones can disappear, leaving them to bear their difficulties in lonely isolation. Social rejection activates the very zones of the brain that generate, among other things, the sting of physical pain. Matthew D. Lieberman and Naomi Eisenberg of U.C.L.A. (writing in a chapter in *Social Neuroscience: People Thinking About People*, M.I.T. Press, 2005) have proposed that the brain's pain centers may have taken on a hypersensitivity to social banishment because exclusion was a death sentence in human prehistory. They note that in many languages the words that describe a "broken heart" from rejection borrow the lexicon of physical hurt.

So when the people who care about a patient fail to show up, it may be a double blow: the pain of rejection and the deprivation of the benefits of loving contact. Sheldon Cohen, a psychologist at Carnegie-Mellon University who studies the effects of personal connections on health, emphasizes that a hospital patient's family and friends help just by visiting, whether or not they quite know what to say.

My friend has reached that point where doctors see nothing else to try. On my last visit, he and his wife told me that he was starting hospice care. One challenge, he told me, will be channeling the river of people who want to visit into the narrow range of hours in a week when he still has the energy to engage them. As he said this, I felt myself tearing up, and responded: "You know, at least it's better to have this problem. So many people go through this all alone."

He was silent for a moment, thoughtful. Then he answered softly, "You're right."

Daniel Goleman is the author of Social Intelligence: The New Science of Human Relationships, Emotional Intelligence, Primal Leadership *and* Ecological Intelligence.

Body and Spirit

By John Hanc

I met Father James Maher, a six foot-one inch tall marathon-running, basketball-playing Catholic priest about ten years ago.

Father Jim, as he is known to the students and staff of St. John's University, was not the frail, bookish ascetic I had come to associate with men of the cloth. Far from it. Eleven years in a row, he ran the New York City Marathon to raise funds for St. John's Bread and Life, a soup kitchen in the Bedford-Stuyvesant section of Brooklyn. Imbued with a good sense of humor as well as a good heart (he jokingly admitted that in his role as the spiritual advisor to the university's basketball team, he occasionally asked God to allow his team to hit a three-pointer when it really counted), Father Jim reminds us that good health is not incompatible with good intentions; that a life devoted to creating a better world can also include a commitment to maintaining a healthier body.

While he personally exemplifies this belief, he is quick to note that this idea—that physical fitness and spiritual growth can go hand in hand—comes from a higher authority. "There was a saying in the early church that 'the glory of God is the human being fully alive,'" he says. "I think that being active and being a person who exercises is a way of accessing that positive energy that comes from God."

It's easy to think otherwise. Athletes are by nature a selfish group; often, they have to be. And what could seem shallower than the larger fitness world, where self-esteem is often measured by the inches of a biceps, or the tone of your tush? Yet, while the fitness and sports world admittedly has its share of self-absorbed knuckleheads, people whose depth can be measured by the thickness of a PowerBar wrapper, we should also recognize

226

that studies have shown that the greatest predictor of exercise participation is education, that the smarter you are, the more likely you are to engage in regular physical activity. Father Jim reminds us that the rewards are far greater than calories burned; activating the body can also help actualize the soul.

Runners often refer to their sojourns on the roads and trails of their neighborhoods as being "their religion." As a veteran of twenty-five marathons, I'm not quite sure that running would pass muster as religion with Father Jim or a theologian of any faith, but it surely is a great way to get in shape and feel better about yourself. And when you feel better about yourself, when you're moving and using the body given to you by nature or God or The Force or whatever higher power you believe in, you appreciate it more, and you might find that some of those bigger questions become clearer.

"If you are seeking the solutions for the Great Whys of your creation, you will have to start with the Little Hows of your day-to-day living," wrote Dr. George Sheehan, in his classic 1978 book on the philosophy of active sport, *Running and Being*. "If you are looking for the answers to the Big Questions about your soul, you'd best begin with the Little Answers about your body. If you would become either saint or metaphysician, you must first become athlete."

That doesn't mean professional athlete or even proficient athlete. That doesn't necessarily mean runner, either; you could be a walker, stationary bicyclist, swimmer or hiker. In the eleven New York City marathons that he completed from 1992 to 2002, Father Jim never ran very fast. That wasn't the point. "The point was really to use running as a spiritual vehicle," said Maher, who continues to train regularly. "The prize was not winning the race; the prize was just being in the race and helping others who couldn't be in the race."

So if you want to change the world, get in the race.

John Hanc is a contributing editor for Runner's World *magazine. His work has appeared in* The New York Times, AARP Bulletin, Family Circle, Smithsonian, Men's Fitness, Newsday *and* Yoga Journal. *Hanc, who teaches writing and journalism at the New York Institute of Technology in Old Westbury, New York, is the author of eight books, the latest of which is* The Coolest Race on Earth: Mud, Madmen, Glaciers and Grannies at the Antarctica Marathon.

Making Love, Not War

By Stella Resnick

No human experience can be more earthy, more grounded in the intimate body yet at the same time more heavenly and transporting, than that of passionate sexual union between two loving people. We don't have to go all the way to feel a jump in energy. A smile, a kiss, or a caring caress has the ability to soothe, reassure, and make us feel alive.

Research shows that emotionally gratifying sexual pleasure is good for us. When feelings of love accompany sexual activity it can release tensions in the heart and chest muscles, and that's good for the heart. Satisfying sex releases endorphins, the body's natural opiates, which are not only capable of reducing pain but also boost the immune system. We don't need scientists to tell us that making love keeps the bond strong in a committed relationship.

Unfortunately, many couples find that while their affection for one another may grow with time, their sex lives begin to diminish. Everything else becomes more important. The focus of their lives becomes work or children or dealing with finances, and the sex becomes an afterthought. When sexual contact always happens at night and in bed, as the last weary act of a long weary day, it loses its appeal.

In fact, a lack of sexual desire is the most common sexual problem in America. According to recent studies, from twenty to thirty percent of men and between thirty to forty-three percent of women report a loss of interest in sex. A lack of sex in marriage is a reliable measure of whether or not the relationship will last.

So what can inspire an individual in a relationship or a couple to give more attention to the physical expression of love? As a psychologist and therapist who has specialized for over thirty years in working with individuals and couples on their love lives, here are a few critical factors to look at in restoring sexual desire in a committed relationship.

One of the hidden dynamics dampening sexual interest for couples is the fact that when two people become emotionally attached they begin to treat each other as "family." As children, however, we learn to turn off our sexual feelings in the presence of family. When we commit to a relationship, we typically project old family patterns onto our new attachments and the same sexual inhibitions we felt for family are reactivated in our adult bodies toward our partner. Once these automatic body-based inhibitions are triggered, they are communicated at an implicit or unspoken level, primarily through body language, such as a dry versus a wet kiss, a parental pat on the back, a sudden discomfort with nudity.

This is especially critical for couples raising children together. So one important way to regain sexual interest in a partner is to find ways to be non-family with each other, to rediscover one another as individuals. I always tell couples I work with that the couple is the nucleus of the nuclear family. Make sure you spend time together as a physically affectionate couple and not just as mommy and daddy to the kids.

Another important factor is taking the time to relax with each other in silence, just holding each other and breathing together, stroking and kissing. Don't think of sex as an act that has a beginning, a middle and an end all within the same twenty minutes. Listen to music together. Massage each other. Let your physical intimacy spread out over several days. Be playfully erotic, even for just a few minutes at a time. Let the journey be more important than the destination.

Finally, recognize that our sexual selves are a valuable part of our true selves. We don't stop growing as adults. Just as we can grow wiser with the years, all aspects of our being can evolve over our lifetimes. This is particularly true of our sexuality, which is a quality of life issue across the lifespan. Sex is not just for young people. There's a good deal of evidence now that most people don't reach their sexual potential until they are well into their sixties. In fact, making love may very well be the best elixir for keeping us young.

As more and more of us master the skills for emotionally gratifying, sexually fulfilling relationships, the cumulative effect can improve more than our sexual health and the stability of our marriages. It can also open the way to our becoming a more intuitive, more compassionate, and more evolved society.

Stella Resnick, PhD, is a clinical psychologist in private practice in Beverly Hills, California, and the author of The Pleasure Zone: Why We Resist Good Feelings & How to Let Go and Be Happy. *She served as president of the Western Region of the Society for the Scientific Study of Sexuality, is an AASECT certified sex therapist, and a Diplomate of the American Board of Sexology.*

Achieving Heaven on Earth Through a Just Cause

By Laurie Norris

Is it possible for a young boy to die because he can't see a dentist? Yes. This was the tragic beginning of the painful realization that most of America's low-income children have poor oral health and no access to dental care. I found myself in a position to make sure that this child, who was my client, did not die in vain.

For almost twenty years, I have worked as an attorney to help low-income people and to right injustices. I used the blunt instrument of the law to fight against the forces of exploitation and bureaucratic ineptitude, and for a better world.

Then along came Alyce Driver and her five boys. When she could no longer afford both to pay her rent and support her children, she lost the family's apartment and the boys were distributed among relatives who agreed to provide them with temporary refuge. At the time, ten-year-old DaShawn was suffering from dental abscesses and pain. Though he was insured through the state's Medicaid program, his mother was unable to find a dentist willing to accept his insurance. I agreed to try to help, but I hit the same brick wall—the first twenty-six dentists on the list of contracted dentists provided by DaShawn's Medicaid managed-care plan no longer participated in the plan. It took six months, but DaShawn ultimately did receive all the dental care he needed after several public health case management professionals and I stepped in to help.

A few months into DaShawn's dental drama, his twelve-year-old brother, Deamonte, began experiencing terrible headaches and showed signs of being disoriented. Doctors at the local hospital emergency room diagnosed a severe brain infection, so he was immediately transferred to a regional children's hospital and

231

rushed into surgery. The neurosurgeon identified a tooth as the source of the infection. Six weeks after the surgery Deamonte seemed on the road to recovery, but suddenly one morning he died from complications of the tooth decay.

While Deamonte appeared to be recuperating, I introduced Alyce Driver to Mary Otto, a *Washington Post* reporter. Otto decided to write a story about Deamonte's illness to highlight the avoidable human and fiscal effects of a lack of access to basic dental care for children insured by Medicaid. But when Deamonte died, the story, published three days afterwards, took on a much larger significance. It caused an immediate shock wave felt across the country and around the world. Everyone was asking how a child could die of tooth decay.

Suddenly, there was an opening for change and everyone was clamoring to be part of the solution. Politicians, government officials, advocates, dentists, public health experts, dental hygienists, pediatricians, academicians, even health insurance companies all spoke up. Traditional divisions between groups (Democrats/Republicans, dentists/dental hygienists, advocates/ health insurance companies) dissolved. Suddenly, we were all on the same page, united in our intention to fix what was broken so no more children would die of this completely preventable condition.

In Maryland, Governor Martin O'Malley and Health Secretary John Colmers led the charge for change. They convened a Dental Action Committee on which I served. We made far-reaching recommendations, ranging from completely restructuring the Medicaid dental delivery system, raising dental reimbursement rates and building more community dental clinics, to launching a comprehensive oral health literacy education campaign targeted to parents and caregivers of low-income children. All the recommendations were accepted by the secretary, and many have been funded and implemented. More children received dental care.

Deamonte's story also spurred action at the national level. My congressman, Elijah Cummings, became an evangelist for children's oral health. He held press conferences, gave speeches, introduced legislation, and facilitated large donations from insurance companies to dental schools. He also co-chaired a congressional investigation into lax federal oversight of state

Medicaid dental programs. I appeared as the lead witness at the first hearing, and said, "Let us not fail to heed the warning Deamonte's death provides. Let us not, by our indifference or our incompetence, have to bear on our consciences the burden of more dead children." For the first time in many years, advocates making the rounds in Washington, D.C., found Congress receptive to their suggestions about how to ensure that all of America's children have access to dental care.

For me as an advocate, there has been a magic to this moment. Rather than having to cajole, persuade or even force reluctant defendants to do something the law requires or stop doing something the law prohibits, I have joined with people from all sides of this issue, unified in outrage at what happened to Deamonte and determined to prevent a recurrence. I was privileged to play a part in letting the world know about Deamonte. That was the first step toward making sure his sacrifice does not go unheeded. Though we have made progress, we still have a long way to go. In order for me to fully honor Deamonte's memory, I have dedicated my work to achieving my dream that every child enjoys good oral health and has access to dental care.

Laurie Norris is a staff attorney with the Public Justice Center in Baltimore.

With Sobriety Anything Is Possible

By Todd Crandell

How did I achieve my heaven on earth? It all started for me on April 15, 1993. No, that is not my original birthday but rather the beginning of a life that I never thought was possible or that I was worthy of having. I had gone from addict to Ironman and was ready to experience all that life had to offer.

My sobriety has given me peace and security, spiritual harmony, freedom, mental and physical health and purpose, all of which I utilize not only to help myself but more importantly to help others, because in the end that is what heaven on earth is all about.

Instead of living in my car and wondering where my next meal was coming from, I no longer have to worry about my safety. Another gift is my continual spiritual growth. As an addict I did not feel I was worthy of God's love, but now I realize my life is a gift from God. As the saying goes, "To those to whom much is given, much is expected in return," a statement I fully endorse and appreciate.

During my addiction I thought my purpose in life was to end up dead from drugs and suicide as did my mother, and I actually welcomed that fate with open arms. Being free of addiction has enabled me to experience the gift of life on many levels, including the ability to cherish every day, and the establishment of Racing for Recovery, an organization to help others, to demonstrate that with sobriety anything is possible. My organization is my passion, not a job, and I am grateful and humbled by the life I have today. Knowing one's purpose in life is truly a gift, and I hope each of us can find it.

The holistic approach that we utilize at Racing for Recovery is simply to take that negative addiction and place it into something productive. It does not have to be the vigorous exercise of an Ironman regimen, although that is encouraged for not only the physical but mental benefits, but it can be education, volunteering, arts, music etc. We focus what passions were lost during addiction and recapture them, while also looking at other ways to fill the day. Getting off drugs and alcohol gives individuals a golden opportunity to experience anything in life that they desire. People who have drug problems simply need to take that addictive state from a destructive standpoint and switch it into something positive.

Todd Crandell, who lives in Sylvania, Ohio, is the founder and executive director of Racing for Recovery, a nonprofit foundation with the mission of preventing all forms of substance abuse by promoting a lifestyle of fitness and health. His own thirteen-year struggle with drugs and alcohol nearly destroyed his life, devastating relationships with family and friends and shattering the promise of a professional hockey career. In the process of rebuilding his life, he realized traditional recovery programs weren't enough, so he began training for the Ironman Triathlon—2.4 mile swim, 112 mile bike ride and 26.2 mile run. He earned a bachelor's degree in business and a master's of counseling, and is the co-author of From Addict to Ironman.

The Mental Health Checkup

By Craig L. Katz, M.D.

In 2005, I was among the many mental health professionals who responded to the massive tsunami which struck South Asia. An experience I had in Sri Lanka taught me a demoralizing lesson about how little disaster psychiatry can often accomplish. My disappointment ultimately gave way to an unexpected inspiration about a much more proactive form of psychiatry and therein lies one path to finding heaven on earth.

We were visiting an elementary school south of the Sri Lankan capital, Colombo. We were the experts, there to train teachers about addressing the tsunami-related mental health needs of their students since there was a shortage of mental health professionals in Sri Lanka under even normal conditions. Not long into the lecture session, one teacher deviated from the cordial nature of things by asking, "We greatly appreciate that you are all here to help us and our country, but where were you before?" Their students needed our attention even before the tsunami.

The teacher unwittingly led me to question my goals and motivations. I came to see how the adrenalin rush of disaster seems to lead us to prioritize the mental health needs of a stricken community when before we lacked the interest, the will or the resources to do so. Disaster survivors' mental health somehow even becomes more important than the mental health of my own patients, whom I leave behind in New York while I go to rescue others.

The truth is that the people who are among the most likely to psychologically suffer after a disaster, perhaps even developing problems like post-traumatic stress disorder or clinical depression, are people who had problems before. Abundant research and experience has shown that people with prior traumas, prior

236

psychiatric problems, and even problems in their personal or work lives are amongst those at highest risk of developing mental health problems after encountering disaster.

Enough grief, horror or loss can strain the mental wellbeing of anyone. But, within a community of people exposed to the same basic effects of disaster, those survivors with prior psychiatric, traumatic or life problems carry among the highest risk for the need to see a mental health professional like me.

So, the teacher in Sri Lanka was perhaps more right than he realized. Not only are pre-disaster mental health problems important in their own right, but also they pave the way for the very mental health problems that eventually receive the ministrations of disaster psychiatrists. I have translated this lesson into my practice—besides still working in disaster response, I now conduct development work around the world, trying to help countries improve the mental health services available to their citizens under normal circumstances. The hope is that these countries will not only help their people feel and function better in general but also better prepare them to cope with the disasters that increasingly dot the globe.

On an individual level, this suggests that attending to your mental wellbeing amid your usual life will help you not only feel better but equip you to better deal with the challenges that come along, whether stresses, personal crises, and even community-wide disasters. That is why I suggest that one path to a heaven on earth is through preventatively checking on one's mental health on a regular basis. It is ingrained in our culture that we should get a medical checkup on an annual basis. Kids get regular checkups for school. But who gets an annual "checkup from the neck up," as a television character once put it?

Psychiatry has not yet researched how to do this, and no guidelines I have ever heard of support seeing a mental health professional on a regular basis for a checkup or a "mental." But you will be ahead of the curve, and undoubtedly happier and more functional, if you find a mental health professional to periodically check you for such common conditions as clinical depression and anxiety. They may be surprised at your proactive stance on the manner, but then you can teach them something, just as that teacher taught me after the tsunami.

Craig L. Katz, M.D., is a clinical assistant professor of psychiatry at the Mount Sinai School of Medicine in New York City. He co-founded Disaster Psychiatry Outreach in 1998 as a charitable organization devoted to the provision of voluntary psychiatric care to people affected by disasters and serves as its president. Dr. Katz has a private practice in general and forensic psychiatry in Manhattan.

Heaven via Bike

By Mark Maccora

One of my favorite aspects of Los Angeles, my hometown for nearly a decade, is that it is a perfect city for bicycles. Los Angeles proper is a nearly-flat desert plain adjacent to the sea. It rarely rains, and the lack of many hills allows most rides to be low impact unless you enjoy a healthy sprint, as I do. Even the Hollywood Hills can be crossed with a bike-friendly subway. Pop knowledge categorizes Los Angeles as the ultimate car culture; the town where your car is both your castle and kingdom, your retreat and status. Most Angelenos commute long-distance or race to accomplish many tasks. While I sometimes felt trapped by vehicles in my career as a filmmaker, I prefer to ride my bike. It is an incredibly enjoyable, stress-relieving exercise which doubles as relatively inexpensive, ecologically responsible transportation. If our society converted from cars to bikes for daily tasks, we would be happier, healthier, safer, and, most importantly, more connected to each other and the environment, all helping to achieve heaven on earth.

Let's start out with the extreme of our transportation concerns, our dependency on oil as fuel. Much world conflict, from Iraq to Sudan, finds basis in the struggle to secure this resource. While we need to create an alternative energy infrastructure, constructing a hydrogen, ethanol, solar, or biodiesel international fuel system will take years and billions of dollars. Riding bikes lowers our oil consumption quickly and cheaply. Decreasing demand will curtail the atrocities committed to control the oil supply, and possibly pause the pump's price hikes. At the very least, it saves gas money.

Riding bicycles also combats one of our nation's gravest epidemics: obesity. Obesity, and the lack of exercise that propels it, is linked to physical and mental illnesses such as heart failure, kidney disorders, stroke and depression. By using our bodies to power a bike, we will add exercise into our days in an efficient and productive manner. Part of what limits our ability to achieve heaven on earth is our laziness. Since technology assisted in making our lives as Americans so effortless, we became comfortable with an inactive lifestyle. Most problems need physical effort to solve them, but obesity more than any.

Bicycling will assist not only our health but also our happiness. The endorphins associated with aerobic exercise regulate the increasing malady of depression. Also, riding a bike is fun! You enjoy the sunshine, the wind whipping by your face, and the nostalgia of childhood's carefree days. Our cars shut us off from the world and each other. While on a bike you notice plants developing across seasons, birds and animals dancing through landscapes, and people moving through their days. Bicyclists enjoy the opportunity to greet and chat at stoplights. Communing with pedestrians, fellow cyclists, and even drivers dispels the alienation of modern urban life.

While bike-riding appears to be an impossibility for some long-distance commuters and those who experience harsh weather, we must consider that even a small change will make a significant shift in our oil consumption. It takes the most gas to start an engine and drive through city traffic. Bicycles avoid traffic. A road bike easily averages fifteen to twenty miles an hour, which paces most city speeds in a car, especially considering stoplights. If urban dwellers used solely bikes to run small errands, such as picking up a few groceries with a backpack, we would make a considerable change in oil consumption.

We really can get to heaven on earth more quickly bicycling. God gave us gifts to solve our problems, and show love and respect to each other and all parts of the universe. These gifts are physical as well as mental. Too often we look to our minds to solve problems and harmonize with the divine. Our bodies are powerful tools and only by using them can we achieve health. Thanks to the miraculous bicycle, we can also use them to lower our oil use, which increases our security and protects the environment. Let's embrace simple solutions to grand dilemmas. We are merely humble beings.

A graduate of Loyola Marymount University, Mark Maccora works on independent and major films as a producer, production manager, cinematographer, and digital composer and provides visual effects. His newest project is documenting American spirituality in The Eternal Love Revolution.

Battling Post-Traumatic Stress Disorder

By Eric Newhouse

We already have been given a map for how we can make this earth more like heaven. According to the Gospel of Matthew, Jesus said: "You shall love the Lord your God with all your heart and with all your soul. This is the first and great commandment. And the second is like it: You shall love your neighbor as yourself. On these two commandments hang all the Law and the Prophets."

Over the next few years, 1.6 million of our neighbors—combat soldiers returning home from Iraq and Afghanistan—will need our love, our compassion and our help.

As a journalist, I'm acutely conscious of the red flags popping up in the aftermath of our wars in Iraq and Afghanistan. They are, ironically, the same red flags we ignored when our troops came home from Vietnam a generation ago. As a nation, we can't make that mistake again.

Whether or not you agree with the waging of this war, the young American men and women fighting it are among its victims. A recent Rand Corporation report estimated that one soldier in three will come home with post-traumatic stress disorder (PTSD), traumatic brain injury or major depression, and it said that figure is a very conservative estimate. Combat vets agree it's low. They say war changes everyone, and that every returning warrior should be presumed to be emotionally disabled, not normal.

Combat is terrifying, facing the certainty that you will die unless you kill your enemy first. It's a white-knuckle, gut-wrenching, heart-pounding flood of adrenaline into the nervous system that focuses a soldier solely on survival. But many soldiers can't shift out of that battlefield mentality when they return home, and that inability defines post-traumatic stress disorder. These vets are

242

scanning the rooftops for snipers, hitting the deck when a car backfires, driving at ninety miles an hour to avoid being an easy target for roadside bombs, and responding to civilian provocations with violence. If a vet ever sleeps, nightmares will blast him awake—flashbacks torment even the waking hours. Frequently, alcohol and drugs are used to blunt the pain. Divorce, joblessness and homelessness are common among vets.

In Montana, a National Guard infantryman named Chris Dana came home and tried to deal with his emotional disorder by toughing it out. As it progressed, he isolated himself from his family and friends. He also couldn't handle going to his weekend drills, so he didn't. The National Guard gave him a less-than-honorable discharge, and he shot himself to death a few days later.

Dana's death caused shock waves in a state with one of the nation's highest numbers of veterans per capita. And it forced us to look closely at what's happening to our returning warriors. The state's governor and its adjutant general took immediate steps to prevent such tragedies from happening again. Montana is now the only state in the nation in which the National Guard does mental health assessments every six months for two years following deployment. It has set up crisis response teams to intervene when its soldiers need help, and those teams, which include chaplains, will show up to talk with soldiers who exhibit problems or don't come to drills. The adjutant general has pledged that no soldier will receive a less-than-honorable discharge until he personally reviews the file and concludes that it is justified.

Our Guard has no mental health counselors, so TriWest Healthcare has initiated and funded a plan to embed counselors with Army and Air Guard units during drill weekends where they can observe and be available for help. And the National Guard is now reaching out to veterans who may be suffering from post-traumatic stress disorder. In a series of meetings in communities across the state, they're describing the symptoms of PTSD to vets and their families and telling them where to find help.

It's a remarkably humane response to a human tragedy, and one that the rest of the nation needs to emulate. I have written about these experiences in my newest book, *Faces of Combat, America's Next Crisis: PTSD.*

I've focused on combat soldiers because our VA hospitals are being filled with combat-traumatized soldiers, but primarily those of the Vietnam era, and I want our government to be prepared to help the Iraq/Afghan-era soldiers who will need treatment once they realize their disabilities. An estimated ten percent of our civilian population also is estimated to suffer from PTSD as a result of tragedies like Hurricane Katrina, violent crime and childhood abuse or neglect. These screening improvements should be used for all major events, but all individuals will benefit from better assessment and immediate treatment.

Eric Newhouse, projects editor for the Great Falls Tribune *(Montana), won the Pulitzer Prize for explanatory journalism in 2000, for a yearlong series of stories on alcoholism. Those articles, "Alcohol: Cradle to Grave," have been adapted into a book by the same name.*

Taste Heaven on Earth

By Poppy Tooker

So many problems of body and soul in Americans today are directly related to the intense disconnect between real food and the average meal. With senses dulled from preservatives, additives and food substitutes, many rush through life with never-satisfied stomachs, settling for ersatz sustenance on demand. Much of this eating is actually done in transport, often alone. And therein lies the final blow to the human spirit—the loss of conviviality in the shared meal. As Creole chef Leah Chase points out, "The problems of the world could be solved over a bowl of gumbo."

The magic solution to the food disconnect is in itself pleasurable. Give yourself the gift of sourcing locally as much as possible. Fresher, more alive food from farmers' markets renews a sense of community as you create a human bond with the man who grew the brilliantly colored, still-warm tomatoes and the woman who weighs out pounds of sweet, freshly-caught shrimp, just off of her husband's trawl. Simple, fresh food is easier to serve, as it needs so little preparation. The intense flavor of the just-harvested often needs little more than salt. And locavores, a new label for those who advocate for locally-produced foods, help reduce the consumption of fossil fuels by reducing transportation needs.

For the last twenty years, the international Slow Food movement has gently guided stomachs and souls across the world in this direction. Eighty-five thousand members are active today in 132 countries, committed to protecting traditional and sustainable quality foods, conserving methods of cultivation and processing and defending the biodiversity of cultivated and wild varieties while always championing the pleasures of the table.

Through an initiative called "Slow Food in Schools" children across the world are gaining taste education and real knowledge about where their food comes from. Over a decade ago, Slow Food champion Alice Waters brought her food revolution to the students at Martin Luther King Middle School in Berkeley, California, where Alice lives and where her visionary restaurant, Chez Panisse, is located. At King Middle School, Alice began the Edible Schoolyard, creating a curriculum where seasonal fresh food is cultivated organically in the school garden, then harvested and prepared in the teaching kitchen—all by students. The program is fully integrated into each grade's class work, reinforcing the lessons of the garden and kitchen, whether the primary subject matter is math, science, social studies or language arts, and it goes without saying that the children are getting plenty of exercise and fresh air.

The New York Times Magazine published a study by Harvard Medical School that found, "After one year, students at King, compared with a control group at a similar middle school, showed improvement in behavior and had fewer emotional problems. They were savvier about ecology, and their overall grade point averages improved." (Source: Edible Schoolyard website)

In the fall of 2006, New Orleans' Samuel Green Charter School became the first sanctioned replica of the original Edible Schoolyard. At Green Charter, the program has expanded on the original concept, completely altering the school breakfast and lunch programs, sourcing local foods through a partnership with the Crescent City Farmers Market. Now regional, seasonal food is prepared fresh daily in the school's cafeteria. The farmers themselves are welcomed into the classroom through special programs that allow the children to put a face on Louisiana's winter citrus and the strawberries and blueberries of spring.

You don't have to be a child to rediscover the wonders of real food. The sense of taste, the sense of smell—these sensations are most evocative to the human spirit. A perfect, juicy peach fills your mouth with sweetness and floods your memory with summers past. Your beloved grandmother's smile rises in your heart as the steamy scent from a warm bowl of vegetable soup fills you with her love. The cultural significance found in a classic hometown dish ties your soul to a place.

Let your taste memory wander back to early food comforts

reminiscent of home and hearth, however metaphorical the latter may be. For those who wandered far, something as simple as a Monday bowl of red beans and rice will transport most New Orleanians home through flavor. Home-cooked meals are not the only solution. From the neighborhood sandwich shop where they know you prefer mustard to mayonnaise to the white table-clothed restaurant where the food is as familiar as home and the well-loved waiter pours your favorite libation before you can even order it, these can all help reconnect the stomach with the soul.

We all have to eat to live, no matter our race, religion or nationality. When life begins to include the element of consciously living to eat, another dimension is added. Join in the delicious revolution. Garden if you can, and reap the benefits of better flavor, fresh air and exercise. Buy locally-produced foods, and contribute to the prosperity of your neighbors while reducing the use of fuel. You'll improve your own health, the health of your community, and, in a small way, the health of the planet.

Slow down and taste a bit of heaven on earth.

Native New Orleanian Poppy Tooker has spent her life immersed in the vibrant colors and flavors of her home town. For over twenty-five years her classes have centered on history and tradition, as well as the food science reasons of why and how while remaining eminently entertaining. As Food & Wine *magazine described, "She may wear ceramic red beans in her ears and make finger puppets out of crawfish, but her class is certainly no joke. Rather, it compels you to take reams of notes so as not to forget a single nugget of her fascinating culinary wisdom."*

In 1999 Poppy brought the international Slow Food movement to New Orleans by founding the local chapter whose efforts helped revive endangered local foods such as Creole cream cheese and rice calas. She has served as an international governor with the movement, heads the US Slow Food Ark and Presidia committee, and most recently has been appointed to the board of the International Slow Food Foundation for Biodiversity.

Fit from the Inside Out

By Chris Bynum

As a newspaper health and fitness writer, I read the workout books that cross my desk every week, and interview people about their lifestyles. Universal fitness goals are measured in crunches or push-ups or miles or laps or weight repetitions or a flowing series of yoga postures. But the underlying motivation behind these efforts is personal time. While "me time" may seem self-indulgent, those who commit to it say it is soulful.

"Your soul is who you inherently are, and is a part of your self that is connected to all of creation. . . . A Fit Soul is one whose meter is usually pointed in a positive direction. It has strength and energy for real purpose in life . . .," writes shaman-healer Brant Secunda. In *Fit Soul, Fit Body*, written with six-time Ironman triathlon world champion Mark Allen, Secunda says, "It sparkles in the presence of others as well as in the silence of one's own solitude."

It is that inner sanctum we find in physical goals that sets us on a healthy path. Studies have shown that when we pursue an activity that calms our minds, we lower blood pressure, stabilize the heart rate, calm the digestive tract, stabilize glucose levels and lower the stress hormone cortisol.

Runners tout being in the zone, walkers talk about the rhythm of being outdoors, yogis talk about "the flow"; even weightlifters describe their inner devotion to this external challenge. Often in group endeavors—in spinning classes where the instructor shouts the pace, in running groups where conversation keeps feet moving, and in cardio classes where loud music moves us—there is a meditative quality to the time we set aside for the mind-body-soul connection. The quiet can filter into our lives when we are not alone.

"Silence isn't about avoiding noise and movement. We can be completely involved in movement with sound all around us, and yet if we are not reacting to it or fighting it, we can be in the stillness or silence within ourselves," Nancy Torcson of Clearwater Wildlife Sanctuary and the Sanctuary for Stillness and Silence in Covington, Louisiana, told me in an interview.

For me, personal time is like sharing a sunset with God. It is silent. But the power is in sensing something greater than self. I can do this as my body moves, even when I am physically challenging it, or I can experience it in the cool-down after a workout. We call this inner silence many things. Busy mothers call it "mommy time." Master multi-taskers call it "down time." Elite athletes think of it as "being in sync." Others simply call it prayer.

What I have come to understand, both personally and professionally, is that when we connect mind, body and soul, the merger challenges us; it feeds us, and in the long run, it nurtures us. The visible benefits are simply an outward manifestation. Our jobs, families and friends also reap the rewards because we perform better, enjoy life more and are more open to joy and optimism.

In my weekly profiles of New Orleanians who practice healthy lifestyles, one man described his pre-dawn run as a readiness run before heading to Mass before work. One woman quoted the scripture about one's body being the temple of God, and her spiritual responsibility to take care of it. Another said regular exercise reminded him that being free to move was a blessing.

Author Julia Cameron spoke of the act of walking not as fitness for the body, but exercise for the soul in her book *Walking in This World*. She gave a nod to St. Augustine ("himself a walker") for his proclamation, "Solviture ambulando" ("It is solved by walking").

In the solace of personal time, we embrace the physical as we seek the spiritual, whether it is the blur of green foliage as we race to the finish line of a 10K race or the wind in our faces as we take part in a sailing regatta. Returning home from an early-morning bike ride, we can look across the table at a child's face and see a healthy future, and take our places in the new communal day.

Chris Bynum has worked as a journalist for almost four decades, as a food editor, a fashion editor, a feature writer, a social columnist and an entertainment magazine editor. She is the health and fitness writer for The Times-Picayune *in New Orleans. But her best work is as an alpha dog whose bark, not bite, entreats her three dogs to allow her daily quiet time.*

Perfectly Broken

By Mark Lundholm

I have a chemically-challenged anatomy, a drug-resistant soul and a penchant for guessing incorrectly when it comes to the betterment of others. And I talk to myself as well. Because I am terminally self-centered, there are certain symptoms I display: I am spiritually retarded, emotionally invisible, financially irresponsible, socially phobic and almost pathological when it comes to lying. And that "almost"? That is my saving grace. See, there is a slim window of truth I gaze through every morning as I wake up. It is the slightest chance that, even with my character defects, broken moral compass and natural ability to sabotage success, I can adjust my perception, manipulate my attitude and walk in the light of health, happiness and hope. I am a recovering drug addict, a product of incarceration, information, education and transformation. These have given me an umpteenth opportunity to avoid ending up in the morgue hopeless, helpless, ruthless, and toothless. I am alive and well. Doesn't seem fair.

If life were fair, I would have been doing forever in prison or buried in my own filth in some alley right now. Fortunately, life is not fair and that simple slice of grace has allowed me more time to discover the truth about a disease that has plagued mankind since the very first cry of a newborn child. Addiction can walk safely among us because it will disguise itself as confidence or focus or passion or persistence. Beautiful words for a brutal condition. In truth, addiction is energy without grace. It is a boundless force of nature that erodes the human heart, wisdom and humility that balanced people seem to use to avoid becoming a willing participant in a lifestyle that says "Me first, second, last and always! You, never!"

Most people have a credo of live and let live or follow the Golden Rule. Most. The rest of us confuse tools that become weapons and the irresistible arrogance of imagining we can out-think a physical disease. Hint: try using willpower, IQ or spirituality to stop diarrhea. Some things in life you just have to surrender to, adjust to, just to survive. I am no longer the willing victim I was in my addiction days of cocaine, speed, alcohol and other clever chemical pursuits. I have been taught by other recovering individuals that addiction to anything—money, power, work, smoking, food, golf, computers, sex, shopping—is treatable. I have been liberated by the knowledge that my liabilities as a practicing addict can now become finely tuned assets that allow me to deftly navigate the foreign terrain of relationships, employment, success and excellence. I am allowed on a daily basis to make a 180 degree rotation toward health even though my primary nature is flawed and my first thought is always wrong. That is my heritage, not my legacy. "First thought wrong" say relapse, dabble, delay, decay, dissolve, destroy and disappear. My second thought (or tenth if I am off my game that day) is "What? Again? How has that worked for you in the past? Yeah, that's what I thought."

Oh, I still talk to myself. But these days I do it when no one else is around and I have deeper, lengthier, healthier discussions. Energy with a little grace.

Clean and sober since 1988, Mark Lundholm is a former criminal, mental patient, homeless wino and halfway house resident. After very humble beginnings, he has taken his successful standup comedy career through all fifty states and ten foreign countries. The New York Times said, "Mr. Lundholm's acerbic powers of observation are quite dark and funny. He is a terrific performer—aggressive, entertaining and charming." Lundholm has had his own Showtime Comedy Special, appeared on A&E, Comedy Central and written and starred in the off-Broadway hit Addicted . . . a comedy of substance. *Mark has also lectured, presented and appeared at over three hundred professional conferences and has never been rated less than excellent. He is the only speaker of his kind in this industry or in this country. He is also the creator of the revolutionary DVD series* Humor in Treatment, *a three DVD box set available for professionals to use as a tool for healing and education.*

Moral Purpose and Meaning

I expect to pass through life but once. If therefore, there be any kindness I can show, or any good thing I can do to any fellow being, let me do it now, and not defer or neglect it, as I shall not pass this way again.

—William Penn

What Our Lives Should Mean

By Danny Wuerffel

When I think about moral purpose and meaning in life, I remember the words of King Solomon. God gave this third king of Israel wisdom when as a youth he requested discernment in administering justice. The Bible documents in Ecclesiastes that Solomon, who was the wisest man who ever lived, had examined the human experience between the horizons of life and death and concluded that everything in life is meaningless—apart from God.

So to find meaning and purpose, we must find God. The Bible says we do that through personally knowing His Son, Jesus Christ. Having been raised in a Christian home, I knew that faith involved being a good and moral person. But in college, I reached the biggest turning point in my life as a Christian through weekly Bible study on the character of God.

The scene from the movie *The Lion King* best illustrates what happened. Simba, a young lion cub, was trapped by the wild and dangerous hyenas. In the face of danger, he did what any lion would: he roared. The only problem was it sounded more like a kitten's purr, and the hyenas got quite a laugh. When he tried again, something incredible happened. Simba's father, Mufasa, the great Lion King, showed up, and his roar was deafening. The demeanor of the hyenas changed in an instant. They were no longer dealing with a small cub; they had the king of the beasts to reckon with!

As my understanding of God grew, I felt like the hyenas that encountered Mufasa. I realized I had encountered greatness—and my demeanor and attitude drastically changed. My new focus became the lesson of Micah 6:8: "He has shown you, O man, what

255

is good and what the Lord requires of you: to do justice, to love mercy, and to walk humbly with your God."

Walking with God is the foundation of a life of meaning and purpose. Apart from Him, we have no hope for life beyond the horizon of death. Through believing that Jesus Christ died to pay God's required price for our sins, we become reconciled to God. We then go forward from that point in a framework of humble reliance and right understanding of God in His greatness. The fruit, then, of a life lived like this is justice and mercy.

For me, justice and mercy are lived out in my calling as executive director of Desire Street Ministries, which exists to revitalize impoverished neighborhoods through spiritual and community development. It was founded in the Ninth Ward of New Orleans in 1990, but in 2005 Hurricane Katrina devastated the Ninth Ward and pushed the ministry to a three-pronged focus: education, replication and redevelopment. We work to redevelop the Ninth Ward, helping residents there and those now scattered elsewhere with affordable housing, economic development opportunities and education. We replicate our model by strategically supporting other urban ministries and by starting new works, such as that in the Eighth Ward where we have begun with a multi-cultural church plant preaching the Gospel in word and deed, intentionally reaching youth and seeking as a body of believers to address the felt needs of the poor. We educate leaders in urban ministry through our Urban Institute, and exist to serve inner city community leaders. We have helped to start a medical clinic and churches, and look to help others do the same in other cities.

As did Solomon, I look over my life between the horizons of birth and death, with God, and I see a life full of meaningful work of justice and mercy. I also see relationships rooted in Christ: a precious family, friends and co-laborers. And I see God, who graciously loves me and allows me to walk humbly with Him in this life and in the life to come.

Danny Wuerffel is perhaps best known for his football career, which included a state championship at Ft. Walton Beach High School in Florida, four Southeastern Conference championships and the national title at the University of Florida, culminating in his winning the

Heisman Trophy in 1996. He also won the Draddy award as the nation's top student-athlete, and set seventeen National Collegiate Athletic Association and university football records. He played professionally with the New Orleans Saints, Green Bay Packers, Chicago Bears and Washington Redskins.

After retiring from pro ball, Danny became the executive director of the Desire Street Ministries in New Orleans. He has written a book, Danny Wuerffel's Tales from the Gator Swamp: Reflections of Faith and Football, *and is working on a second. He and his wife, Jessica, have two sons, Jonah and Joshua.*

Dreaming Heroic

By Lolis Eric Elie

When we were children we pasted our pictures in that magazine. Then the daddy looked like me and the mama looked like you. And in that world between naptime and animal crackers we were who we thought we would be.

Later, you were the distressed damsel and I rescued you from all the fairy tale tormentors we knew by heart. And when those savages tied up poor Pocahontas, wasn't I right on time with my brand new cowboy hat and all the scary noises a pop gun could make?

Sometimes I wonder what I was thinking. I think I figured if I played courageous often enough, pretended I was ready to be right and ready to kill because I was right, then when something did happen I would know what to do. The heroes never died in the movies in my mind.

We played these games before, but have you ever played one alone? I keep getting pulled back into them, only now it's not imagination but introspection.

I see this photograph in a book. There are three men. Their shirts are bloody. Their necks are broken. They're hanging from a tree, dead. All around them are these other men smiling and posing and celebrating. And we have to paste our pictures into that picture, but where? Who will look like you and who will look like me? Will we be hanging or smiling? Or will we be hiding beyond the camera's range?

This girl is on television, living in an attic, writing in a diary, scared of every knock at the door. I'm her neighbor. She's so scary, I laugh. Then a real scary knock comes and they ask me where she is, tell me to take them to her and I freeze. This dragon doesn't breathe fire.

It has polished military shoes and asks simple, direct questions.

What if we played this game with our history? Suppose we really learned the history of our country? Not just the textbook history about how God has chosen us to do what we want to do to whomever, but suppose we actually looked at the blood and the money and the lies of it. And suppose, with the comfort of distance, we asked ourselves what characters we would have played in our national morality plays?

Not just the easy questions like would we have owned slaves. Suppose we asked whether we would have stolen the land from that black farmer knowing that the judge would never make us give it back. Or, if we know our great-grandfather stole the land, would we now, in full knowledge, give it back. With interest.

Or when the Japanese family was marched off to Manzanar*, would we have protested or participated? Would we have stolen their property or kept it secure?

And standing beside that ditch at My Lai, would we have followed orders? Would we have killed? Or would we have preferred to face the taunts and ridicule of the men who had what it took to kill babies, parents, grandparents and whoever else was there and happened to look like them.

***

I write about history, often about painful, brutal, bloody history in which the righteous are vanquished and the wicked lord over their corpses and wear evil grins. I don't like sad stories—there is so much tragedy in the morning newspaper that I feel little need to look for reasons to be depressed.

When I started writing such stories in newspaper columns and barbecue books, it seemed enough just to keep them alive. But Larry Powell, Tulane University professor and historian of slavery and the Holocaust, was organizing a conference that would look at the civil rights movement, and I wanted to write about it in my column in *The Times-Picayune*. I already knew what angry readers would say when they called me.

Why bring up these painful memories, some readers would wonder, when you know that they are going to cause unrest and stir up racial antipathy? Can't we just leave these things alone, and not disturb everyone else's domestic tranquility? Powell didn't refer to Santayana's quote about being doomed to repeat history, yet he made me understand that quote for the first time.

In considering these episodes, we have an opportunity to imagine ourselves as characters in these histories, Powell explained and I had learned. We can imagine ourselves to be members of the lynch mob, or wearers of the noose, victims of the Holocaust or perpetrators of it, the killers at My Lai or the massacred. We can water board or be water boarded.

We can imagine these scenarios in private, away from the mob or the army or the ignorance that might otherwise replace our sober deliberations with the drunkenness of the group. Imagining ourselves in these histories is a way of exercising our moral muscles. It's a way of preparing ourselves to resist when the gang tells us to rape, or the mob tells us to lynch.

If we are to make this world a better place, I believe that we must make history personal. We must imagine ourselves in the positions of the hungry, the downtrodden and the wrongly accused. We must imagine ourselves in positions of power, able to decide to alleviate suffering rather than inflict cruelty. The road to a heaven on earth requires an understanding of history and a determination to change its future course, in large ways and small.

We must study history, not as an exercise in memory, but as a preparation for action.

*Manzanar was one of ten "relocation camps" where U. S. citizens of Japanese extraction were held from the beginning of World War II.

Born in New Orleans and educated in Philadelphia, New York and Charlottesville, Lolis Eric Elie is a staff writer at The Times-Picayune, *the author of* Smokestack Lightning: Adventures in the Heart of Barbecue Country, *and editor of an anthology,* Cornbread Nation II: The United States of Barbecue. *He has produced two documentaries, one based on his barbecue book, and another,* Faubourg Tremé: The Untold Story of Black New Orleans, *which has been selected for screening in New York's TriBeCa Film Festival and the San Francisco International Film Festival. He is at work on another book about the legacy of the Atlantic slave trade.*

Billy Graham: God's Ambassador

By William Griffin

What's wrong with the photograph? Billy Graham never preached in a Catholic church, and yet, according to the caption, he was doing precisely that. Obviously, someone had doctored the photograph or messed around with it digitally. Protestant and Evangelical churches don't usually have choir lofts, but this photograph was taken from one. Hanging from the ceiling is a huge crucifix; not just a bare cross, but one with a huge corpus on it. There's an altar rail and behind it an altar. It's definitely a Catholic church, but, according to the caption, the congregation of ten thousand was mostly Protestant. The flyspeck at the upper right hand corner was supposed to be Graham. But what was he doing preaching in Poland?

Therein lies a tale. In its short and inglorious history the Communist Party made at least two catastrophic mistakes. In the 1920s they kicked religion out. In the 1970s, they invited religion back. To help keep the non-Communist masses in Eastern Europe in line, they gave visas to itinerant preachers such as Billy Graham. After all, what harm could they possibly do?

In 1978, as Graham's plane was landing in Cracow, another was taking off for Rome. It seemed that his host, Karol Cardinal Wojtyla, with whom he was supposed to have tea that afternoon, was flying to Rome. Pope John Paul had died, and the cardinals were assembling to elect his successor. Wojtyla never came home; he was elected and chose the name John Paul II.

Yes, the Communists allowed Graham to preach, but not on public property. Knowing that, the Catholic hierarchy who had owned property all over Poland for centuries offered their churches. That explains why Graham was introduced to the crowd by a Catholic bishop and preached Christ crucified in the Cathedral of Christ the King in the coal-mining city of Katowice. Inside, the crowd stood, crammed like North Sea sardines, drinking in every sight and sound. Outside, an overflow crowd was listening to and watching the events on several huge mobile televisions. Surrounding them as crowd control was a massive Communist military force ready to retaliate, should Graham give the signal to charge.

In 1989 the Berlin wall came down. Apparently, the mortar had turned to powder. Most gave credit to the United States; some to Pope John Paul II; a few to Billy Graham. Having preached all over Communist-occupied Europe and given hope to all the Christians living in those countries, he was a major player in the final demise of the Communist party.

How did Graham pull this off? He's a jumble of virtues, public and private, although he'd deny them all. He's easy-going, but at the same time taut as a bowstring. To those who know him, he's witty and sometimes funny to a hilarious degree.

During his career he practiced the theological virtues of faith, hope and charity, and observed such moral virtues as prudence, justice, fortitude and temperance. In addition to these last, Graham sported a number of minor moral virtues. They're hard to spot because he wore them like comfortable old clothes. I might mention a few.

With world leaders such as England's Queen Elizabeth II, Jawaharlal Nehru of India, Golda Meir of Israel, and King Hussein of Jordan, he was diplomatic. With dictators such as Alfredo Stroessner of Paraguay, Haile Selassie of Ethiopia, and Kim II Sung of North Korea, he was courteous. With American presidents from Dwight D. Eisenhower to George Walker Bush, he was trustworthy. With religious leaders such as the Pope, the Archbishop of Canterbury, and the Chief Rabbi of Israel, he was respectful. With the generations of sinners who attended his crusades and came forward at the invitation, he was compassionate.

This isn't to say that Graham has been without imperfections; but it is to say that he treated everyone with respect and dignity. Virtually everyone he ever met returned the compliment. One dictator was so charmed by the evangelist that he invited him back one day to go fishing.

No wonder Graham found doors opened where others found doors firmly closed. He had a constant message, a clear voice, a firm hand, and a forgiving heart. In his ninety-first year he's still a most beloved man. As someone put it, he's been God's ambassador.

We who have admired him over the decades would do well to imitate his virtues. We too will find closed doors opening to us as we attempt in our own generation to bring peace to the world.

William Griffin is a writer and translator who has done major biographical work on Billy Graham, C. S. Lewis, G. K. Chesterton, Augustine of Hippo, and Thomas à Kempis. He lives with his wife, the writer Emilie Griffin, in Alexandria, Louisiana.

Healing Holes in Hearts

By Darlene MacInnis

I have always known that having a good mother is a very special gift. My maternal grandmother Marjorie died at the very young age of thirty-two, leaving behind eleven children between the ages of three months and thirteen years. My mother Norma was just nine years old. The family looked after one another, with my mother's sister Josie taking over the role of mother. Then, three years later when she married, my mother took over for her, assisted by members of the extended family who did whatever they could to help nurture the children. I am proud to say that I grew up in a home where there was always room at the table for one more person.

I was in the first grade the first time I met a child who was in the foster care program, Ruth, who became a wonderful, caring friend. One spring day all of us children were sent outside when a social worker came to our one-room schoolhouse to talk to our teacher about Ruth. All of us, including Ruth, feared that the social worker was there to whisk her away, and vowed that we were not going to let this happen. We loved Ruth and did not want to lose her.

The social worker's car was covered in mud. We wrote "Do Not Take Ruth" all over it, and for good measure tied tin cans to the rear bumper. The social worker did not take Ruth away that day, and we were able to enjoy her friendship for a few more years until, sadly, the inevitable occurred and she had to move away.

It was then that I knew that I was going to be a foster parent some day. I understood that not everyone was as lucky as I, and I knew that I could help. Over the years I have had many children other than my own call my house home, and I have also been a group home worker. I have had the pleasure of tucking in many different children at night, and I hope that I have made some small difference in their lives. I know that they have made a difference in mine.

An eight-year-old girl with whom I worked described the longing to have someone who cares as "a hole in the heart that cannot be healed." I believe that it can, with love, be healed. We need to create a world where every child has someone to be there through good times and bad. We can each do our part by doing small or large things to improve the life of a child. We need to see all the goodness and potential inside each child. We need to believe in the child until he can believe in himself.

By sharing our blessings, everyone has the opportunity to touch and change a child's life forever. This support can be provided in many different ways, and everyone can take part in helping create heaven on earth.

Some of us may feel inspired to become foster parents. There are many children waiting to be welcomed into a loving home. Children may have been neglected and abused. Foster homes give them a safe place to heal and grow, and often offer the first glimpse of healthy family relationships. Sadly, many never experience the care and security of a foster home and grow up in group homes, which are the modern answer to orphanages.

For those unable to foster on a full time basis, opening one's home as a respite is a way to support foster families, allowing foster families a well-deserved break. The commitment could be as small as an occasional weekend. Foster children often lag behind in school, but for a commitment of only a few hours a week, the one-on-one attention of a retired person volunteering at a school to help with schoolwork could reap a huge result. The commitment of only a few hours a week could develop a relationship that is a gift to both.

Others may decide to volunteer with Big Brothers and Big Sisters, a wonderful organization always looking for new people to meet children's needs.

On a global scale, for as little as a dollar a day, anyone can sponsor a child and make a tangible and lasting difference in a world where life is often a struggle. Sponsorship provides medical and dental care, education, clothing and leadership skills. It also assists the communities where these children live in many ways. One of these is by bringing precious fresh water to the villages. Imagine how your support can change the world and help to break the bonds of poverty.

By opening our hearts and lives to children in need, we can help change the world, because the child who is nurtured and believed in will pass self-esteem and love on to the next generation. Your home could be a refuge and you could be the person who the child knows can help him face whatever difficulties occur in life. Set an extra place at the supper table. Get to know a child and find out what she likes or dislikes. Try asking what constitutes his heaven on earth.

Darlene MacInnis is a child and youth care worker and a family service worker with Child and Family Services. She lives in Charlottetown, Prince Edward Island, Canada, with her husband Trevor and daughter Sophie. Her daughter Alecia, son Mitchel, and stepson Craig, are adults, living on their own.

Where Is Your Treasure?

By Dan Amos

As the CEO of a Fortune 200 company, I am often asked a lot of questions. And I ask a lot of questions. Through the years, there's one question that I've asked when given the opportunity to speak to groups. The question is simple and I encourage both young and the not-so-young to find the answer to it. The question: "Where is your treasure?"

It is a question that I was asked early in my life. The origin is one of my favorite Bible verses. It's found in Matthew 6:21 and it says, "Where your treasure is, there your heart will be also." Many people in life believe that their treasure can only be found in the work they do every day. They're understandably focused on their jobs, because of the financial responsibilities we all face. We all have people whom we must please.

In my case, I have to please a lot of different groups. Shareholders want to see a company prosper and its stock grow. Customers want the best products, and rightly demand great customer service. And employees want good wages, benefits and working conditions. We all know that good companies deliver on those expectations, so the pressure to succeed can seem somewhat daunting at times. That's why you have to be committed to doing a good job. But while you may treasure a job, it may not be your treasure.

So how do you find your treasure?

The map begins with passion. A half-hearted approach will leave both you and your endeavor lacking. Whether your calling is helping others through a charitable mission or running a major corporation, if you're passionate about it, you'll be successful.

As a company, Aflac has been very successful. We have

thousands of employees who are passionate about their jobs. They believe in what they do and our results reflect their commitment. Success brings great rewards, but also tremendous responsibility. A corporation must strive to increase profits and build shareholder value, but successful companies also have a responsibility to give back to the community. At Aflac, we take our social responsibility very seriously.

While we give to dozens of worthy causes, our primary philanthropic focus is the Aflac Cancer Center and Blood Disorders Service at Children's Healthcare of Atlanta. It's a world-class hospital for the research and treatment of childhood cancer, along with sickle cell disease, hemophilia and other blood disorders. Including donations from our employees and sales associates, Aflac has contributed over $35 million to the Aflac Cancer Center.

In return, we have found our treasure, and it lies in knowing that someday childhood cancer will be cured. And in the meantime we are trying to make a difference in the lives of children and their families. A while back, the mother of a little girl with cancer wrote a letter to our local newspaper about our company.

She wrote, "I don't know how many of you realize how Aflac has touched the lives of so many children with cancer. Nor did I, until my then eighteen-month-old daughter was diagnosed with cancer in September of last year. Aflac has transformed a traditional hospital floor into a place she and her friends from throughout the Southeast consider home. Because of Aflac, our devastating situation has turned into a rewarding experience."

The heartfelt words in the letter meant as much to me as any of the great financial quarters we've had. And it's something I'll always treasure.

Dan Amos is chairman and chief executive officer of Aflac Incorporated. Aflac, a Fortune 200 company, insures more than 40 million people worldwide. It is the leading provider of individual insurance policies offered at the worksite in the United States and is the largest life insurer in Japan in terms of individual policies in force.

He joined Aflac in 1973 and worked in the sales area for ten years. He was named president of Aflac in 1983, chief operating officer in 1987, chief executive officer of Aflac Incorporated in 1990, and chairman in 2001. Mr. Amos also is responsible for launching the company's national advertising program that features the popular Aflac Duck.

We Urgently Need an Academic Revolution

By Nicholas Maxwell

The crisis of our times—the one that's behind all the other crises—is that we have scientific knowledge without wisdom. Population growth; the lethal character of modern war and terrorism; immense discrepancies of wealth worldwide; annihilation of indigenous peoples, cultures and languages; impending depletion of natural resources; destruction of tropical rainforests and other natural habitats; rapid extinction of species; pollution of sea, earth and air; and global warming: all these relatively recent crises have been made possible by modern science and technology.

Successful science produces knowledge and technological know-how, which in turn enormously increases our power to act. It is to be expected that this power will be used beneficially (as it has been used) to cure disease, feed people, and in general enhance the quality of human life. But it is also to be expected, in the absence of wisdom, that such an abrupt, massive increase in power will be used to cause harm, whether unintentionally, as in the case (initially at least) of environmental damage, or intentionally, as in war and terror.

Before the advent of modern science, lack of wisdom did not matter too much; we lacked the means to do too much damage to ourselves and the planet. But now, in possession of unprecedented powers bequeathed to us by science, lack of wisdom has become a menace. The crucial question becomes: How can we learn to become wiser?

The answer is staring us in the face: we need traditions and institutions of learning rationally designed to help us acquire wisdom, which at present we do not have. Academic inquiry as it now exists, devoted primarily to the pursuit of knowledge and

269

technological know-how, is grossly and damagingly irrational when assessed from the standpoint of helping humanity acquire wisdom, for wisdom is much more than knowledge, understanding and technological know-how, but includes the capacity to realize what is of value for oneself and others.

Two elementary, banal rules of rational problem solving are to articulate the problem to be solved, and then to propose and critically assess possible solutions. A kind of academic inquiry rationally devoted to helping humanity solve its problems of living so that that which is of value may be realized (thus enhancing wisdom) would put these rules into practice. Such inquiry occurs, at present, within academia, but only on the fringes, for the primary intellectual activity is to solve problems of knowledge, not problems of living. To pursue knowledge more or less dissociated from the attempt to help humanity resolve its conflicts and problems of living in more just and cooperative ways than at present is not only irrational, it is a recipe for disaster, as we have seen. It is this that has led to our distinctively modern global problems.

We need to bring about a revolution in the academic enterprise so that the basic aim becomes to promote wisdom rather than just acquire knowledge. Social inquiry needs to change, so that it gives intellectual priority to problems of living over problems of knowledge about the social world. The relationship between social inquiry and natural science needs to change, the new kind of social inquiry becoming more fundamental intellectually than natural science. The natural sciences need to change so that three domains of discussion are recognized: namely evidence, theory, and aims, the last involving problematic issues about what is unknown, and values. Education needs to change. The whole relationship between academia and the social world needs to change, so that academia does not just study the social world, but rather is in two-way debate—with itself, ideas, experiences and arguments flowing in both directions. Academia needs to become a kind of people's civil service, doing openly for the public what actual civil services are supposed to do in secret for governments.

Academics today have a profound responsibility before humanity to put their houses in order, intellectually and morally, and create a kind of inquiry rationally devoted to helping humanity learn how to resolve its conflicts and problems of living in more just, cooperative ways than at present.

Nicholas Maxwell has for years argued for revolutionary changes in universities so that they promote wisdom, not merely the acquisition of knowledge. He has published five books on this theme: What's Wrong With Science?, From Knowledge to Wisdom, The Comprehensibility of the Universe, The Human World in the Physical Universe, *and* Is Science Neurotic? *For nearly thirty years he taught philosophy of science at University College in London, where he is now Emeritus Reader.*

Mother Teresa: An Ordinary Woman of Extraordinary Compassion

By Emilie Griffin

One day in the late 1970s I met Mother Teresa of Calcutta. With one of her sisters she came floating down an office corridor, wearing lovely white garments with blue stripes. I knew exactly who she was, for she had just appeared on the cover of *Time*. Her reputation was huge even then, and I was in awe as she took my hand in a warm gesture.

The place was the office of the New York City Archdiocese. I had been meeting with Father Pat Sullivan, SJ, who ran the Catholic Office for Motion Pictures. He insisted that I be introduced to her—a not-so-random brush with an internationally famous humanitarian, on an ordinary afternoon.

As Mother Teresa and her companion walked away, Father Sullivan grinned. "Now you can't wash your hand," he said, jokingly. He meant, I suppose, that I had been physically touched by a saint.

Now, whenever I remember that moment, I think about the good one person can do. And I want to bring Mother Teresa, as it were, down to size. She was slight, slender and plain. Her face was creased with wrinkles. She did not seem even slightly heroic, but her sincerity was obvious and inspiring. She was not cutting a figure, striking an attitude or putting on airs. She was just herself and very much at ease, yet this small, determined woman had done amazing things.

Born Agnes Gonxha Bojaxhiu, in 1910, of Albanian descent, she was raised Roman Catholic, and left home at eighteen to join the missionary Sisters of Loreto. Serving at a convent school in India, she took solemn vows in 1937, and then received "a call within a call." Jesus, she felt, was directing her to leave the convent and serve among the poor. "To fail would have been to break the faith," she later explained.

She began this new mission in 1948, adopting Indian citizenship and assuming native dress: a white cotton garment with a blue border. Going into the slums, she began to help the destitute, and gained admiration from Indian officials, even a commendation from the prime minister. Yet in her first year she was little more than a beggar herself, cadging food and supplies. By 1950 she received Vatican permission to form a new community, the Missionaries of Charity. From thirteen members in Calcutta, her group grew to four thousand worldwide, running orphanages, hospices and centers for the disabled, displaced, homeless, terminally ill, aged and blind, AIDS cases, victims of hunger, epidemics and disasters. From 1952, at their Home for the Dying in an abandoned Hindu temple, Mother Teresa's sisters comforted Muslims, Hindus, and Christians, offering them the solace of the Koran, the Bible, or the dignity of their chosen religions.

They established a home for leprosy patients called The City of Peace and a children's home for abandoned youth. When she received the Nobel Peace Prize in 1979 Mother Teresa refused the ceremonial banquet, asking that the funds be donated to the poor. During the 1982 Siege of Beirut she personally rescued thirty-seven children by brokering a temporary cease-fire between Israeli and Palestinian combatants. In the 1980s and 1990s her efforts extended to former Communist countries, including radiation victims at Chernobyl. Her sisters' work continues today.

Mother Teresa focused not on social change but on transformation of the heart. Asked frequently, "How can we promote world peace?" she gave a gospel answer: "Love each other." For this simplicity she was denounced by some who felt she did little to relieve oppression. Among her detractors is British journalist Christopher Hitchens, who was invited by the Vatican to name her failings when she was being considered for beatification after her death in 1997. Hitchens considered her a fraud because she told him, "I am not a social worker." He suspected her stated motive: "I do it for Christ. I do it for the church."

Mother Teresa's newly published diaries reveal years of spiritual darkness. Still, she persevered, believing that suffering could transform the human heart. Pope Benedict XVI has noted

274   HOW TO ACHIEVE A HEAVEN ON EARTH

the connection between her sustained prayer life and her earnest desire to comfort and console.

Can we be like her? Can she move us? "Just go home and love your family," she often advised. Mother Teresa was an ordinary woman who inspired millions through service and love. She opens our hearts to those most in need and close at hand. Such intense, lived compassion is a force that can transform the world.

Emilie Griffin, known to college friends as Russell Dietrich, won awards as an advertising executive in major firms in New York City and New Orleans. She is also an award-winning playwright and the author of sixteen books on Christian spiritual life. Now living in Alexandria, Louisiana, she travels to speak and lead workshops nationally and internationally.

Pilgrims' Pointers

By N. H. Atthreya

What are heaven and hell like?

To this question of mine, when I was ten, my mother's answer was a story.

"A young man asked God the same question," she began. "And God said, 'I will take you to heaven and hell. Find out for yourself.' The young man discovered much in both heaven and hell. However in heaven he found people well fed, but in hell they were famished.

My mother pointed out that an operating constraint and the approach to it made the difference. "The constraint? People could not bend their arms. The approach? In hell, they tried to feed themselves, but in heaven, they fed each other!"

I learned that one way to achieve heaven on earth then is to feed each other. But can my "other" go beyond my dear and near? Yes, say some, and they treat all humanity as near and dear. What makes them do so? They have graduated from passing physical and economic realities to perennial social and spiritual realities. They are beneficiaries of what one of the spiritual leaders in an Indian ashram called " a supreme discovery."

She said that the self and the great universal are one, an idea expressed in different ways by all the great teachers throughout the ages all over the world. The divine presence is within every part of each living thing, and it is up to humankind to manifest it. To do that, she taught, we must all become aware of that spark of divinity within ourselves, for in so doing we shall feel the presence of the divine in every other being and feel at one with the universe.

Of the same phenomenon, Gautama Buddha said, "In the end

275

we can choose to continue to believe that we are local, isolated, doomed creatures, confined to time and the body and set apart from all other human beings, or elect to open our eyes to our immortal omnipresent nature and the One Mind of which we each are a part. If we choose the former nothing will save us. If, however, we choose to awaken to our divine Self, we face a new dawn."

When we ignore this supreme discovery, we give ourselves an evolutionary downside. When we live this reality, we nurture heaven on earth for ourselves and others. This aspect of reality has been spotted and eloquently spelled out by hundreds of pilgrims of truth—call them saints or scientists.

It is one thing to know this secret and it is another to put it into practice.

An invocation from the ancient Vedas texts, here translated from the Sanskrit, gives us a guideline. It reads, "Let us learn together, let us nourish ourselves together, let us strengthen ourselves, and let us not hurt anyone by thought, word or deed."

Central to one's own well-being and the well-being of all of us is the message: hurt none, a message echoed by masters and mystics of all ages and climes. For example, Jesus said, "You have heard it said, 'Love your friends and hate your enemies.' But now I tell you, 'Love your enemies.'" A complementary discipline to achieve heaven on earth is that I take care of you and you take care of me. To quote Jesus again, "Love one another. As I have loved you, so must you love one another." When I take care of myself, I have only one to help me. When we take care of others mutually, I have many to take care of me!

Achieving heaven on earth is a human privilege for which pilgrims have provided pointers. A strategic opportunity lies in childhood. Let us inform our children that they possess sparks of divinity, and share these pointers with them, so they can develop needed habits of feeling, thinking and doing, for exercising the privilege of being human, being divine.

N. H. Atthreya, PhD, is the author of Spiritual Culture in the Corporate Drama, Practice of Excellence, *and* Towards Heaven on Earth. *He lives in Mumbai.*

The Kindness of Strangers

By Chris Rose

© 2008 The Times-Picayune Publishing Co. All rights reserved. Used with permission of The Times-Picayune.

"Jammin' generosity of two families places guitars in the hands of young rockers."

Let us pause to consider, once again, the kindness of strangers.

There is a young woman in the North Chicago suburbs—Wilmette, Illinois, to be exact—who cooked up a rather unorthodox plan to celebrate a hallowed rite of passage in her life.

Her name is Mel Racenstein and, as her bat mitzvah approached this past May 31, she told her parents that she would like to forgo the bundle of cash and gifts that generally attend the Jewish celebration of a young woman's entrance into adulthood and, instead, would like to buy—of all things—a bunch of guitars for kids in New Orleans.

At the very same time, a couple of kids from the Discher family in Wheaton, a western suburb of Chicago, decided to canvass their neighborhood residents and businesses, soliciting donations for a trip they planned to take with their family to New Orleans this month.

It's part of a Discher family tradition, something they call their annual Donation Vacation, wherein they pick a troubled spot in the world—hopefully one that's nice to visit, as well—and they go there not only to sightsee but to help out in any way they can.

What both of these kids' families had in common—other than the obvious Chicago link—was that the parents in each case went online in search of a worthy recipient of their generosity.

Both considered but eventually eschewed the big dogs of the rebuilding effort—the Red Cross, Habitat for Humanity, etc.—and looked for something more grassroots. Since music was a common tie among all parties involved—the two kids in Wheaton are both musicians—they both happened upon the New Orleans Musicians Relief Fund.

To add to the serendipity of it all, the New Orleans Musicians Relief Fund is headquartered in Illinois, south of Chicago in Bloomington. It was founded by a former New Orleans couple, Jeff and Karen Beninato, who evacuated there for Hurricane Katrina and remained.

The timing was just too exquisite. The Racenstein family bought fourteen Fender Squire electric guitars. The Dischers asked the Beninatos what they needed most, so they made a list of accessories—guitar cases, straps, strings, amps, picks, etc.

Put in touch with each other by Karen Beninato, the two families met last month in Rosemont, Ill., for the guitar handoff. Then the Dischers headed south for New Orleans. They arrived last week and, on Thursday afternoon, fourteen New Orleans kids got outfitted with brand new guitars.

The giveaway was a little unusual not just because of the very poignant details of the donations, but because most music charities around here tend to focus on horns and other staples of the brass, jazz and marching band traditions.

"We didn't want to leave out the rock-and-rollers," Karen Beninato told me with a laugh at the Parkway Bakery in Mid-City, where the giveaway was held. "We're what you'd call an 'instant charity'—what people donate to us, we immediately deliver to New Orleans. And we've brought down everything from saxophones to cellos, but this is the first time we delivered a bunch of axes."

The Parkway Bakery courtyard was abuzz with activity Thursday afternoon as the chosen recipients picked out their guitars from the selection of black, turquoise and even pink Squire models.

What most of the kids had in common is that they are the children of New Orleans musicians; this is one way to keep the music flames burning here. Eleven-year-old Olivia Huston, the daughter of local sax player Derek Huston, hugged her turquoise model to her chest like it was a favorite doll or stuffed animal.

It's her first instrument. She was wearing a Ramones T-shirt. I asked her what kind of music she planned on learning on it and she told me: "The guitar kind." Yeah, you right.

Eight-year-old Dinneral Shavers Jr., the son of the slain New Orleans brass band leader, leaned on his new ax with a big smile. "This is my first real guitar," he said. I asked him what his music ambition was. He said: "Like, I don't know. Jazz?"

Other Squire recipients hailed from equally notable New Orleans musical families—the Frenches, the Andrews, the Allens and the Clemenses. Also, six guitars were being donated to the Lusher Charter School—"the school of rock," Karen Beninato called it, a reference to the inordinately large number of musicians' children who go there.

Carson and Emma Discher watched it all with satisfaction. He's twelve; she's fourteen.

They're the two kids who solicited their neighbors up north. She wore peace sign earrings and told me: "It's cool to help people." Their mother, Deb Discher, said: "We live by the motto: To whom much is given, much is expected."

And what we can expect around here now is the sound of ringing guitars. Courtesy of our friends in Illinois, strangers no more.

Chris Rose began his journalism career at The Washington Post, *and in 1984 became a columnist for* The New Orleans Times-Picayune. *He says, judging from this progression, his next paper will be a weekly somewhere in the middle of the Kansas wheat fields. After Hurricane Katrina and the devastating breaks in the Corps of Engineers levees, the most prevalent topic of his column became, rather than Britney Spears trivia, how Orleanians dealt (or failed to deal) with all the losses. In early 2006, he compiled many of his first post-storm columns into a book,* One Dead in Attic, *which was picked up and expanded by Simon & Schuster in 2007, an extraordinary occurrence for a self-published work. The book was nominated for a Pulitzer Prize, and Rose won a Pulitzer for his contributions to* The Times-Picayune's *Public Service Award. He retired from the paper in 2009.*

A Thing New, Meaningful and Dangerous

By Robert D. Gamble

I have always held firmly to the thought that each one of us can do a little to bring some portion of misery to an end.

—Albert Schweitzer

Sunset. We are roaring about the city under streetlights and in the darkness, our driver leaning forward with a grim look, shifting, grinding, braking, honking, swerving. No one wears belts. We have a first aid kit, a deep pot full of beef and hot noodles, and tea to drink. I grasp a metal pole, holding my camera case in my lap. We pull to the curb; children stand on a raised platform of concrete with two round steel-rimmed holes and ladders that lead below.

I see Jana. She wears a T-shirt and jeans that are gathered by a belt. I can see her dirty hands, the black beneath her fingernails. Up close, her breath reeks of glue.

She leaps to the platform and disappears down a hole. I hoist myself up, grab the rails and descend. The stench of rotten beef, sausage, and potatoes, of moldy bread, urine and feces rises slowly with the hot air from below. I see several massive steel sewage pipes with mattresses laid across them and smaller pipes with valve handles the size of steering wheels. There is no visible floor, only garbage—cans, cups, plastic bottles and bags, cardboard containers and the remains of food and milk. I think of the Apostle's Creed: "He descended into hell. . . ."

My camera—the massive digital Fuji Fine Pix S2—sounds like a film camera: the swish and clop of the mirror inside as it lifts and falls to expose the light to the delicate sensor. The first shot and her head turns back toward me; the second is her face full on; the third and fourth can be less than a second apart and still show

280

a difference—the eyes darkening or filling with light. Street kids fear you, need you, trust you and doubt you. I fear they cannot love. They can gaze at and through you.

Almost all squirt glue into a plastic bag and huff it. "Why do you do it? Why do you sniff the glue?" one journalist asked. "It makes us feel lighter in our souls, to forget about and escape what is all around us." But the chemicals in glue and the injected Baltushka stop the growth process so that at fifteen or sixteen, they look twelve. In this time they are attempting to kill the pain of a life in which no adult seems to love them; they inflict pain on themselves by slicing their wrists repeatedly. When they share needles, they share the virus that leads to AIDS.

I am not a photographer by profession; I am a minister of the Presbyterian Church (USA). In Odessa, I am not a pastor; I work with street children and with the "social orphans." I raise funds to provide not only needed items such as food, clothing, medicine and eye care, but also tutors for college bound education, a program of horse therapy and counseling for at-risk kids in school. Photography helps me tell their story.

Why Ukraine?

In the summer of 2005, my church gave me a sabbatical. I believe that in order to find new direction in life, one must do a thing that is new, meaningful and a little bit dangerous. I decided to visit street kids in Ukraine. A year later, shocked by what I saw, I raised the money, started a nonprofit called This Child Here, and moved to Odessa.

I have climbed down holes, scaled walls, crawled through air ventilation holes on the sides of apartment buildings; I have walked on mounds of garbage and stepped through holes in brick walls to reach children. The sight of children coming out of a hole or huddled in the corners of abandoned buildings, the feel of cold steel ladders that took me beneath the streets, the weight of the camera in my hand, the view of a child's face filling the viewfinder—these are the details of my life. I know I am doing not only a thing of purpose that meets a need in our dark world, but also a work that meets a need deep within myself.

Sometimes, you can do a simple thing to make ours a better world: donate money, purchase a goat, adopt a child you never meet, or start a nonprofit for a worthy cause. Sometimes, your life has to change completely. Sometimes, you feel you are called and you know you are sent. Sometimes, to achieve something of heaven on earth, you must go to a place not far from hell.

Robert Gamble is the director of This Child Here, a nonprofit supported largely by Presbyterians and Presbyterian Churches (USA). A graduate of the Coast Guard Academy, he served as an officer for five years. He earned a doctor of ministry degree from Columbia Theological Seminary and a master of theology degree at Princeton Theological Seminary, and served as a pastor of Presbyterian churches in Tennessee, New Mexico and Florida. In 2006, he left the parish ministry to work with street kids and social orphans in Odessa, Ukraine.

Won't You Be My Neighbor?

By Peter Lovenheim

From *The New York Times,* June 23, 2008 © 2008 The New York Times. All rights reserved. Used by permission and protected by the Copyright Laws of the United States. The printing, copying, redistribution, or retransmission of the Material without express written permission is prohibited.

The alarm on my cell phone rang at 5:50 A.M., and I awoke to find myself in a twin bed in a spare room at my neighbor Lou's house. Lou was eighty-one. His six children were grown and scattered around the country, and he lived alone, two doors down from me. His wife, Edie, had died five years earlier. "When people learn you've lost your wife," he told me, "they all ask the same question. 'How long were you married?' And when you tell them fifty-two years, they say, 'Isn't that wonderful!' But I tell them no, it isn't. I was just getting to know her."

Lou had said he gets up at six, but after ten more minutes, I heard nothing from his room down the hall. Had he died? He had a heart ailment, but generally was in good health. With a full head of silver-gray hair, bright hazel-blue eyes and a broad chest, he walked with the confident bearing of a man who had enjoyed a long and satisfying career as a surgeon.

The previous evening, as I'd left home, the last words I heard before I shut the door had been, "Dad, you're crazy!" from my teenage daughter. Sure, the sight of your fifty-year-old father leaving with an overnight bag to sleep at a neighbor's house would embarrass any teenager, but "crazy"? I didn't think so.

There's talk today about how as a society we've become fragmented by ethnicity, income, city versus suburb, red state versus blue. But we also divide ourselves with invisible dotted lines. I'm talking about the property lines that isolate us from the people we are physically closest to: our neighbors.

It was a calamity on my street, in a middle-class suburb of Rochester, several years ago that got me thinking about this. One night, a neighbor shot and killed his wife and then himself; their two middle-school-age children ran screaming into the night. Though the couple had lived on our street for seven years, my wife and I hardly knew them. We'd see them jogging together. Sometimes our children would carpool.

Some of the neighbors attended the funerals and called on relatives. Someone laid a single bunch of yellow flowers at the family's front door, but nothing else was done to mark the loss. Within weeks, the children had moved with their grandparents to another part of town. The only indication that anything had changed was the "For Sale" sign on the lawn.

A family had vanished, yet the impact on our neighborhood was slight. How could that be? Did I live in a community or just in a house on a street surrounded by people whose lives were entirely separate? Few of my neighbors, I later learned, knew others on the street more than casually; many didn't know even the names of those a few doors down.

According to social scientists, from 1974 to 1998, the frequency with which Americans spent a social evening with neighbors fell by about one-third. Robert Putnam, the author of *Bowling Alone*, a groundbreaking study of the disintegration of the American social fabric, suggests that the decline actually began twenty years earlier, so that neighborhood ties today are less than half as strong as they were in the 1950s.

Why is it that in an age of cheap long-distance rates, discount airlines and the Internet, when we can create community anywhere, we often don't know the people who live next door?

Maybe my neighbors didn't mind living this way, but I did. I wanted to get to know the people whose houses I passed each day—not just what they do for a living and how many children they have, but the depth of their experience and what kind of people they are.

What would it take, I wondered, to penetrate the barriers between us? I thought about childhood sleepovers and the insight

I used to get from waking up inside a friend's home. Would my neighbors let me sleep over and write about their lives from inside their own houses?

A little more than a year after the murder-suicide, I began to telephone my neighbors and send e-mail messages; in some cases, I just walked up to the door and rang the bell. The first one turned me down, but then I called Lou. "You can write about me, but it will be boring," he warned. "I have nothing going on in my life—nothing. My life is zero. I don't do anything."

That turned out not to be true. When Lou finally awoke that morning at 6:18, he and I shared breakfast. Then he lay on a couch in his study and, skipping his morning nap, told me about his grandparents' immigration, his Catholic upbringing, his admission to medical school despite anti-Italian quotas, and how he met and courted his wife, built a career and raised a family.

Later, we went to the Y.M.C.A. for his regular workout; he mostly just kibitzed with friends. We ate lunch. He took a nap. We watched the business news. That evening, he made us dinner and talked of friends he'd lost, his concerns for his children's futures and his own mortality.

Before I left, Lou told me how to get into his house in case of an emergency, and I told him where I hide my spare key. That evening, as I carried my bag home, I felt that in my neighbor's house lived a person I actually knew.

I was privileged to be his friend until he died, just this past spring.

Remarkably, of the eighteen or so neighbors I eventually approached about sleeping over, more than half said yes. There was the recently married young couple, both working in business; the real estate agent and her two small children; the pathologist married to a pediatrician who specializes in autism.

Eventually, I met a woman living three doors away, the opposite direction from Lou, who was seriously ill with breast cancer and in need of help. My goal shifted: could we build a supportive community around her—in effect, patch together a real neighborhood? Lou and I and some of the other neighbors ended up taking turns driving her to doctors' appointments and watching her children.

Our political leaders speak of crossing party lines to achieve

286   HOW TO ACHIEVE A HEAVEN ON EARTH

greater unity. Maybe we should all cross the invisible lines between our homes and achieve greater unity in the places we live. Probably we don't need to sleep over; all it might take is to make a phone call, send a note, or ring a bell. Why not try it today?

Peter Lovenheim is the author of Portrait of a Burger as a Young Calf: The Story of One Man, Two Cows, *and* The Feeding of a Nation; *his next book is about neighborhoods. He is also a professional mediator, and while wearing that hat he wrote* How to Mediate Your Dispute *and* Mediate Don't Litigate. *A graduate of Cornell Law School, he has served as legal counsel and director of program development for the Center for Dispute Settlement in Rochester, New York, and was the founding president of Empire Mediation and Arbitration, a private dispute resolution company.*

Changing the World with Kindness

By David E. Crosby

Adapted from an opinion piece in New Orleans' *The Times-Picayune.* © 2008 The Times-Picayune Publishing Co. All rights reserved. Used with permission of The Times-Picayune.

A former president in his mid-eighties is entitled to do whatever he wishes with his time. So I wrinkled my brow to see President Jimmy Carter and his wife, Rosalyn, on their knees affixing boards to a porch in the Upper Ninth Ward last week. I decided, watching them work, that this presidential couple really believe they are changing the world with these small acts of kindness. Looking around, I saw many of the hundreds of volunteers who graced our city last week pausing in their own work to observe this famous man and woman accomplishing their humble service. These young faces, eyes shining, are portraits and symbols of faith and hope. They come to our city with the express purpose of lifting our spirits, holding up our arms, and joining us in the grunt work that moves our community forward.

The former president and his wife were all smiles as they greeted people, grabbed tools, and hit the deck with gusto. They request routinely that admirers not interrupt their construction time so that they can get something done. Harry Connick, Jr., and Ellis Marsalis dropped by to greet the volunteers and visit with the Carters. I thanked Harry for giving high visibility to our work of rebuilding, but he turned that thank you right back on me. The Carters did the same, and instructed me to pass on their gratitude to my congregation. Sometimes, around some people, it is hard to get a thank you in edgewise. I suspect that people who are busy trying to change their world are also very grateful as a matter of disposition.

Our environment here in New Orleans is being changed one hammer stroke at a time. For us, the progress is visible and palpable. It may be hard to extrapolate our progress to the rest of the world, but all the same principles apply whether we are looking at changing a city or changing a world. The accumulated effect of millions of tiny hammer strokes, and the faith and love that prompt them, is the rebuilding of a devastated region.

If multiplied throughout the world, the goal of eradicating poverty housing seems truly within reach. Hope springs eternal when we are busy building what we hope, because if despair or resignation were to bench us, our inactivity would reinforce the despair and quell the hope. Of course, it's not only people who are swinging hammers who hope for and expect such a transformation—achieving such goals also relies on the dreamers who come up with the concepts, the visionaries who promote the causes, the magnanimous donors who purchase or give materials, and the organizers who keep the projects running.

But lowly labor by individuals of every rank is the final step in putting the dreams into action. Billy Puckett, construction manager for the New Orleans Area Habitat for Humanity, challenged a thousand volunteers one morning this week to persevere in their good work. Perseverance, he said, would build character. And character produces hope. When you see the Carters kneeling at their work, your own heart swells. You start to imagine a world where people give of themselves in this way. You begin to believe that people can make a difference. Their determination and courage ignite hope in you, the observer. Maybe genuine hope has always traveled on these arcs of imagination and admiration that connect people.

Hope can derive from stirring words of encouragement and gentle acts of kindness, from a smile of sympathy and a look of understanding. Hope can also emanate from the sweat of honest labor and the embrace of active love.

David Crosby, the son of a pastor, was one of twelve children. He received a BA from Baylor University, a master of divinity from New Orleans Baptist Theological Seminary, and a PhD from Baylor University. For a time he was a reporter on the city desk of The Times-Picayune, *and now serves as senior pastor of New Orleans' First Baptist Church. He and his wife have three grown children and four grandchildren. He wrote* First Principles: Basics of Biblical Faith, *published by Pelican Publishing Company, Inc.*

Individual Paths to Heaven on Earth

Do not go where the path may lead, go instead where there is no path and leave a trail.
—Ralph Waldo Emerson

The Golden Rule and Other True Truisms

By Albinas Prizgintas

If I were making a list of steps toward creation of a heaven on earth, the first item would be to follow the Golden Rule: "Do unto others as you would have others do unto you." But to be useful, that admonition might need to be broken into smaller bites.

One of my duties as music director of my church is directing the choir, and I have found that people feel better when they sing. Events that include singing—religious ceremonies, state occasions, any kind of festive events that mark special moments in our lives—are uplifted by singing. It has been said that our eternal occupation in heaven will be singing, suggesting that singing and heaven are closely connected.

Now to sing well, one needs to be totally involved in the act of singing. There is no room to wonder what somebody thinks of you, or what you think about someone else. You have to play your own game as best you can. I learned this lesson a long time ago, and the reason is that because singing encompasses much: you need to focus, practice, perfect, meditate and so on. Taken to a logical conclusion, one must become one with what one is doing. No mean feat, even for an Einstein.

So my first addition to the golden rule is the observation that everyone minding his own business and doing his own thing may very well help the world along on the path toward achieving a heaven on earth.

In high school metal shop, if a student was caught doing something wrong, he had to scrape off a large area of gray paint applied to the blackboard, using a very fine piece of steel wool. After an hour or two of observing absolutely no progress, the teacher suggested concentrating on the minutest area

291

imaginable, and soon the student obtained results, though the task still required some time to accomplish. Patience was the lesson of the day. I think if we would all be a little more patient with ourselves, our tasks and with each other, we would discover what a wonderful world this can be.

On the first day of kindergarten at St. Mary's School in Bound Brook, New Jersey, a nun told the class a story about the rising sun instructing the flowers to shake the bugs off their petals early in the morning. All the little flowers obeyed, with the exception of one, which shook off all the nasty bugs, but not the little cute one with pretty colors and a funny little nose. Well, it turned out it was that cute bug that ate the flower up. T. S. Eliot complained of "innocent pleasures." I believe that real evil is insidious and often seemingly harmless. The occasional drink is not harmless, nor is the extra piece of cake or serving of fatty food. Nor is the off-color remark said in jest. I think an analysis of our "innocent pleasures" would do much to help us on the road to building a heaven on earth.

While one might argue that one glass of wine is not going to hurt anyone, drinking is drinking and alcohol is alcohol regardless of the quantity consumed. One needs to enter into it accordingly: it really has little to recommend it. As Bobby Short wrote in his biography, if an establishment serves alcohol, it is a saloon. I try to keep my own drinking down to a roar, but I know I'm better off without it. I've learned never to make a judgment or decision of any kind, even after a single glass of wine.

There is a Steve Winwood song that includes the line, "Come down off your throne and leave your body alone." I find that idea very helpful. We often abuse our bodies—and I include myself here—which can lead to addictions, poor eating habits, insufficient rest, and generally unsatisfactory behavior. I suggest yoga as a path toward getting in touch with the body, and, by extension, with the universe. This wisdom was imparted to me by an Indian doctor, and I often recall that proper exercise of the body can lead us a long way along the path to a better life.

Shakespeare writes in *Hamlet*, "To thine own self be true," which I understand to mean that one should meditate enough to know how to be true to oneself. I believe too often we find ourselves not in control of our lives, and out of touch with ourselves and with each other. To be at one with one's self and to know one's own hidden motives and agendas is a marvelous feat that too few people accomplish. Not to be in touch with one's self is a tragedy. In this state, to borrow from Langston Hughes, "we dry up and fester . . . like a raisin in the sun."

We might also follow Confucius' advice to respect our ancestors. Following the Ten Commandments is always a good idea. All these sound like a lot of rules and regulations, but they're all good. I also strongly recommend a lot of reading. All kinds of reading. I adhere to what some literary critics call "promiscuous reading." Read anything, so long as it's got words. Reading has made my life truly richer and a lot less disruptive to myself and to others. As the composer Arnold Schonberg pointed out, great art always existed that just needs to be discovered. I feel this statement is also true of the self. Thank God for Sigmund Freud. I think a minimum of five years of psychoanalysis should be required of everyone. Like Dante, it might take us through Hell, but the rewards may be worth it.

Albinas Prizgintas was born in a Schweinfurt, Germany, camp for displaced persons shortly after World War II, and grew up in Bound Brook, New Jersey, where he began playing the organ for daily church services while in the fifth grade. After earning two degrees from Julliard he was awarded a Fulbright Scholarship to study in Munich. He eventually settled in New Orleans, where he has been music director at Trinity Episcopal Church. His musical interests include blues as well as all facets of classical music. Besides the weekly Trinity Artists Series, Prizgintas developed Bach Around the Clock, the annual twenty-eight hour presentation that has garnered many prizes.

The Centrality of Wisdom

By Copthorne Macdonald

Considering the complexity of the world situation and the large number of problems that humanity faces, the task of achieving a heaven on earth seems daunting. Where does one start?

Is there by any chance a simplifying element, a focal point, a center from which the needed changes can flow? I believe there is. That point of origin, that central source which allows us to address any problem optimally, is wisdom. Wisdom is an all-purpose aid to creating heaven on earth. Whatever our life-focus happens to be among those ten essential heaven-on-earth elements, wisdom raises the level of our contribution.

Research has shed light on what wisdom is and what it is not.[1] There is a growing consensus that wisdom is a state of personal development which involves the acquisition of knowledge, but goes beyond it. Words of wisdom and wise behavior arise from wisdom, but wisdom is not the product of wisdom. Wisdom is a mode of cognition—one rooted in perspectives, interpretations, and values. Wisdom is not about facts per se; it is about the meaning of facts. It is about the significance of facts and their implications. Wisdom is a kind of meta-knowledge that helps us to make better sense of the rest of our knowledge and to apply that knowledge in appropriate ways. Wisdom does this by relating our ordinary everyday knowledge to a variety of contexts, by viewing it from various illuminating perspectives, and by bringing into the decision-making process a set of values that seeks the good of the whole and well-being writ large.

Values are at the heart of the matter. In an April, 1977, article in *American Psychologist*, Nobel laureate Roger Sperry put it bluntly: "Human value priorities . . . stand out as the most strategically powerful causal control now shaping world events. More than any other causal system with which science now concerns itself, it is variables in human value systems that will determine the future." As we know, human values are a very mixed bag. They range from selfishness, hate, greed, envy and revenge to wisdom-associated values such as empathy, truth, honesty, justice, cooperation, peace, compassion, universal well-being, creativity and comprehensive knowledge.

None of us is totally wise or totally unwise. Even among children we see differences—some kids are reactive and mean while others are calm and caring. In the past, most people considered the development of wisdom to be totally uncontrollable. A few people became wise. Most didn't. It doesn't have to be that way. We now know that wisdom can be developed intentionally. Research reveals a strong correlation between psychological/spiritual development and wisdom. Both psychological therapies and spiritual practices can help us become wiser, and in Ken Wilber's assessment of the research, meditation has been shown to be the most powerful single tool for advanced inner development.[2] The exploration of our own psyche through investigative kinds of meditation leads not only to a quiet, receptive mind, but also to an appreciation of the laws by which our subjective life operates, ethical understanding, moral behavior, and the expansion of our circle of caring in both space and time.

Age itself doesn't guarantee wisdom. Monika Ardelt's research[3] reveals great differences among the elderly. It has also shown that dealing effectively with life's difficult situations can help develop wisdom. Many wise people have a history of overcoming adversity. Like many others, they have faced great challenges in their lives. But instead of feeling diminished and victimized by their circumstances, they dealt with them in positive ways and grew past them.

There are also numerous efforts these days to introduce education-for-wisdom into schools from kindergarten through university.

So how do we move from personal wisdom to heaven on earth? In my view, we can do so by introducing "the values of the wise" into the internal guidance systems of society's institutions. Groups of wise individuals would implant those values (and other aspects of the wisdom process) in ways that ensure, as far as possible, the continuing of wise institutional behavior into the future.

I close with a question. Because the quality of our *doing* can only reflect the quality of our *understanding*, isn't the widespread cultivation of wisdom absolutely essential for achieving a heaven on earth?

[1] See, for example, Richard Trowbridge's comprehensive review of wisdom research at http://www.wisdompage.com/TheScientific ApproachtoWisdom.doc
[2] See Ken Wilber's comments at http://wilber.shambhala.com/html/books/formation_int_inst.cfm/xid,8287/yid,9296268
[3] Information about Monika Ardelt and access to her publications can be found at http://www.wisdompage.com/WisdomResearchers/MonikaArdelt.html

Copthorne Macdonald is a writer and independent scholar. Among his eight published books are three that deal with aspects of wisdom: Toward Wisdom, Getting a Life, *and* Matters of Consequence. *Since 1995 he has tended a website that provides Internet access to wisdom-related resources.*

How to Create a Heaven on Earth

By Chris Wood

A critical element in the creation of a heaven on earth is the visualization of a detailed plan and an end result. Very few lofty goals are ever met by mere happenstance. As a teacher and coach of adolescents, I truly believe that the movement toward a more perfect world must be embraced by our youth. People must, at an early age, begin to conceptualize each of the necessary elements of achieving a heaven on earth. In addition, it will take bold leadership to instill a confidence that never waivers in such a vision.

I can remember various mentors in my life who spoke of the importance of defining one's goals, but until I gained experience working with young men and women, I never fully understood the power of visualization. As an athletic director at a small, private school in Alabama, my first major undertaking was to hire a coach to revive the school's fledgling football program. After interviewing several candidates, I decided to take a chance on a relatively unproven candidate. Coach Felder was a young man who had spent the first five or six years of his career at large, public schools with very athletic student bodies. Even though he'd made himself familiar with the history of our football program— the team had not won a single game in the previous season—he adamantly proclaimed that his goal was for our school to win a state championship.

As much as we tried to make him understand that, at the moment, we would simply like to see enough participation to allow us to field a team, he was insistent upon this vision of creating a winning program. Coach discussed the characteristics of championship teams and mapped out a very detailed plan to create one at our school. While I was somewhat skeptical, his enthusiasm was indeed contagious. As the new school year approached, I became more and more eager to see how the students would react to his confidence and his expectations for the program.

As promised, Coach began to implement his plan to turn ours into a championship program. Each and every day he spoke to his players about being champions. His expectations, at first, were laughed off as the empty rhetoric of an eager young coach. But as the season approached, you could see an excitement and confidence in the boys that had never been there before. However, in spite of all the pre-season hype, the team posted its second winless season in a row. Even still, Coach never stopped talking about the vision. This was going to be a championship program. The message was to stay the course. Set your goals high. Keep working. Keep believing.

We finished our second season with five wins and five losses and a playoff berth. Though we were eliminated in the first round, the students were starting to see the fruits of their hard work. The vision of their head coach that once seemed like a fantasy suddenly looked attainable. Many of the team leaders heading into the third season had a very clear vision of the possibilities. They'd been listening to the coach illustrate his vision for over two years now, and it became their vision. In addition, the growing spirit and optimism began to win over the parents and faculty. It was refreshing to see such excitement among adults who had initially expressed skepticism and apathy.

Season three brought a perfect regular season, ten wins, no losses and an area championship. In the playoffs, we were a mere field goal away from advancing to the state championship. The students who made this unbelievable improvement possible were able to embrace an amazing vision of the future with an almost naïve optimism.

I believe that it takes a special person to lead such a movement. A movement that builds a championship football program. Or a movement to create a heaven on earth. Coach Felder was able boldly to state an objective, inspire others to join him and see his vision realized. Through this book, my father-in-law, John Wade, is hoping to do the same on a larger scale. And while these adults clearly have a passion for what they do, I believe the vision of a heaven on earth must be clearly and enthusiastically illustrated for our youth, for they have a wonderfully high capacity for embracing dreams and working toward lofty goals with confidence and energy. They should be encouraged to discuss, debate and analyze the various elements involved in creating a heaven on earth. And as the vision becomes their vision, even the most cynical will begin to see what is possible. I truly believe that as more and more people begin to share in this grand vision, progress toward its fruition is inevitable.

Chris Wood earned a bachelor of science in business administration from Auburn University, and is pursuing a master's degree in education. He has taught and coached grades seven through twelve in public and private schools in Anniston, Alabama.

How to Achieve a Heaven on Earth in Marriage

By Anne Teachworth

We all know the story of the Garden of Eden in the Bible. Adam and Eve began their lives together in a heaven on earth, but their failures as the first couple cost them paradise, and set an example for human couples to follow over the eons.

And what a bad example it was. According to the account, God gave Adam and Eve only one rule to follow: "Do not eat of the fruit of the Tree of Knowledge of Good and Evil." But our first parents not only broke the commandment, they hid from God afterwards. When God asked them what had happened, Eve blamed the snake for tempting her and Adam blamed his wife for tempting him. As a result, they were banished from the Garden. To this day, their descendants are still struggling to regain a heaven on earth in marriage.

Now with fifty-five percent of all first marriages and sixty-five percent of second ones ending in divorce, large numbers of married couples are seriously seeking advice on how to live "happily ever after." As a therapist specializing in trans-generational couple counseling, it is timely for me to remind couples that centuries after Adam and Eve, God gave humans a few more rules to guide us back to paradise.

Ten to be exact. Statistics have proven that couples who follow His Ten Commandments consistently achieve a higher degree of happiness together than those who don't. "Love is patient, love is kind, love is not jealous," adds Paul in his letter to the Corinthians. Most Christian marriage vows today include a promise to "love, honor and respect." Updated to substitute "respect" for the politically incorrect "obey," the traditional vow also includes ". . . in sickness and in health, for richer and poorer, keeping myself only onto thee as long as we both shall live." All good promises to keep.

However, as a marriage counselor, I would suggest couples agree to more specific behaviors from the beginning. My Ten Commandments for Couples to Live By are based on God's original Ten.

1. Put your spiritual relationship with God as the top priority in your married life and regularly pray together, preferably at family mealtimes.

2. Speak to each other in a kind, considerate and respectful manner, being willing to be at peace, forgive and/or apologize if someone's feelings are hurt.

3. Set aside one day a week as your special couple time to keep your friendship alive; have fun, play together, talk privately, listen, laugh, resolve any differences or misunderstandings, and confide in each other anew.

4. Make every effort to honor, befriend and be at peace with all the relatives in both your childhood families and the new family—children and friends—you have created together.

5. Be loving and cooperative as parents who nurture, support, and protect your children, and provide a home that is a refuge, a safe place where they can grow, increase their self-esteem, practice compassion for each other and imprint positive family values by your example.

6. Remain sexually faithful, physically considerate and emotionally responsive in your relationship, respecting each other's need for time together and time apart without possessiveness or jealousy.

7. Be generous in both giving and receiving, sharing time, tasks, obligations and belongings with each other equally without selfishness or resentment, being fair, considerate and responsible in decision-making, living arrangements, housekeeping and lifestyles.

8. Stay open, trusting and pleasant in your communication, reliable in your promises, truthful in sharing your feelings, admitting your mistakes, and giving feedback without criticizing, accusing, intimidating, abusing, lying, insulting or betraying each other's confidences or secrets.

9. Demonstrate your attention, affection and appreciation by regularly reaffirming your spouse as your lover, your partner for life and your best friend.
10. Express your gratitude to God and each other for the gifts you have received by enjoying the home, money and possessions you two own, without being dissatisfied, unhappy or envious of anyone else's lifestyle.

Wow, you might think, if we would do all those, we could actually create a heaven on earth in our marriage, wouldn't we? Yes, you would. Especially if you two agree from the very beginning your goal is "to live happily ever after."

Anne Teachworth is the author of the popular book, Why We Pick The Mates We Do, *and the developer of The Psychogenetic System, her own trans-generational approach to couple, parenting and family counseling. She is the founder and director of the Gestalt Institute of New Orleans/New York, and a Certified Gestalt Counselor, Certified Psychogenetic Trainer, Certified Matchmaker and Fellow of the American Psychotherapy Association, and teaches at conferences all over the world.*

Lesson of the Ants

By Yashodhara Raje Scindia

There is a stream of worker-ants that I encounter as I take my morning walk. Each one is furiously committed to feeding its subterranean colony, an endless stream going nowhere but somewhere. Or am I missing something? The worker-ants go about their business instinctually and live their lives not questioning the right or wrong of things. Not even why these giant monster feet that come their way one day crush them with impunity, and on another step by the side like a gentle earthquake, sparing their lives. I wonder what an interesting world it would be if God gave us the power to switch into the consciousness of these fellow co-habitants and experience their world. Would we begin to see heaven in another light?

Aren't we all just those worker-ants in a different manifestation? The animal kingdom inhabits the same earth as we. Have we humans been given the power to make the necessary corrections that will keep the world as we know it in the right balance? The balance that has existed among all things since the creation of the universe. A balance that maintains a certain status quo in the system of life.

Just as solar systems and galaxies are in perfect balance for life to develop, so must all living things exist in perfect balance and mutual respect for life to thrive. But the balance is often upset by hatred, global warming, extinction of species and unmitigated greed in an endless spiral. We need to give each other and others—ants, dolphins, tigers, spiders, colored people, white people, poor people, and yes, even jihadists—the respect to find ours and their own space in this small planet, a space as much theirs as ours.

Humility will give the human mind the understanding and

303

ability to metamorphose itself into the minds of all living beings by stepping outside self into those of others—worker-ant, head of state, Mumbai slumdog, even the fanatic jihadist—for us to be able to truly understand the meaning and value of a respect that allows us all to be patient with each other, to understand, appreciate and work with each other.

Maybe technology such as Google Earth has given us the means of looking down into our collective lives from a different perspective, to realize how insignificant we are in the larger scheme of things. But that viewpoint can also show us how the infinitesimally small can collectively achieve a much larger good.

As a politician and social worker in my tiny sphere, I need to respect the position I am in with regard to those around me. From my workers, peers and supporters to my opponents and the common man there needs to be an awareness that we are working toward a common good, knowing that each one, friend or foe, is working towards a common purpose.

The humility to give each living being the respect to have its own rightful space will only come from an education that inculcates these values as an integral part of its curriculum. Parents and educational institutions alike need to help one another and our children to understand the concept of a life lived with respect for ourselves, each other and all living beings.

Therefore whether it is between a prisoner and jailor, a parent and child, president and his people, slumdog and his peers, or Muslim fundamentalist and moderate, respect will play the part in turning our earth into a heaven that is within our reach. But it has to begin with me. I will educate myself and those around me. I will respect you.

Born in London, Princess Yashodhara Raje Scindia is the daughter of the late Jivajirao Scindia, Maharaja of Gwalior. She was educated in India, and lived in the United States for a number of years, but returned to India in 1994, when she entered politics. She served in the State Legislative Assembly of Madhya Pradesh and as Cabinet Minister for tourism, sports and youth welfare, and in 2007 was elected to represent the Gwalior constituency of Madhya Pradesh in Parliament. She is a member of the Parliament Standing Committee on Health and a member of the Parliament Consultative Committee on Tourism.

The Age of Ambition

By Nicholas D. Kristof

From *The New York Times*, January 27, 2008 © 2008 The New York Times. All rights reserved. Used by permission and protected by the Copyright Laws of the United States. The printing, copying, redistribution, or retransmission of the Material without express written permission is prohibited.

With the American presidential campaign in full swing, the obvious way to change the world might seem to be through politics.

But growing numbers of young people are leaping into the fray and doing the job themselves. These are the social entrepreneurs, the 21st-century answer to the student protesters of the 1960s, and they are some of the most interesting people here at the World Economic Forum (not only because they're half the age of everyone else).

Andrew Klaber, a 26-year-old playing hooky from Harvard Business School to come here (don't tell his professors!), is an example of the social entrepreneur. He spent the summer after his sophomore year in college in Thailand and was aghast to see teenage girls being forced into prostitution after their parents had died of AIDS.

So he started Orphans Against AIDS (www.orphansagainstaids. org), which pays school-related expenses for hundreds of children who have been orphaned or otherwise affected by AIDS in poor countries. He and his friends volunteer their time and pay administrative costs out of their own pockets so that every penny goes to the children.

Mr. Klaber was able to expand the nonprofit organization in Africa through introductions made by Jennifer Staple, who was a year ahead of him when they were in college. When she was a sopho-more, Ms. Staple founded an organization in her dorm room to collect old reading glasses in the United States and ship them to poor countries. That group, Unite for Sight, has ballooned, and last year it provided eye care to 200,000 people (www.uniteforsight.org).

In the '60s, perhaps the most remarkable Americans were the civil rights workers and antiwar protesters who started movements that transformed the country. In the 1980s, the most fascinating people were entrepreneurs like Steve Jobs and Bill Gates, who started companies and ended up revolutionizing the way we use technology.

Today the most remarkable young people are the social entrepreneurs, those who see a problem in society and roll up their sleeves to address it in new ways. Bill Drayton, the chief executive of an organization called Ashoka that supports social entrepreneurs, likes to say that such people neither hand out fish nor teach people to fish; their aim is to revolutionize the fishing industry. If that sounds insanely ambitious, it is. John Elkington and Pamela Hartigan title their new book on social entrepreneurs *The Power of Unreasonable People*.

Universities are now offering classes in social entrepreneurship, and there are a growing number of role models. Wendy Kopp turned her thesis at Princeton into Teach for America and has had far more impact on schools than the average secretary of education.

One of the social entrepreneurs here is Soraya Salti, a 37-year-old Jordanian woman who is trying to transform the Arab world by teaching entrepreneurship in schools. Her organization, Injaz, is now training 100,000 Arab students each year to find a market niche, construct a business plan and then launch and nurture a business. The program (www.injaz.org.jo) has spread to twelve Arab countries and is aiming to teach one million students a year. Ms. Salti argues that entrepreneurs can stimulate the economy, give young people a purpose and revitalize the Arab world. Girls in particular have flourished in the program, which has had excellent reviews and is getting support from the U.S. Agency for International Development. My hunch is that Ms. Salti will contribute more to stability and peace in the Middle East than any number of tanks in Iraq, U.N. resolutions or summit meetings.

"If you can capture the youth and change the way they think, then you can change the future," she said.

Another young person on a mission is Ariel Zylbersztejn, a 27-year-old Mexican who founded and runs a company called Cinepop, which projects movies onto inflatable screens and shows them free in public parks. Mr. Zylbersztejn realized that ninety percent of Mexicans can't afford to go to movies, so he started his own business model: He sells sponsorships to companies to advertise to the thousands of viewers who come to watch the free entertainment.

Mr. Zylbersztejn works with microcredit agencies and social welfare groups to engage the families that come to his movies and help them start businesses or try other strategies to overcome poverty. Cinepop is only three years old, but already 250,000 people a year watch movies on his screens—and his goal is to take the model to Brazil, India, China and other countries.

So as we follow the presidential campaign, let's not forget that the winner isn't the only one who will shape the world. Only one person can become president of the United States, but there's no limit to the number of social entrepreneurs who can make this planet a better place.

Nicholas D. Kristof was educated at Harvard and Oxford Universities, the latter as a Rhodes Scholar. A native of Oregon, he has traveled extensively and writes bi-weekly op-ed columns for The New York Times. *With his wife, also a* Times *journalist, he won a Pulitzer Prize for coverage of the events at Tiananmen Square, and he won a second in 2006 for his columns on the genocide in Darfur.*

Four Hurdles to Success

By Dale Brown

There is a very thin line separating winners from losers—total dedication and commitment. Our ability to set goals and then dedicate ourselves to reaching those goals is imperative for us to be successful. Oftentimes a person establishes goals but then falls short in making the kind of commitment and perseverance necessary to reach them, and at the other end of the spectrum is the person who is very dedicated and committed but hasn't established goals or laid out a map to reach the desired destination. So my advice is to set a goal first, then dedicate yourself to that goal and the goal will never let you go.

I have discovered four obstacles to reaching our goals; I call them the four hurdles to success.

The first hurdle is "I can't." The power inside each of us is incredible if we allow it to be released. I remember a small boy in Georgia with a near-fatal kidney problem. He set a goal to become the strongest person in his class and dedicated himself to that goal. He was not tied down with "I can't" even though the doctors told his parents he probably would not live past the age of twelve. This young man, Paul Anderson, then set a goal to become the strongest man in Georgia and accomplished that also. He went on to become a super heavyweight Olympic goal medalist, set nine world records and became the strongest man in the history of the world.

Paul did not stop there, however, and in 1957 a miracle occurred. There is an event called the back lift, in which the individual gets under the weight and lifts it off the ground. Since 1896, a French-Canadian had owned the back lift record of 4,300 pounds. Paul Anderson shattered that record by lifting 6,270 pounds, over three tons! Your life is a product of your thoughts. The only way to alter your life is to alter your thinking.

The second hurdle is "afraid to fail." How many times do we not even attempt to accomplish something because we are afraid to fail? It is frightening to think what might have happened to history had one man been afraid to fail.

This one man lost his job, had a business fall apart, his sweetheart died, and he suffered a nervous breakdown. His political life consisted of losses as he ran for the legislature, House Speaker, Congress and Senate, and then for vice-president. Yet in 1860, that same man became the sixteenth president of the United States. After many heartbreaks and defeats, Abraham Lincoln went on to change the course of history and our lives— because he was not afraid to fail.

The third hurdle is "handicaps." Many of us are constantly looking for excuses for lack of success and why we shouldn't even try. There are some who need only one excuse not to attempt to be successful, yet any time this hurdle confronts me I find it easy to overcome by thinking of Kay Vandiveer.

In 1959, in a bowling tournament, Kay rolled a strike on her last ball, resulting in a perfect game. Hours after this fantastic moment, her car was hit by a train. It took four and a half hours to remove her car from the wreckage, and the call was made to her family to get to the hospital as she probably would not live through the night. Her body was so badly injured that the doctors were forced to amputate her right arm. Kay lived through the night, though she did remain in a coma for three months, and for over two years never set foot on the hospital floor. Still, she clung to life.

Then, in a remarkably courageous comeback, Kay returned to bowling. Formerly right handed, she taught herself to bowl with her left arm. Five years from the date of her accident, Kay entered the North Dakota state woman's tournament, and on her last ball rolled a strike, giving her a game of 295 and the state championship.

"Know yourself" describes the fourth hurdle. It can be deceiving, though, as it is not expressed in the same manners as the others. It's the most difficult one we face, and we face it every day, for if we don't know ourselves, we can never be truly happy or find true success.

Picture this: a capacity crowd at the stadium, a hundred thousand strong, standing, cheering a runner in his victory lap after capturing the Olympic gold medal. He had set a goal and dedicated himself to reaching that goal and then there it was—a gold medal proclaiming him the very best in the world in his event. Yet six months later this same athlete took his life by slashing his wrists. He never knew himself. He had beaten the first three hurdles, but he could not get over the final one.

Real confidence comes from knowing and accepting yourself, your strengths and your limitations, in contrast to depending on affirmation from others. The beginning of wisdom is being honest with yourself. The most noble and perfect victory is the triumph over oneself.

Always try to do your best, never give up, and God will take care of everything else.

Dale Brown began his career in North Dakota, where he coached basketball, wrestling, football and track and field. After serving as assistant coach at Utah State University for five years and one year at Washington State, he became the head basketball coach at Louisiana State University in 1972, leading the Tigers to 448 wins, thirteen NCAA tournaments, and two Final Four appearances. He is now a motivational speaker and author.

Can Fire and Water Make Peace?

By Hans Ucko

However we formulate it, we would like things to go better, not only for ourselves but for the planet we inhabit and its people. Although not everyone might be comfortable speaking of heaven on earth, many are curious about what it means in real terms. But how does one attain heaven on earth? We might be able to say what heaven on earth should not consist of: no war, no hunger, no insecurity, no dictatorship, no poverty, etc. It would be much more difficult to agree on what heaven on earth should include. We are different and we think differently, particularly when it comes to the big concepts: peace, justice, freedom, etc. Many of these ideas have also lost their power of inspiration, having been overused as slogans and catchphrases. They have become empty words and we look at them without knowing what to do with them. How could we achieve heaven on earth? It is a good question indeed.

The words "heaven on earth" echo The Lord's Prayer: "Your will be done, on earth as in heaven," and the Jewish prayer called Kaddish: "May there be much peace from Heaven." The question arose among the rabbis, "How is then peace in heaven, since it is to be a model for peace on earth? What is the quality of peace in heaven?" Discussing among themselves, the rabbis looked into the very word for "heaven," which in Hebrew is shamayim. And the rabbis discovered that they could recognize two words hidden in "shamayim." These two words are each other's absolute opposite: "(e)sh" is fire and "mayim" is water. And the rabbis understood one important dimension of the characteristics of heavenly peace. In heaven, peace is the living together and the communion of opposites, fire and water. Fire and water are one in heaven but

311

312   HOW TO ACHIEVE A HEAVEN ON EARTH

the water doesn't quench the fire and the fire doesn't vaporize the water. It is not a zero-sum game, a balance of terror or the tentative peace of a balance of power. There is also no fence of separation between fire and water. Fire and water are reconciled in diversity. And yet there is no fusion. They are different and together they make up what peace is really about. If heaven on earth is to be achieved, the dimension of paradox is necessary to break new ground and to get the new perspectives needed. We must break out from a mindset, where, if I am right you must be wrong.

A man came to a judge complaining about his neighbor, and the judge said: "You are right." Then came the neighbor and complained. The judge said: "You are right." The judge's wife, having listened to the rulings of her husband, asked, "How can they both be right? It is not possible." And the judge said: "You are right."

This is as incomprehensible as fire and water in the same word—heaven. And yet, the judge has a point; he offered a space where contradicting elements, contradicting views, contradicting statements and contradicting claims could be heard together. It is in these spaces and crossroads that material for another kind of thinking and discourse is born, in affinity with our time of continuous change of reality and knowledge and where concrete experience matters more than many fixed abstract principles. It will affect how we look upon ourselves and the other, the one who is unlike us, different in faith, in culture, in nationality, in gender, etc. We will see that we often have projected a view of the other because we feared putting fire and water in the same room; we feared more than one opinion being considered right. The moral of the story about heaven holding both fire and water was to make us aware of the dangers of abstract and static understandings of self and other. We will come to realize that the one we call "the other" is often our own projection and construction.

To achieve heaven on earth requires dialogue between self and other. It is not an option but a way of life. Dialogue implies a new kind of listening to the other. Such listening is much more than just waiting for one's own cue. It allows the encounter itself to set the agenda. In this perspective, dialogue is not self-gratification or an *a priori* affirmation of one's own position or thinking. Dialogue between self and other is the only way to achieve heaven on earth.

Rev. Dr. Hans Ucko is from Sweden, and has for many years been involved in interreligious relations and dialogue, most of the time on the staff of the World Council of Churches. He is now an affiliate of the Center for Faith and Practice at Hartford Seminary in Connecticut.

Insight Through the Blue Dog

By George Rodrigue

All my life I have answered the question, "What is your favorite painting?" with "The one I'm working on now." And so it is tempting for me to describe "heaven on earth" as that moment when my paintbrush hits the canvas. It is the act of painting that drives me. It is the reason that when I'm standing at the latest fundraiser cocktail party and am explaining whatever abbreviated Blue Dog history I've latched onto for the evening, when the inevitable "When do you have time to work?" arises, my seemingly sarcastic, yet utterly honest response should be, "This is work. If you mean to ask me when I will return to my easel, well, that's not work, that's living, that's ecstasy, that's my heaven on earth."

Furthermore, the phrase "heaven on earth" is to me a cliché, so it is tempting for me to respond in that way as well. We all want peace on earth, healthy children, better schools, safe streets and clean water. We want to feed the hungry and clothe the naked and comfort the downtrodden. We want to embrace compassion in our daily lives, to believe in ourselves, to believe in others, to believe in God.

But how do we, how do I, find these things as an individual? How do I make a difference and achieve my own heaven on earth against the impossible odds associated with something like "save the planet"?

The answer to that challenge lies for me right back at my easel. As content as I am in seeing a blank canvas transform beneath my brush, however, that specific joy is not heaven on earth. Rather, the secret to heaven on earth lies in my ability to change the world in my own way because of that deliberate act.

In the 1970s I set out to "save the Cajun culture." I had read an article that said that just before a culture dies, it erupts with one last burst, after which it is assimilated into the bigger influence, in this case the melting pot that is the United States. I mourned my heritage, and I made the decision to interpret it graphically, to preserve it with symbolic interpretations of light and oak trees and ghostly subjects. I painted festivals, industry, folklore and scenes from daily life. And I honestly thought I was recording the end, preserving it so that future generations could understand what we had lost. Now, forty years later, as I look back on a body of work that says something, maybe I did exactly what I set out to do. Maybe I made a difference.

The Blue Dog grew out of these paintings, as a Cajun myth called the loup-garou, a scary wolf-dog that, in my interpretation, was blue beneath a midnight sky. Like the Cajun paintings, the Blue Dog evolved into something that allowed me to deliver a message. Through these paintings I no longer comment on the past, but rather on today. I can reach thousands of people with a message in one painting, and whether it is romantic, spiritual, political or humorous, it has the ability to inspire. Through the Blue Dog I remind people that they don't have to interpret a situation (or a dog) exactly as it is on the surface, but they can use their mood and imagination to look deeper and interpret it anyway they want. They can open their minds to a new way of seeing, and they can approach life with an openness that can rise above past negative experiences, with a belief in humankind that surpasses the one they've been trained to see.

Because of my art, I've encountered betrayal, bitterness and jealousy. And yet, because of my art, I've remained trusting, confident and calm. I still believe in people.

And so herein lies heaven on earth. I have found and nurtured that thing we all have—a gift that is unique to each of us—and I use that gift to remain grounded, to remember where I come from, and to remember that not everything (or everyone) is as it appears on the surface. The more we can all, deep inside us and intensely, remember these things while remaining open to experiences and trusting of each other, the more likely we are to make each day on this earth better than the one before.

George Rodrigue is a Cajun artist originally from New Iberia,

Louisiana, best known for his paintings of Cajun folk life until his Blue Dog paintings catapulted him to worldwide fame in the 1990s. He has written and been the subject of numerous books on his art including The Cajuns of George Rodrigue, Blue Dog Man, The Art of George Rodrigue, *and* Blue Dog Speaks, *as well as a children's book,* Why Is Blue Dog Blue? *He and his wife, Wendy, live in New Orleans' historic Faubourg Marigny. He was named Louisiana Artist Laureate in October, 2008.*

Heaven on Earth Is a Choice

By Lenny Ravich

In order to achieve heaven on earth, you have to make the decision to do just exactly that. Say out loud, "I am now experiencing heaven on earth." It is a choice.

Albert Einstein said, "One must experience everything as a miracle or nothing as a miracle." Begin to see everything that has happened to you as a gift from God, even though it may not seem so at the time. Those who attain heaven on earth know that "everything happens for the best." Whatever happens, do believe in God or a higher power.

In addition, stay on the positive side. You must start looking at "what is" and never look at "what isn't." The moment you try to find what is missing from your life, your current existence becomes hell. Let me give you an example. What is omitted from this list of numbers: 1, 6, 7, 8 and 10? Some of you might guess 2, 3, 4, 5 and 9. But the truth is, nothing is absent. What appears is "what is." What is missing is only in your mind.

Never view the world with judgment, comparison or criticism. Looking at the world according to the way things "should be" will definitely cause suffering. Expecting certain outcomes only leads to disappointment. Looking at the world as an observer, and not being involved in the drama, guides you to inner peace.

In the Jewish tradition, one rises in the morning in prayer, "Thank you, Oh Lord, for returning my soul to my body." Thanking God for another day while realizing that untold millions never got to experience this day helps you develop an attitude of gratitude. By giving thanks for everything that happens, even the so-called bad things, which will eventually realize themselves as the best that could have happened in the

317

particular circumstances, offers a glimpse of heaven on earth.

Once the entire cosmos is viewed as conspiring to support you, you begin to feel first-rate. The law of attraction works by bringing into your life more of what you have. Have you ever heard the sayings, "money attracts money," or "the rich get richer"? That's because if you will your life to be abundant in money, love, powerful relationships, good health, well-being and joy, you will attract more of that. The same is true for negative thinking.

Take total responsibility for how your life looks at this point in time. Holding others responsible leads to victim-hood and there are no victims in heaven. Life is one great university. Every person and thing that comes into your life is a lesson on how to become a better human being. If you meet a monster, embrace him/her because what you are witnessing is yourself. By observing the world as a mirror, a projection of your own inner world, you begin to make choices that improve your life and create happiness.

Dr. Bernie Segal once said, "As a general rule, happy people don't get sick." One way to do this is not to allow a negative thought into your mind. Train yourself to watch your thoughts, and when you catch yourself thinking negatively, say, "I delete that thought." You delete it over and over until it disappears and then you replace it with a positive thought. This takes time and practice, but it's worth it. Find your signature strength and use it to serve society. Your signature strength is your core passion which only you can do your own special way. This is the path to living your dreams by doing what you love and being paid handsomely for it. This adds meaning to your life.

Lastly, practice aerobic exercises, e.g. cycling, swimming, walking or Aerobic Laughter™, one-half hour at least three times a week. When you are physically active, endorphins are released in your body, which causes you to feel a natural high and at the same time releases tension and lowers blood pressure. Smile and the world smiles with you.

Lenny Ravich lives in Israel. A humor expert who facilitates workshops and presentations throughout the world, he is the author of the bestselling book, A Funny Thing Happened on the Way to Enlightenment.

Many Mothers

By Maida Rogerson

Imagine. You've just had your first baby. Your husband is in a new job and doesn't have a lot of time for you. You've moved away from your extended family. Suddenly, there you are, you and your beautiful baby, home, alone. Your baby starts to cry, and you're dead tired and all you want to do is cry yourself, and you have no one to turn to.

Or, maybe you're older and you've just had your third child. The birth was hard and you're exhausted. Your husband helps as best he can, but he works during the day and you now have three children, each demanding your attention and you don't know where to turn. What do you do? How can you get to spend some one-on-one time with your new baby?

These are a couple of the situations that an obstetric nurse brought to the attention of Anne McCormick several years ago. Anne was working at a family center in Santa Fe, New Mexico, and soon turned her attention to creating a program to help these kinds of new mothers. The program was called Many Mothers.

I found out about the program when I moved to Santa Fe fifteen years ago. I saw an ad for volunteers to work with new mothers and I thought it would be a wonderful way to start interacting with my new community.

Anne came to interview me and told me about the philosophy of Many Mothers. She believed that new babies thrive on love, care and attention and so do new mothers. Because extended family support is often absent, Many Mothers attempts to fill that role by using volunteers: grandmothers, aunts, businesswomen, and often other mothers who want to give their time to help a family get off to a good start. Knowing that bonding and attachment in infancy are necessary to create healthy adults, Many Mothers believes that in nurturing the mother, you nurture the newborn, the family and the whole community.

Service to a new family is given free of charge to all income levels. A new mother may need help with grocery shopping, housecleaning, laundry, entertaining a sibling, or rocking a baby so she can simply take a rest or a shower. We honor the work it takes to care for a new baby and we care for the one who does it.

At some point every volunteer learns this secret—you always get more than you give. That was certainly my experience with Many Mothers. I entered the program with visions of coming into a neat, tidy home, rocking a perfectly clean, sleeping baby for a couple of hours and then leaving. It hasn't been like that. I've spent a lot of time playing with jealous siblings so mom can spend some alone time with her new baby. I've done laundry; scrubbed floors; attended doctor's and court appointments; researched resources; cooked; cleaned, and cleaned, and cleaned. What I did most, and what made all the other chores bearable, was listen. I got to know the joy and terrors of my new mothers. I was able to assure them of the normalcy of their feelings, and on a couple of occasions alert the community when I felt a mom might be slipping into depression. I was deeply appreciative of the trust these mothers gave me in sharing their children and their lives with me, and I was happy to be able to contribute in such a tender and loving way toward a healthier community.

The thing I like best about Many Mothers is that the program meets a need on both sides of the volunteer experience. We volunteers meet monthly to discuss our experiences and to receive advice and help, and it's very clear that many of us are also distanced from our own extended families. Volunteering with new mothers satisfies our longing to be in family, to be "with" and "for" someone.

And I did get my experience of rocking a beautiful baby. My own mother died during a time when I was volunteering for a family. She lived abroad and I flew to her funeral. The day after I returned was the day I was to volunteer with my family. I didn't know if I could make it. I was tired and grief-stricken, but I decided to go. The mother met me at the door, baby in arms, and said she'd been up all night and asked if I would mind rocking the baby while she had a nap. Would I mind! I pulled the rocker to the window where I could look out to the trees. I held that baby to my heart, and we rocked and rocked, and I reveled in holding this new life and in knowing that life goes on and love is constant.

Anne McCormick died in the spring of 2008, but Many Mothers continues. She left us a manual she had written on how to create a similar organization in other communities. For me, heaven on earth includes being able to provide loving support for families with new babies so that everyone involved—the givers and receivers—experiences the joy of rearing healthy children.

Maida Rogerson is an actor, writer, speaker and seminar leader. She uses the power of storytelling to move people to greater compassion, creativity and joy in their work and in their lives. Co-author of The New York Times *Business Bestseller,* Chicken Soup for the Soul at Work, *Maida delights in sharing its inspirational stories and positive messages. Her particular focus is on acknowledgment, creativity and balance.*

The Word Is the Way

By Sage Cohen

We all walk our own paths to discover heaven on earth. My portal has always been poetry. At the borrowed retreat house, I place the blue mug on the red counter, lay the dog bed down. How little it takes for me to make a house a home.

As each turn in my travels reveals a new landscape rising up, I recognize the patterns of yesterday. There is a kind of belonging to seeing the same sight twice. How easily we nestle into a new life with just a few repetitions. The way practicing music makes the scales a part of you, this drive belongs to me. In the driving of it, I will embed Route 53 into the hardwiring of my non-thinking, the backbone of my memory.

Here I can simply climb the loft into my quiet mind, let the rising heat warm me, let the dishes turned upside down dry in their own time because slowness has its own rhythm, as do wood gathering, closing the gate, firing the alarm with the doors closed, the mind alert. I love my little nest of covers framed in sky. I like sleeping above the sleep of my dogs, as if my beneficence might pour down over them like starlight.

I love my dogs: Henry curled into a little knot like the heart of cherry wood, Hamachi stretched long and lean like a fallen branch too full of the weight of its own potential to stay suspended above the earth.

The worn chairs with their slumped pillows feel something like a family, a circle of friends, witnesses. I feel the sitting, the thinking, the gathering of the women who have been here before, receiving words through their wide nets of butterfly catching: mash of bananas and beer. Attracting the spirits with the song of the river, with the receptivity of the dictionary. She waits for me to open her. She is alive with an orderly thinking, a waking of the mind that can be activated with any interpretation. As if there were such a thing as definition.

This must be how electricity was discovered: a charge we all know but have not figured out how to tap. Like music, captured and channeled into individual songs, when the truth of music is everywhere, swarming us in our inability to listen. The gift of the musician is to untangle a melody, a harmony and a base line and feed those to us bit by bit so we can learn how to digest them.

And this is what the poet does: relieve the heat of its burdens; send it into the atmosphere to mingle with the particles of words that are accumulating there, waiting to fall down upon us, fat as bread crumbs whose trail we follow into the darkness.

Sage Cohen is author of Writing the Life Poetic: An Invitation to Read and Write Poetry, *and the poetry collection* Like the Heart, the World.

The Invisible Element

By Gabriel Lang

Of the ten elements needed to create a heaven on earth, which is the most important? The answer is subjective and any one of them could be posited as the most important, or we could ask Mr. Wade. After all, he is the builder and conductor of this train. But in actuality, I believe the most important element is one that's not even mentioned. It's the one that's always there but never really recognized. It's an invisible little piece of all the elements and something that keeps us from taking ourselves too seriously—a sense of humor.

The first time I met a former girlfriend, a close family friend of hers had just died. In a message to her I offered my condolences, an ear if she needed someone to talk to, and a dirty joke. She took me up on all of them and later told me that the joke was the thing that at that moment made her feel better. To this day, even though we're just friends now, she occasionally gives me a call when she needs cheering up and asks me to tell her a joke. I always oblige and hearing her laugh makes me feel better too.

The reason I know so many jokes is that while dealing with a bout of adolescent depression during high school I found a book called *Truly Tasteless Jokes*. I read it from cover to cover in one sitting. When those two hours were over my mood had drastically changed from one of slight despair and not caring about anything to cheerful and optimistic demeanor. There was nothing life affirming or lessons learned in those old dirty jokes; it was the laughter they elicited that brought me out of my funk and made me realize I didn't really have it that bad. I still own six of those old joke books from different times when I'd have to get out of the house, drive to the book store and pick one up to get myself to laugh again.

More recently I was at the funeral of a friend's grandfather with whom I was also close. Many people think funerals are no laughing matter, but I think the opposite is true. In my opinion if you can't laugh at a funeral, when can you laugh? This man was loved by many, which was obvious by the fact that there were literally hundreds of people at the Mass. The eulogy was given by one of his sons, and it was filled with hilarious stories of when they were young, plus humorous and heartfelt things this man said and did throughout his life. I wouldn't go as far as to say people were rolling in the aisles, but it was a wonderful speech and all the people in the church were constantly laughing out loud. A eulogy filled with humor not only helped him deal with his father's death, but also made everyone there feel better and more able to deal with their loss. He received a standing ovation from almost five hundred people and was embraced by his family members.

A couple of months later, as I was working at the deceased man's estate cleaning his office, I came across a couple of three-ring binders with the word "Humor" written on the spines. When I opened them up I realized they were full of emails from friends, associates and family members—all were jokes, or fictional and non-fictional anecdotes that he had printed out and saved. I sat there for hours and read them. Needless to say, I laughed constantly. Another thing I realized about these emails was that the earliest ones were dated shortly after he was diagnosed with cancer. The people who sent him these emails knew that laughter was going to help him get through his rigorous chemo and radiation treatments a little bit easier. Even though he eventually succumbed to his illness, he lasted almost a year longer than his doctors had predicted. I firmly believe it was the laughter that helped him spend one last Christmas with his family.

A sense of humor is one of the most important things we possess. I equate it with faith, love or happiness; you can't see any of those things either, but we all know they exist and we all know they are good.

Originally from Cincinnati, Ohio, Gabriel Lang is a graduate of Loyola Marymount University. Recently his transient lifestyle brought him to reside temporarily in Uptown New Orleans. If you or someone you know is in the area, look him up and he'll tell you a dirty joke.

Relationship: A Means to Consciousness

By Sat-Kaur Khalsa

Consciousness to me is the key to creating a heaven on earth. It is the state in which the ten elements identified in this book can be achieved. It is the foundation on which all else is built. It is the purpose of our soul's incarnation on this planet at this time. Given its importance for humankind and the future of our world, how can we expand and elevate our consciousness?

From my vantage point as a psychotherapist in private practice, one of the most powerful tools of consciousness we have is relationship. Everything in our lives is colored by relationship. Think about it. We have our relationship with our little self (ego, personality, identity), higher self (higher consciousness, spirit, God, universe, cosmos—however you label it), our significant other, family, and our inner circle of friends, community, state, country, environment, globe and universe. All of these relationships impact the quality and experience of our lives.

Human beings have the capacity to be self-aware. We place value on this awareness and label it self-esteem. We judge whether we are capable and confident within ourselves to meet the requirements of life and whether we are worthy of what life has to offer. The problem with this identification and definition is that it is focused from the outside in. That is, we make our worth and value attached to a role, job, spouse or a response from another person in our outer world. Unfortunately these things change over time and are unstable. As our outer world fluctuates, so does our sense of self-esteem. People are constantly in reaction to that which is around them. When you invest your worth and value in that which is not infinite, you build your foundation on shaky ground. It is liable to crumble.

326

Take the example of a man who is the CEO of a major corporation. If his company is bought out, he may find himself unemployed. It is likely that he will feel lost and worthless. But in reality, did he die? Is he less human? Is he less than who he was before the takeover? Of course not. He just doesn't have that label or social identity that he had when he was CEO. He is still very much the person God created him to be.

What then is our true identity? What is infinite and lasts forever? It is the radiance of our soul, which is intact at all times. This is the relationship with Self. It is the God essence in each and every one of us. As my spiritual teacher Yogi Bhajan often said, "If you can't see God in all you can't see God at all." This is a profound concept to contemplate. Can you imagine a world that operates from this belief system? What a magnificent world it would be! Clearly, the relationship with Self is the most important relationship of all. If your relationship with your higher Self is strong you will evolve in consciousness and that will affect all the other relationships in your life.

How can we nurture a relationship with our Self? There are many ways: meditation, prayer, communion with nature, yoga, love, music, art, dance and sex, just to name a few. As we experience this consciousness and operate from our higher Self, we will have the means to transform our world into a magnificent place. New operating systems, structures and vehicles for change can emerge. Global peace and harmony can prevail. Joyful, graceful and respectful interpersonal relationships can be the norm. We will indeed achieve a heaven on earth.

Dr. Sat-Kaur Khalsa received her master of education from Northeastern University, Boston, in 1972, and her doctorate of education from the University of California at Berkley in 1990. She is a licensed psychotherapist and counselor in Los Angeles and Santa Fe, a certified Kundalini Yoga teacher, Secretary of Religion of Sikh Dharma International, and author of Sacred Sexual Bliss. She specializes in relationships and personal growth. With her spiritual perspective together with the tools of traditional psychotherapy, she has worked with thousands of people to help improve their lives and relationships.

Paradise Now

By Lili Lakich

In art, as in life,
Paradise is in your head
   —Lili Lakich

One of the more charming aspects of visiting Bali in the 1980s was learning that the Balinese believe that when they die they go to a place exactly like Bali. They truly believed that they were, in fact, living in heaven on earth.

I had to agree. When I was there twenty years ago, Bali was a lush, egalitarian and art-rich island paradise where several generations of a family lived together in equality and mutual respect. The Balinese believe that demons live in the ocean and the gods live in the mountains, so they leave the coastline to the tourists and build their houses in the interior of the island, where everyone, it seemed, pursued an artistic vision. One may have been a rice farmer by day, but in the evening he demonstrated his skills as a player in the village dance company or gamelan orchestra—or a painter, woodcarver or mask maker.

With great generosity of spirit, the Balinese invited tourists to their weddings and their funerals. Life and death were to be celebrated—even with perfect strangers. All they asked is that we wear a temple sash, or maybe a sarong. And so we traipsed around the countryside in our sashes, sarongs and high-top Reeboks visiting many of their 9,000 temples and being enchanted by the elaborate productions of their dance companies. Crime was virtually non-existent. Shopkeepers would leave their goods displayed outside their shops when they left for the day. What about the tourists, one might ask? Wouldn't they take advantage of the inherent goodness of the natives? Miraculously, tourists were transformed when they got to Bali, leaving treachery behind on the mainland.

My own vision of heaven in my island studio involves neon— yes, that screaming harlot of the urban landscape. Developed in 1910 by Frenchman Georges Claude as a byproduct of distilling air to produce oxygen for medical and welding purposes, neon soon became the light of the American dream, selling everything from girdles and liquor to religion with giant "JESUS SAVES" signs in several major cities.

The Pioneer Club's glowing neon cowboy, looming over downtown Las Vegas for more than half a century, points to himself with one hand and to the club with the other. He is our secular society's interpretation of the luminous painted images of Christ pointing to himself with one hand and upwards to heaven with the other. Simon and Garfunkel's caustic song lyric—"and the people bowed and prayed to the neon god they made"— ironically points to the connection that neon has to religious iconography. The colored auras, the sinewy lines, the ability of the medium to depict imagery that glows from within—neon is a contemporary manifestation in the attempt to make our saints and icons glow. Depicting subjects with halos around their heads, shimmering luminosity projecting from their bodies, or flames of fire enveloping their beings, artists have used these and other techniques in their struggle to portray the metaphysical. Neon makes the metaphors real.

This iconoclastic relation between neon and religious experience has not been lost on contemporary neon sculpture artists. Most of us were drawn to the medium because of its alluring references to the magical, the metaphysical and the spiritual. We are modern-day alchemists transforming a denigrated material that has been stigmatized by a wrong-side-of-the-tracks reputation into vibrant artworks of radiant and jewel-like beauty. While commercial neon signs may be comprised of only two to eight colors, there are actually more than 250 colors available that artists may employ. Neon (bright orange), which gives the medium its name, is only one gas among several that include argon (lavender), helium (peach), krypton (silvery white) and xenon (pale bluish).

No doubt I was drawn to the medium because, having been

brought up in the Serbian Orthodox faith, in observance of my family's patron saint's day I burned votive candles before a small brass relief icon in a monastery built of marble from my grandfather's quarries in Serbia. I have visited all the monasteries built of marble from those quarries, as well as the major Serbian Christian churches and Muslim mosques, and was powerfully drawn to them and to that icon, now in my possession. I consider its beauty and emotional pull the reason for my interest in bas relief metal sculpture, which forms the basis for my neon works.

I am incapable of understanding how this incredible world came to be—it boggles my mind. Although life and love and God are far too mysterious for my limited intelligence, I see neon art as my contribution to the world and its beauty. But on the evening of the very first exhibition of my neon sculpture, the heavens put forth the most gorgeous sunset anybody had ever seen, as if to prove that artists should always remember their place.

My studio in downtown Los Angeles is filled with more than fifty of my own neon sculptures that I have created over four decades, many of them large-scale. One time a woman came into the Museum of Neon Art and, seeing my work, said, "For years I have been giving money to the peace movement; this is what peace is for." I love what she said, because for me, this work, whether in my studio or a museum, is my heaven.

And when I die, I hope to go to a neon-lit paradise just like my studio.

Lili Lakich is internationally recognized as a pioneer in the art of neon sculpture. She is the author of Neon Lovers Glow in the Dark *and* LAKICH: For Light. For Love. For Life. *In 1981, she founded the Museum of Neon Art in Los Angeles and served as its artistic director through 1999.*

What Is Heaven on Earth?

By Jeff Teachworth

One must approach the definition of "heaven on earth" in a philosophical way. We know what earth is, but what truly is heaven? To some, heaven is a land of free-flowing milk and honey, to some it is connecting with a higher power, while to others it is simply a well-deserved rest. There are many meanings of the concept in many religions, but always heaven is deeply rewarding to the individual.

In the simplest logical sense, heaven is freedom from want or need. Conversely, if you define what heaven on earth really is, you will have a life of pure fulfillment, whether or not you have many possessions. How is this manifest for the common man? It becomes a state of mind. When someone is in this state of mind it is similar to the feeling we have after a great sexual experience, or after a delicious meal—we are fulfilled and at peace. Material wealth is not needed in that moment.

Enlightenment is a state in which the mystic is free from want or need, and content on the planet. He is solidly connected to his higher power, radiating inside and throughout himself. His mind is clear and his emotions are calm yet vivid.

So if we are to have a heaven while still on this earth, it needs to be achieved on a personal internal level; each person realizing it for himself. According to this theory, we need to slow down and get in deep touch with ourselves. How many times do we look at material goods and think we are lacking? Or do we look at others' skills and feel a pang of jealousy? Sometimes we fall into belief systems that make us think we are part of a certain group of people that excludes others. Terrorists are taught to feel this sense of exclusion and hate certain other groups of people

332 HOW TO ACHIEVE A HEAVEN ON EARTH

enough to kill them. We could also look at people with a different skin color as threatening, and then our eyes betray us and we feel insecure. Any belief system that has strong personification of an evil, tempting devil existing to scare us makes us insecure, so we cannot achieve lasting peacefulness. There are many belief systems that lower thinking and feeling and put us in a state of anxiety and separation from our natural inner state of heavenly peace.

So the trick is to stop everything for a moment and take a deep breath, then realize that heaven is a personal concept. We can either create or destroy it from within, or seek to feel around and find it inside. Sitting or lying still and calm will help us imagine this inner state of sacred peace. Taking several deep breaths in a row will help our bodies loosen up and allow oxygenated blood to circulate to our brains. Know that we are high beings upon a planet that has been here for thousands of lifetimes, floating through space, space that is composed of solar systems around clusters of stars forming mighty galaxies that are themselves part of thousands of repetitions throughout limitless space. This is justification that we deserve to be here and deserve to maintain a higher form of reason and being.

The highest form of reason and being possible has one incredible feature at its base: love. Love is the unifying force that counteracts all of the abusive learning systems listed above. Land, color of skin, religious dogma, material things, personal characteristics, fear and the devil—all these concepts cannot exist for any individual in the face of overwhelming love flowing out of his or her heart. Forgiveness and unity, sharing and brotherhood—all these fly forth like angels from love. They shatter the voodoo of separatist thinking and flood the individual with warm, divine peace and satisfaction.

Heaven on earth is simple and attainable—focus on and emanate deep spiritual love in everything you do and toward everyone with whom you deal. That is a true heaven on earth available for the taking.

Jeff Teachworth is a certified Transformational Life Coach and has been certified as a Gestalt therapist since 1987. He studied with Richard Bandler, co-founder with John Grinder of Neuro-Linguistic

Programming, and has been a certified NLP practitioner since 1989. Over the last three decades, Jeff has researched the philosophy of religion, radical Zen, Jungian psychology, lucid dreaming, transformational breathwork, and metaphysics.

Turning Our Dream of Heaven on Earth into Reality

By Martin Rutte

There is a desire, a longing, in each of us for a world that works. We want to end the immoral and recurring problems of the planet, such as war, hunger, disease and hatred. We want our soul's dream of a world that inspires hope, engagement and creativity to flourish. We want heaven on earth.

We've already proven that humanity can accomplish the extraordinary. We've returned a human from the moon, we've extended life by transplanting hearts, and we've brought democracy to South Africa.

But our human story also contains suffering, fear, prejudice and horror. The apparent strength of these negatives contributes to our feeling powerless and believing that we are unable to make a true, deep and lasting difference in the world. Yet even through these sufferings, we still experience times of heaven on earth, times of beauty, love and tranquility.

How do we nourish and support this collective project? We establish a new model of existence, a new collective purpose, a new civilization-fueling vision. We expand the idea of what is possible, focus on and multiply what works, and confront and reduce what doesn't work. We join with others to make the creation of heaven on earth the new story of what it means to be human and what it means to be humanity.

I've asked many hundreds of people to tell me a time when they've experienced heaven on earth. They don't hesitate or ask me what I mean, but immediately tell me about a moment when they've experienced it. They answer with clarity and certainty, sharing moments ranging from the birth of a child, to an

334

appreciation of nature, to a moment of deep communion. Heaven on earth, like love, peace and joy, is hard-wired into us, an eternal, innate truth, one that we want to extend from a moment to always. Ask yourself this question, "What is heaven on earth?" Just sit quietly now and answer.

The Oxford English Dictionary defines "heaven" as both a noun and a verb. It says that heaven is not only an abstract concept of the afterlife, it is also a transitive verb, "to heaven." This means we can go around heavening all day. We can heaven our relationship with problems. We can heaven our relationship with life itself.

Here's one simple way you can begin. Speak to two people in the next twenty-four hours about creating heaven on earth and ask each of them to speak to two other people the next day, and so on. If everyone does his part, it would take just thirty-two days to reach all 6.5 billion people on earth—a small act, a huge impact.

Your contribution is vital to this building process. Author Frances Hodgson Burnett said, "At first people refuse to believe that a strange new thing can be done, and then they begin to hope it can be done, then they see it can be done—then it is done . . . and all the world wonders why it was not done centuries ago."

There are many other ways to bring about a heaven on earth. Here are some:

- Discover and live your life's purpose and vision.
- Be true to your values.
- Express the beauty of life through music, art, writing, photography, dance, etc.
- Experience the Divine.
- Be aware of the presence of heaven on earth in every moment.
- Create enlivening affirmations.
- Build a better future by contributing your gifts.
- Take on one of the world's major sufferings and be part of ending it.
- Encourage our institutions to take their rightful place in creating heaven on earth.
- Identify an issue that needs resolving in your nation and help resolve it.
- Create a vision for your nation.
- Describe your vision for the world community.

I believe the vast majority of the world's people want to participate and play their part in a new global vision, a new human story of hope and momentum. United, we can and will create a grand and global planetary chorus, each person adding his voice, his gift, his inspiration. Through our intentions, our actions and the circumstances that provide the opportunities to move in a more expansive world, a heaven on earth can be created. This truly is the work of humanity. This truly is fulfilling the longing for the world we want.

Perhaps best known as co-author of Chicken Soup for the Soul at Work, *a* New York Times *bestseller, Martin Rutte is the president of Livelihood, a management consulting firm in Santa Fe, New Mexico, that explores the deeper meaning of work and its contribution to society. He founded and is chairman of the board of Canada's Centre for Spirituality and the Workplace at the Sobey School of Business, Saint Mary's University, Halifax. Rutte is in demand throughout the world as a speaker and consultant.*

UNICEF at Work

By Lisa Szarkowski

At this moment, a global network of people is working around the clock to help achieve a version of heaven on earth. They represent every country, religion, race and belief system. Though diverse as the world we inhabit, together, this team moves mountains towards a common ideal.

What is this network? What is this ideal? Who are these people?

We are UNICEF, and we believe that every child is equally deserving of protection, health and education, regardless of race, nationality, religion, gender or politics. UNICEF has saved the lives of more children than any organization in history. We have not done this by ourselves. Our work is funded and implemented by people just like you.

You may already be a part of the network that is UNICEF. We are rock stars and volunteers; scholars and economists; teachers and students; CEOs and religious leaders; socialites, celebrities and millions of ordinary people. You may find us as easily in Kansas City, Missouri, as in Banda Aceh, Indonesia. Together we form a pipeline that enables children's lives to be saved and improved.

Here's how it works: UNICEF is funded entirely by voluntary donations. Without resources, UNICEF literally could not save or help children. Countless individuals have donated to UNICEF, trusting us to help children they have never seen and will never meet, half a world away.

Some of my most rewarding moments have come when opening mail from the public—people who've taken the time to write about their hopes and fears for the world's children. One single mother who was barely making ends meet sent $1.20, because she heard that was enough to vaccinate a mother against tetanus. She

337

actually apologized that it was not more. An elderly couple on a fixed income sent what they could, after seeing a young Pakistani girl who reminded them of their own granddaughter. "We want her to be able to go to school, like our granddaughter does," they said. "We wish it could be more."

Then there are the thousands of children who initiate bake sales, carwashes and collections to be used when there is an emergency. They spring to their feet without being asked, eager to help. As do teachers, who for years have incorporated UNICEF themes and content into their lesson plans, helping to instill a sense of global awareness and citizenship in their students. Many have championed our Trick-or-Treat for UNICEF program which soon will celebrate its sixtieth anniversary.

We also have volunteers, some who've been with us decades. They tirelessly speak out on behalf of children, and educate their communities and political leaders about our work. Others are board members, college students and working moms who donate their precious time to advance our cause.

That's just the beginning of the pipeline, for on the other end you will find astonishing networks of people coalescing to save children's lives. UNICEF partners with village elders, tribal leaders, governments, non-governmental organizations, children, Rotarians, Kiwanians, doctors, sister UN agencies, and religious organizations, foundations, universities, corporations and millions of other ordinary citizens.

This network works on a shoestring budget, leveraging every nickel to save the estimated nine million children under age five who die each year of preventable causes. We use bicycles, camels, donkeys, trains, trucks and boats to transport supplies and people, whatever it takes.

We work in dangerous places to make sure children are protected. We persuade governments to put more resources towards helping children. And we have negotiated ceasefires between warring parties for the purpose of delivering aid to children. Even bitter enemies can sometimes agree to put their children's needs first.

Along the way, we encounter excruciating realities that some children endure. There are moments of doubt and heartache. But no one quits. We understand that transformation takes time and many footsteps forward.

This diverse network of people, staff, governments, donors and organizations is called UNICEF. And whatever our backgrounds, we are aligned towards the day when no children's lives are squandered or extinguished.

The work we do takes time but ultimately lifts people and nations out of poverty, towards prosperity, security and health. That would be heaven on earth.

Lisa Szarkowski, the vice president of public relations for the U.S. Fund for UNICEF, manages its Emergency Response, Celebrity Ambassador and Media Relations programs. For the past ten years, she has been part of a team that has increased organizational revenue by more than six hundred percent and helped to develop and launch brand and positioning campaigns. She has traveled extensively within the United States and internationally, in pursuit of zero.

Appendix A
Soldiers of Love

Half my royalties from this book will go to Soldiers of Love, a charity I founded in 2006. Its goal is to try to guide the world toward a heaven on earth, based on the pledge I conceived, "I will try to love and help create a heaven on earth."

Our general philosophy is to teach people to fish rather than giving them fish. One key idea is that Soldiers of Love does not intend to "reinvent the wheel," but instead partner with fellow nonprofit entities. To date we have worked with three other charities:

1. Desire Street Ministries: We've made contributions to Desire Street Academy, a school for African-American youth that stressed academics, athletics and Christian education.
2. Junior Achievement: In 2008 we twice partnered with Lafayette Academy Charter School in New Orleans to present the Junior Achievement curriculum.
3. Depression and Bipolar Support Alliance: In 2008 we sponsored two peer specialist training sessions. These seminars taught persons in recovery from mental illness how to coach or mentor others experiencing mental illness. We recruited participants especially from New Orleans because of the dire need in our city. A lack of professionals and facilities coupled with Katrina-related illnesses made our effort important.

Someday I want to see Soldiers of Love play a vital role in raising money to fund charities and operations that promote the ten elements of a heaven on earth: peace, security, freedom,

341

342   HOW TO ACHIEVE A HEAVEN ON EARTH

democracies, prosperity, spiritual harmony, racial harmony, ecological harmony and health as well as moral purpose and meaning (doing the right thing in word and deed).

The vision for Soldiers of Love comprises two things:

1. Promotion of the goal of a heaven on earth as described by the ten elements and the Soldiers of Love pledge.
2. Performance of acts of charity, such as those accomplished in 2008, and funding of other worthy partners.

Promotion of the ten elements will continue through soldiersoflove.org. We may also form committees to pursue these elements individually or in appropriate groups, and build on our three existing partners. Financial support for these partners would come first, with operating activities coming as funding allows. Further partners would be added as our means permit.

In 2009 Soldiers of Love will continue to operate on a sound, responsible, sustainable financial basis. In accordance with this policy, we will not actively participate in the activities sponsored in 2008, but instead concentrate on contributing financially to the same three partners—Desire Street Ministries, Junior Achievement and the Depression and Bipolar Support Alliance. Thus, financial support for these partners will come first, with operating activities resuming as funding allows, and further partners added as our means permit.

John E. Wade II, a retired certified public accountant, author, investor and philanthropist, is the editor of this book and the founder and president of Soldiers of Love, a 501(c)(3) Louisiana nonprofit corporation.

Appendix B
For Additional Reading

Agatino, Daniel *The Tao of Ronald Reagan: Common Sense from an Uncommon Man*

Ashton, John and Whyte, Tom *The Quest for Paradise: Visions of Heaven and Eternity in the World's Myths and Religions*

Baker, James A. III; Hamilton, Lee H.; Eagleburger, Lawrence S. *The Iraq Study Group Reprint*

Barnett, Thomas P.M. *Blueprint for Action*

Beneke, Chris *Beyond Toleration: The Religious Origins of American Pluralism*

Block, Ralph L. *Investing in REITs: Real Estate Investment Trusts*

Bolles, Richard N. *How to Find Your Mission in Life*

Bowker, John *World Religions: The Great Faiths Explored & Explained*

Brinkley, Douglas *The Reagan Diaries*

Brockman, John *The Next Fifty Years: Science in the First Half of the Twenty-First Century*

Buckingham, Marcus and Coffman, Curt *First, Break All the Rules*

Bush, Jenna *Ana's Story: A Journey of Hope*

Chang, Richard *The Passion Plan*

Claeys, Gregory, and Sargent, Lyman Tower *The Utopia Reader*

Connell, John R.; Gordon, Paul R.; Porter, Thomas,; Zobez, Robert E. *The Touché Ross Personal Financial Management and Investment Workbook*

Cota-Robles, Patricia Diane *Home: Heaven on Mother Earth*

Delumeau, Jean *History of Paradise*

DePree, Max *Leadership Is an Art*

———. *Leadership Jazz*

Dyer, Wayne *The Power of Intention*

Easterbrook, Gregg *The Progress Paradox*

Friedman, Thomas L. *The World Is Flat*

Gandhi, Mohandas K. and Attenborough, Richard *The Words of Gandhi*

Gandhi, Mohandas K. *Gandhi's Autobiography: The Story of My Experiments with Truth*

Gartner, John D. *The Hypomanic Edge*

Gillis, Chester *Pluralism: A New Paradigm for Theology*

Goleman, Daniel *Emotional Intelligence*

———. *Social Intelligence: The New Science of Human Relationships, Emotional Intelligence*

Goodwin, Stephen *World Christianity in Local Context, World Christianity in Muslim Encounter, In the Silence Is a Presence*

Gray, John *Men Are From Mars, Women Are From Venus*

Greenspan, Alan *The Age of Turbulence*

Gyatso, Tenzin, His Holiness the 14th Dalai Lama *The Art of Happiness*

Heller, Dagmar and Raiser, Konrad *"Mache Dich auf und werde licht!" "Arise, shine!"*

Hitchcock, Susan Tyler and Esposito, John L. *Geography of Religion: Where God Lives, Where Pilgrims Walk*

Humes, James C. *The Wit and Wisdom of Ronald Reagan*

Jacoby, Mario *A Longing for Paradise: Psychological Perspectives on an Archetype*

Jamison, Kay R. *An Unquiet Mind*

Jenka *A Heaven on Earth: Human Alchemy Through the Practical Use of Universal Principles*

Kaye, Beverly and Sharon Jordan-Evans *Love 'Em or Lose 'Em: Getting Good People to Stay*

———. *Love It, Don't Leave It: 26 Ways to Get What You Want at Work*

Khalsa, Sat-Kaur *Sacred Sexual Bliss: A Technology for Ecstasy*

Kidder, Tracy *Mountains Beyond Mountains: The Quest of Dr. Paul Farmer, a Man Who Would Cure the World*

Kingwell, Mark *The World We Want: Virtue, Vice, and the Good Citizen*

Klembith, George and Tammy *The Key Bridging The Millenniums*

Kreeft, Peter *Heaven: The Heart's Deepest Longing*

Laffer, Arthur B., PhD.; Moore Stephen; Tanous, Peter J. *The End of Prosperity: How Higher Taxes Will Doom the Economy—If We Let It Happen*

Lakich, Lili *For Light. For Love. For Life*

Lundin, Stephen C. and John Christensen *FISH! Catch the Energy and Release the Potential*

Luskin, Dr. Fred *Forgive for Good: A Proven Prescription for Health and Happiness*

Macdonald, Copthorne *Getting A Life: Strategies for Joyful and Effective Living*

———. *Matters of Consequence: Creating a Meaningful Life and a World that Works*

———. *Toward Wisdom: Finding Our Way to Inner Peace, Love & Happiness*

MacLean, Norm *A River Runs Through It*

Manuel, Frank E. and Manuel, Fritzie P. *Utopian Thought in the Western World*

McCain, John *Hard Call*

McDannell, Colleen and Lang, Bernhard *Heaven: A History*

McFaul, Thomas R. *The Future of Peace and Justice in the Global Village*

———. *Transformation Ethics: Developing the Christian Moral Imagination*

Merchey, Jason A. *Living a Life of Value: A Unique Anthology of Essays on Values & Ethics by Contemporary Writers*

Mondimore, Francis Mark, M.D. *Bipolar Disorder*

Muller, Robert *New Genesis: Shaping a Global Spirituality.*

Naisbitt, John *Megatrends: Ten New Directions Transforming Our Lives*

———. *Mind Set!*

Nierenberg, Gerard I. *The Art of Negotiating*

Obama, Barack *The Audacity of Hope*

O'Neil, William J. *How to Make Money in Stocks*

Pearce, Terry *Leading Out Loud: The Authentic Speaker, the Credible Leader*

Peck, M. Scott, M.D. *The Road Less Traveled*

Pelosi, Peggie *Corporate Karma*
Porter, Kate *Life in Beauty*
Psaki, F. Regina, ed. *The Earthly Paradise: The Garden of Eden from Antiquity to Modernity*
Rand, Ayn *Atlas Shrugged*
Rath, Tom *Strengthsfinder 2.0*
Ravich, Lenny *A Funny Thing Happened on the Way to Enlightenment*
Reagan, Michael *In the Words of Ronald Reagan*
Richardson, Cheryl *The Unmistakable Touch of Grace*
Sachs, Jeffery D. *The End of Poverty*
Schneerson, Menachem Mendel *Bringing Down Heaven to Earth: 365 Meditations*
Schultz, George P. and others *Reagan, In His Own Hand: The Writings of Ronald Reagan that Reveal His Revolutionary Vision for America*
Schultz, George P. and others *Stories in His Own Hand: The Everyday Wisdom of Ronald Reagan*
Seligman, Martin *Learned Optimism*
Sharansky, Natan *The Case for Democracy: The Power of Freedom to Overcome Tyranny and Terror*
Shawn, Wallace *The Fever*
Siegel, Jeremy J. *Stocks for the Long Run*
Singer, Pete *One World: The Ethics of Globalization*
Slaughter, Anne-Marie *A New World Order*
Smith, Bruce *Soul Storm*
Stanley, Thomas J. and Danko, William D., Ph.D. *The Millionaire Next Door: The Surprising Secrets of America's Wealth*
Stewart, John *Evolution's Arrow: The Direction of Evolution and the Future of Humanity*
Tooker, Poppy *The Crescent City Farmers Market*
Teachworth, Anne *Why We Pick the Mates We Do: A Step-By-Step Program to Select a Better Partner or Improve the Relationship You're Already In*
Tyson, Eric *Investing for Dummies*
Ucko, Hans *The People and the People of God*
———. *Changing the Present, Dreaming the Future*
Van Gelder, Sarah Ruth *Saying Yes!: Conversations on a World that Works for All*

Van Scott, Miriam *Encyclopedia of Heaven*
Virtue, Doreen *The Lightworkers Way*
Wade, John E. II *Deep Within my Heart*
Williamson, Marianne *A Return to Love*
Zakaria, Fareed *The Future of Freedom*
Zaleski, Carol and Zaleski, Philip *The Book of Heaven*
Zweig, Martin *Winning on Wall Street*